The Ghost Whisperer

The Ghost Whisperer

A Real-life Psychic's Stories

KATIE COUTTS

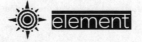

Element
An Imprint of HarperCollins*Publishers*
77–85 Fulham Palace Road,
Hammersmith, London W6 8JB

The Element website address is:
www.thorsonselement.com

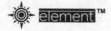

and *Element* are trademarks of
HarperCollins*Publishers* Ltd

Published by Element 2003

1 3 5 7 9 10 8 6 4 2

A catalogue record of this book
is available from the British Library

ISBN 0 00 716323 1

Printed and bound in Great Britain by
Clays Ltd, St Ives PLC, Bungay, Suffolk

Contents

Acknowledgements vi
Introduction: My Story viii

1 By Appointment: Ghostly Experiences of My Clients 1

2 Picture the Scene: My Own Ghostly Encounters 54

3 Over to You: Ghosts Stories from My Readers 119

4 Famous Ghosts 181

Index 286

Acknowledgements

My work commitments leave me very little time for family and friends. I apologize to you all for neglecting you while I've been writing. Thank you for standing by me, for being supportive and for not dumping me after I repeatedly failed to return your calls. I love you all dearly – I hope you know that.

To Davina, for saving me from many a nervous breakdown during problems with my computer. Your knowledge astounds me.

To my darling daughters, Natalie and Athena. You are my whole world and I love and adore you. I'm so proud of you both.

A huge thank you to Bill for everything he has done for me and my family.

To my Mazzie (Marion Quinn, my wonderful co-writer). None of this would have been possible without you. This is it honey!

And to Mum – our ship is on its way. I love you.

I would also like to thank everyone who participated in the writing of this book.

Death is nothing at all –
I have only slipped away into the next room.
I am I – and you are you.
Whatever we were to each other,
that we are still.
Call me by my old familiar name,
speak to me in the easy way which you always used.
Put no difference into your tone:
wear no formal air of solemnity or sorrow.
Laugh as we always laughed at the little jokes we enjoyed together.
Play, smile, think of me ... pray for me.
Let my name be the household word that it always was.
Let it be spoken without effort, without the ghost of a shadow on it.
Let it be spoken without a tear.
Life means all that it ever meant.
It is the same as it ever was;
there is absolutely unbroken continuity.
What is death but a negligible accident?
Why should I be out of your mind
because I am out of your sight?
I am but waiting for you, for an interval,
somewhere just around the corner.
All is well. Nothing is past. Nothing is lost.
One brief moment and all will be as it was before –
only better, infinitely happier ... and forever.
We will all be one together.

author unknown

Introduction: My Story

I was born in Glasgow in 1965, the youngest of three siblings. I believe I 'inherited' my psychic ability from my maternal grandmother, my beloved nana. My mum, Annemarie, is also very psychic, although her visions and premonitions come mainly from dreams. Nana was a hard-working lady, Irish by birth and very down-to-earth. She would often read tea leaves, and I still recall her accuracy. She wasn't a confident woman and she would do this as a favour to family and friends, but I don't think she ever took her ability seriously. I often wonder how she and I would interact if she were alive today. It's a great source of regret for me that she's not here to discuss her beliefs (although I believe Athena, my youngest daughter, is my nana reincarnated).

Although my childhood was happy and secure, I hated school from day one till the day I left. After leaving school I worked briefly as a telephonist, but soon gave birth to my first daughter, Natalie. She was my pride and joy.

When Natalie was four, I met my St Andrews-born husband, and Natalie and I left Glasgow for a new life in Fife. A mere hundred miles away, this place was worlds apart. We settled very quickly and I loved the picturesque village with its stunning views over the River Tay. Within a couple of years, one of my two brothers and my mum had followed me here to Fife, and together we've grown to love the area.

During the early years of my marriage, I did many varied jobs, ranging from sales to running my own business. The common denominator was that I was my own boss in every single job. Although I always knew what I really wanted to do, I was loath to follow my dream for some mysterious reason.

I have always been ambitious – a typical Leo trait – but during the early years of motherhood, my main aim was to be a good mother to my beautiful daughter. My happiness was made complete in 1997 when, right out of the blue and much to my shock and delight, I discovered I was expecting my second daughter, the gorgeous and hugely independent Athena. The girls were born *exactly* 15-and-a-half years apart, both on Thursdays and both at six o'clock.

And, if I had nothing else in my life (except mum of course), I would still be the happiest, proudest person in the world. I have the most beautiful daughters in the universe!

How it All Began

My most famous documented quote is that at the age of six, I suddenly announced Prince Charles would never be king. I don't personally recall saying this but I've been assured I did. I still believe this to be the case.

I was around seven or eight when I had my first psychic experiences. While playing upstairs, I became aware of being watched by a lady. Later I was to learn she was my great-grandmother. I regularly felt a hand on my shoulder or heard my name being whispered. But I was so young I genuinely didn't think this was anything unusual. I was never afraid.

I never knew my granny (my mum's granny) but I seemed to connect strongly with her and always have done.

As a child I preferred to play with tarot cards than dollies. I had a few experiences with Ouija boards but can remember a couple of frightening incidents. In fact, I haven't touched an Ouija board since the age of eight. The friends involved, to this day, remember this experience with horror. I would never encourage or endorse the use of Ouija boards to anyone.

At primary school, my friends and I would lark about, telling each other ghost stories, most of them fabricated. Again, I didn't take any of this seriously, but over the years I've been told by old school friends that I used to freak them out with the things I would say. Coincidence or not, many remembered what I said about the future, their marriages, children, careers etc., and much of what I apparently said has come to fruition.

From the age of 14, I began to take my ability a little more seriously. I would read palms, do psychometry and basically just blurt out whatever came into my head.

Then, after many years of being nagged by family and friends to take my ability more seriously and do something with it, I was given a pack of tarot cards as a gift. I loved them and studied them thoroughly, engrossed in their origin and the myths behind each individual card. My passion for Greek mythology was born.

A friend asked me to visit and bring my tarot cards. When I arrived, she had at least a dozen other people waiting for readings. The rest really is history because word of mouth soon spread and my phone began ringing off the hook. That was in 1991 and it hasn't stopped since!

So What Do I Do?

The one thing I utterly despise is being called a fortune-teller. I'm not really a believer in fortune-telling – seeing the future accurately is not always possible. However, I know there are some very gifted people out there. I'm just terribly aware, and equally saddened by, just how vulnerable the public can be. I am renowned for 'telling it how it is' but I would never violate anyone who asked for my help. I'm sickened by those charlatans who prey on the vulnerable, and we all know there are many out there.

I'm often told I am fairly unique in that I don't 'predict', but rather advise clients on how they can kick-start their lives again. Often this advice pertains to career moves, relationships and so on, but can often be as diverse as overcoming phobias and coming to terms with being abused as a child.

A great deal of my work involves healing, which I often combine with a marvellous treatment called laser therapy. This is similar to acupuncture, minus needles.

Someone recently described me as a 'fate-teller', which I thought was a rather lovely, fundamental way of summing up exactly what I'm all about. I have the ability to tell my clients what fate intends for them – which path they should be on. I only wish I could do this for myself but, alas, I cannot.

We often use the phrase 'what's for you won't go past you', but I totally disagree with this. If it were true, none of us would ever be unhappy, dissatisfied or unfulfilled. And I would be out of a job! The truth is, what's for us goes speeding by all the time, and my job involves telling my clients where they need to be in life and how to make their lives the best they can (and should) be.

In my 13 years as a professional, not one of my clients has ever been surprised by what I've told them, even though the majority are not doing what I advise. I think most people would agree that our lives are mapped out for us. I guess I merely point out the woods from the trees and guide my clients onto the path fate intends for them as individuals.

I advise and guide my clients – the rest is up to them. I don't necessarily take credit for the advice I give them. The way I see it, fate, whom I describe as my boss, shows me the way forward for clients. If they fail to follow the advice then their lives will continue as before – often stagnant, mundane and very much second-best.

My job is similar to that of a doctor in that my clients pose the 'symptoms' and I then make a diagnosis and advise them what they must do in order to make it better. If they don't follow that advice, their lives will not improve.

Fate only ever offers the very best for us. If we want the very best badly enough, then in my opinion it is imperative to follow whatever fate intends for us.

I adore all aspects of the paranormal, even embracing complementary medicines and therapies, but my greatest love is ghosts. I just love to see the pleasure in a bereaved client's face when I pass on a message proving that their loved ones are with them. It doesn't always make sense to me but the important thing is that it makes sense to them.

I disagree with most mediums who say there are several different levels or stages to death. I simply believe in heaven and earth. In fact, I believe strongly that heaven is not somewhere 'up there' but is in fact simply an unseen parallel of earth. I believe that is how close our dearly departed are to us.

ONE

By Appointment: Ghostly Experiences of My Clients

In this chapter, I describe many experiences I've had with spirits during consultations with my clients. Consultations are possibly one of the easiest means of contacting a spirit – I have the client in front of me and, as I tune in to their energies, so the spirits come over. Most of my contact with spirits comes from these consultations. Of course, it doesn't happen every time. Believe it or not, it's usually more difficult if the client has arranged the consultation for the sole purpose of contacting their dearly departed. I don't know about other mediums, but I find it easier just to feel what I feel, see what I see and pass on the ghostly news. I could write 10 books with the experiences I've had thus far in my 13-year career. I feel very privileged and also very respectful of the spirit world. To be given an insight into life after death is truly a gift *to* me as opposed to a gift *from* me.

The Vase

Jane from Perth had a very interesting story to tell me. Her main reason for arranging the consultation with me was a far more personal one, but when she began to relate the following, I found myself utterly engrossed.

Jane and her husband moved into their first home in the spring of 1997. They had been married only a matter of weeks, and naturally the young couple were busy making their new house a home.

Utterly exhausted one evening, the pair decided to have an early night. They both lay in bed reading when, out of the blue, an enormous thud could be heard from downstairs. At this point, the exact location of the noise wasn't clear but as they tentatively descended the stairs, they were both drawn to the lounge. This room was the only one they had so far finished decorating.

Jane remembers that, despite the room being in pitch darkness, she did not feel afraid. During a later discussion, her husband was to admit to the same feeling. This was, of course, very strange. By all accounts it sounded as if there was someone in their lounge – and the most likely candidate was a burglar. However, at no time did either one feel afraid. They tell me they simply didn't think along those lines.

As Frank, Jane's husband, switched on the light, Jane was devastated to see one of her most loved belongings, an ancient crystal vase, lying on the floor. After an inspection, however, they discovered the vase had escaped the incident without the merest scratch – a miracle in itself as the vase was huge and the thud they heard as it fell had been resounding. Still, counting their blessings, they replaced the undamaged vase and returned to bed.

The following evening, Frank was in his study working and Jane was ironing in their bedroom. And, once again, **thud!** Both ran to the lounge and were met with the exact same scene from the night before. And, once again, the vase was intact.

Again, they replaced the vase and returned to the jobs they were doing prior to this incident.

The following evening, at the same time, it happened again. Assuming vibrations of some sort were causing the vase to fall to the floor, they decided not to push their luck. The vase couldn't possibly continue to fall and remain unscathed each time so they moved it to a safer location.

The next day was Jane's birthday. Frank sent her a beautiful bouquet of flowers, very fitting for such a priceless and sentimental vase. Forgetting about the three falls, Jane arranged the flowers in the vase and replaced it in its new location.

Ten full nights passed without incident.

After this time, the flowers began to die and so Jane threw them out, washed the vase and again replaced it.

That evening, the vase fell to the floor – undamaged once again. At last, the young newlyweds began to think there was something amiss here.

The exact same incident happened night after night. Jane was so afraid the vase would break that she moved it around the room many times, leaving a cushion directly underneath.

A few weeks passed and Jane, as planned, bid farewell to her colleagues as she began a new career elsewhere. She was showered with gifts, cards and flowers.

Arriving home that evening, Jane put the flowers in the vase. That night, nothing happened. In fact, the next 16 nights were quiet – the vase never once fell to the ground.

The next time it happened was the very evening when Jane once again discarded the dead flowers.

Becoming increasingly suspicious, Jane would alternate between having the vase filled with flowers and having the vase completely empty. The vase, she stressed to me, was solid, a good weight, so she had ruled out the possibility that the weightlessness caused by the lack of flowers could be responsible for the vase's continuous falling.

This is all a few years ago now, but the answer to this query was straightforward.

When Jane related the events to her parents she was told that the vase had belonged to Jane's grandmother, who in turn had inherited it from her mother – Jane's great-grandmother. She had never met the old lady but was told that she loved her garden, flowers and plants, and was more often than not seen out in her garden picking the huge variety of blooms she had grown over the years.

It was clear, to me anyway, that Jane and her husband were not alone in their new marital home, but they had a spirit with them – the spirit of Jane's great-grandmother. And her way of proving she was with them was to cause the vase to fall.

Breaking Jane's vase wasn't her intention. She just loved to see the vase filled with flowers, as it was while she was alive. Jane now ensures the vase is never empty.

Could the moral of this story be that heaven does not have a florist's shop?

Alec's Exam

Years ago, I had a friend called Alec, whom I still think about with fondness. I remember an amazing story he told me – one of my first experiences of someone relating an encounter to me. We were only teenagers but Alec's story has remained in my mind all these years.

When he was only 13 or 14, Alec lost his father. He had adored his dad, although I believe their relationship was less than affectionate. I know my friend just wanted to be loved by his dad, or at least to hear the words that his dad loved him. Alec senior wasn't a demonstrative man – in fact, as a very young child, I was always slightly frightened of him!

A few years after his father's death, Alec called me and we met, as we often did, for a chat. I immediately noticed there was something different about my friend. He looked happy. He had a glow I'd never really seen before, not before his father's death and certainly not since.

Alec excitedly began to tell me what had happened. He told me his father had come to him, firstly in a dream. For days he remembered the dream but thought little of its meaning. A dream to him was a dream. However, arriving home from school one day after a particularly difficult exam, Alec flopped onto the sofa with his feet up. Suddenly he sat bolt upright – he just sensed his father was around and knew he'd get a telling off for sprawling. It had become a bit of a private joke between Alec and his siblings. When dad was out, they'd sprawl. When he was home, they would sit upright. As soon as their father left the room, they'd laugh and resume sprawl position.

Alec looked over to where his father usually sat and was dumbfounded to see his father sitting there. He described his dad as 'looking perfectly alive'. There was no grey mist around him. He was not opaque. He was just normal, just as he had been when he was alive.

Alec senior began to talk. He told Alec how proud he was of him and that, despite feeling nervous about the day's exam, he had in fact passed with flying colours. He even told him the exact score he would receive.

At this point I was still a little sceptical but Alec continued. He told me his father went on to say he had been with him during the exam. In fact, he had sat right next to him – the *only* empty seat in the classroom. That seat, his father continued, should have been filled by a fellow pupil, but the pupil had received bad news that day regarding his grandmother. Alec had wondered why his pal hadn't turned up for the exam.

Alec's father apologized to him for not showing how much he loved him. He assured him he had always loved him and had, so many times, wanted to say the words but just couldn't. He knew this had affected Alec but he was hoping that, as a full adult, he might understand his dad's shortcomings. He leaned over as if to reach out for Alec but then sat back again.

The whole incident apparently lasted only a few minutes. However, Alec was to discover afterwards that these few minutes would change his life forever. He had finally heard the words he had so desperately wanted to hear his father say. He had also learned that his dad was proud of him. Gone was the insecure Alec and in his place was a young man with confidence and an air about him everyone noticed – although very few knew the reason.

Oh, and the empty seat during the exam… Alec discovered the following day that his pal's grandmother had died and that's why he was absent from the exam.

The Yellow Bubble Car

Fiona was a client who saw a yellow bubble car. A phantom one, of course, or I wouldn't be telling her story! And, as you'll see, it wasn't just a car that she saw but also someone very close and dear, which gives one hope of an afterlife. We just don't know if this is the way we'd spend it!

Fiona's beloved father died very suddenly. Her mum struggled to pick up the pieces after 40 years of marriage. One of the things Fiona's mum was determined to do was learn to drive. She found it a huge struggle. She wasn't young, and the average road – even for the most hardened of drivers – can be a ghastly place.

All the time Fiona's mum was learning, she talked of one thing – the bubble car she was going to buy herself. Fiona didn't like to tell her such things had gone out with the ark. She just smiled fondly and thought this was a wonderful thing, and she'd have to guide her mum to a Mini when the time came.

The time didn't come, however. Fiona's mum died, and Fiona was doubly distressed to lose both parents in so short a time. For a while, Fiona couldn't bring herself to think or speak of anything. Bubble cars in particular. The more she thought about what her mum was hiding, about how she had pretended that all was well since the sad loss of the man who had shared her life for all those years, the more upsetting it was to be reminded of those efforts to put on a brave face. Because that was all they were.

So about six weeks after her mum's death, Fiona was greatly surprised to be forced to brake suddenly because of the car that had just swerved into her path. A yellow bubble car, no less. Fiona was intrigued. How very strange to see it there, right in her path, when she and her mum had talked about it so often. Of course, Fiona was a little angry too. After all, she'd had to brake suddenly. And all because of the silly elderly woman driver who didn't know how to stop in a side street. 'Wait a moment,' Fiona now said to herself. 'That wasn't just any elderly lady at the wheel.' It was her mum!

As the car sped off, the woman even gave Fiona a cheeky wave. Fiona, her heart pounding in her ears, sped off after her. For these seconds, her mum had come back to life and she had such a wish to talk to her.

All the way along a straight stretch of road, Fiona could see her mum, always just ahead but not quite near enough to catch. Then, all of a sudden, she was near enough. Fiona knew the moment was coming. Both cars pulled up towards the corner. The yellow bubble car went roaring round. Fiona followed suit. Then there was nothing. The yellow car had gone. Fiona stopped. The road was perfectly straight – no other bends for a good mile ahead, or side roads, or anywhere a car could have pulled off. Yet the little bubble car was gone, as completely, Fiona recounted, as if it had vanished into oblivion, gone up in a puff of smoke. Fiona was aghast. That was perhaps for all of two minutes. Then she realized that this was a sign, a very special sign from her mum to show her all was well. There was no need to be distressed.

At last the dream had been achieved. And not just achieved. Fiona's mum was driving in a way that would have done credit to Le Mans. She hadn't just succeeded. She had succeeded with a will. And that was what counted.

'The Pregnancy'

Very early on in my career, I nearly packed the whole thing in! Why? Because I thought I had got it all wrong. The client in question wishes to keep her identity a secret. However, she has allowed me to use her story as it is such a concrete piece of evidence that life does indeed go on after death. This particular story has been told several times but, even after all these years, I clearly remember the details and the devastating effect it had on my client – not to mention almost on my career!

We'll call her Fiona and she lives in St Andrews, not far from my home. When Fiona first came to me, probably around 1990, she was aged 46 and was pretty certain she was menopausal. She was experiencing many changes in her body, her menstrual cycle had completely ceased and she didn't feel well within herself. She didn't mention any of this to me but I picked up on how she was feeling. She came to see me because she wanted me to confirm what was wrong with her.

It's often the case that I actually feel physically the client's symptoms and pains – not a pleasant experience! When I described these feelings to Fiona, she looked at me a little strangely and agreed that she was feeling exactly that way. She didn't seem too perturbed and quite blithely told me she was on 'the change'.

At that point, I became very aware of a spirit. I heard the name Isobel and could feel the presence of a female spirit. It was a male spirit's voice, however, that spoke to me. The man proceeded to tell me that Fiona was pregnant but that she didn't know.

Without thinking, I blurted out what I was hearing. I could see Fiona was very agitated by what I was saying – in fact, she was downright annoyed. I passed on several messages from this man, most of which allowed her to identify the spirit as that of her father. She agreed with everything I was saying, *except* for the bit about the pregnancy.

The spirit clearly told me that he had the child in his arms. I found this interesting because I had always believed that life begins at the moment of conception. In my view, even the earliest of foetus is a human being. So I was confused as to what I was being told. If Fiona was pregnant, then surely the foetus was inside her – it couldn't be in two places, so how could it also be in heaven? I've since seen many scenarios in which the spirit of the baby, if it's not to be born – whether that be due to miscarriage or abortion – remains in heaven. I should point out here that I have never had any sign that this is the case with stillbirths.

After talking some more, the consultation ended. I knew Fiona was not one bit happy with me. As I didn't have much confidence in myself or my work at that early stage of my career, I took Fiona's annoyance personally. I was deeply upset that perhaps I had got it wrong. Days went by and I still couldn't shake this dreadful mistake from my mind. However, I had to keep to my diary so I followed my normal routine. Although my confidence had been knocked, I didn't cancel one single appointment.

It was almost three months before I heard from Fiona again. She asked for another appointment as soon as possible. Of course I agreed, and we arranged to meet again two days later. Those two days were a living hell for me. I was so afraid that this was it for my career – the end had come before it had even properly started.

Very nervously, I answered the door to Fiona and we walked, without conversation, to my office. We sat down. I took a deep breath.

'You were right, Katie – I was pregnant! Forty-six years old and pregnant. I genuinely thought I was beginning the change of life.'

Fiona then apologized and admitted that she hadn't been terribly flattering about me and my work (and that's putting it mildly), and had told a number of people what I had told her and how wrong I was. To this day I can still see her face and how genuinely sorry she was.

Fiona explained that she'd had a termination as she was just too overwhelmed by the fact that she was pregnant. Her children were almost grown and the last thing she wanted was another baby. She also told me that she had always been so against abortion but that she felt it wouldn't have been fair to bring an unwanted baby into the world. I knew from her eyes how sad she was about her decision, but I also knew she felt she had done the right thing.

And it is for that reason that Fiona wishes her identity to be protected.

We spoke more about the spirit of her father, who was there that day too. This time I couldn't only hear him, I could also see his face vividly, as if he were alive. I remember thinking how large his nose was! Again, he had the baby in his arms, so I was able to reassure Fiona that her baby was in capable hands. At that point in time, this was something I merely surmised and hoped was true. I didn't have the experience or the knowledge I do now to know that this was very much the case.

The most amazing thing for me that day was when Fiona's father began to leave. I swear he winked at me – a sort of 'knowing' wink, as if telling me something with his eyes.

I now firmly believe what he was trying to say was that the baby *was* safe and that she was in good hands.

The Piper Alpha

As a nation, we will never forget the dreadful tragedy on the oil rig, Piper Alpha. So many lives were lost and so many lives were changed forever by the enormity of the tragedy.

I was carrying out consultations for a group of three women. The first two were completed with relative ease and without complication. When the third girl came in, however, I immediately saw a heart-shaped pendant around her neck. Like a rabbit in the headlights of a car, I almost froze as I watched the pendant grow larger and larger. I know it was only increasing in size in my mind, but it was quite a harrowing experience. I knew instantly that the pendant had some significance on my client, and that the significance was enormous.

I didn't hesitate in telling my client what I had seen but her reaction wasn't that unusual. I did, however, notice that she became very sad-looking. Her eyes took on a faraway look – hard to describe, but they just looked so terribly sad.

As I began tuning into my client, making small talk as is often the case at this stage in the consultation, I became aware of the smell of smoke. I was frightened when I then began to see flames – huge flames – all blowing in different directions. The flames grew larger and, as they did so, I also became aware of the sound of waves. The sound grew in intensity, as did the flames. I was thoroughly confused. How could I see fire and yet also hear water? I began to feel a sense of overwhelming fear and panic. I knew my face was breaking out in a sweat as I sat in front of my client.

I knew I couldn't go on. Something dreadful was happening. I could hear screams, and terror was building up inside me. The entire scenario in front of me was one I'll never forget. The only word to describe it was horrifying, quite, quite horrifying.

It was then that I began to hear a voice, 'Peter … is … in … a … safe … place!' The voice was, in my mind, very staggered and difficult to understand, but I realized this was due to the other noises I was hearing. It wasn't that the spirit was speaking oddly, more that I was hearing so many other things at the same time.

I was so taken up with what was going on that I never noticed the tears pouring down my client's face. I was talking quickly, my fear evident. The whole scene vanished very suddenly, despite appearing in a much more progressive manner.

'Peter is in a safe place,' I told my client. I asked her if she knew what I was talking about. The poor girl cried harder at that point. Clearly she was devastated over something.

As it transpired, Peter was my client's husband. She was widowed some two years earlier when her husband was one of the many victims on board the Piper Alpha platform. Peter's body was never found (to my knowledge it still hasn't been found), and my client's biggest fear, she told me, was that if her husband's body hadn't been found, would that mean he wasn't at peace – wasn't in heaven?

I was able to reassure her (and myself) that Peter must surely be in heaven. The spirit clearly gave me Peter's name and the message that he was in a safe place.

And the locket? The locket contained a photograph of my client and Peter on their wedding day.

The Brooch

Is it possible for items to attract a spiritual presence? I'd say it was, given the amount of stories that come my way about messages being passed on through them. I can even think of one where someone picked up a violin and proceeded, out the blue, to play the owner's favourite tune – the deceased owner that is! But the following story is quite unusual in that the item concerned had such a strong presence attached to it.

Mrs Gair came to me for a reading. I could instantly see she was a very sad lady. Her husband had been working over-seas, in Germany, and she had been expecting him home. But he didn't come. Instead, the day before he was due to return home, he suffered a fatal heart attack in the street. This happened outside a jeweller's shop. Earlier he had gone on a shopping trip, hoping to buy something for his wife – a special present to make up for having been away so long.

Almost as soon as Mrs Gair came into the room, I could sense there was a powerful male presence with her. There was no doubt from the way I described him to her that this was her husband, and she was pleased – as pleased as she could be under the circumstances. She seemed comforted to know he was with her still, and in many ways was still see-ing to her welfare. But an even stronger feeling enveloped me as I began to see a brooch.

To see spirits is one thing, but the 'ghost' of a brooch didn't seem quite right. It was, however, a beautiful piece of jewellery, quite highly detailed, in an unusual shape and set with a variety of stones. To be honest, it wasn't like anything I'd ever seen before, and I told her so. I sensed Mrs Gair had been given the brooch quite recently. Her husband was showing it to me very clearly and it was obvious he was the one who had given her the brooch. What I couldn't under-stand was how she was in possession of the brooch and yet her husband was able to show it to me. So I asked her.

The answer to this was simple. Mr Gair had bought the brooch especially for her. He had gone shopping with a col-league but they had split up. Mr Gair went into the jeweller's and his colleague went into an adjacent shop. When his colleague came out of the shop, he was shocked to see Mr Gair lying on the ground. He was alive, but only just. He died minutes later.

At the hospital, the staff gave Mr Gair's colleague the brooch, along with his other possessions. And upon his arrival home, explaining what had happened, he gave the brooch to Mrs Gair. It was a gift from her husband but he, of course, was unable to give it to her himself.

Mrs Gair had not felt able to wear the brooch. Numb with shock, she had put it in a drawer. After leaving my office, having received the message from her husband and realizing how near he was to her, she went home, took the brooch out of its box, unhooked the clasp and pinned it on.

The Wheelchair

A client came to see me for a reading and had only stepped in the door when it became obvious to me that she had brought along a 'friend'. It was a spirit who in turn was dragging an empty wheelchair. This seemed quite unusual – ridiculous in fact – even for my line of work. So I asked her, 'Who's the person with the wheelchair?' She didn't know. She couldn't think of anyone – family member or friend – who even pushed a wheelchair, let alone sat in one.

The only connection she could make with my outrageous remark was that her mother used a wheelchair but she was very much alive. Not in the best of health, it was true, but alive and in a nursing home.

'Well, that's very strange,' I said. 'This person is quite impatient. They're obviously waiting for someone.'

This still wasn't much help to the client, so we moved on. We talked about a number of things to do with her life, and as we did the spirit vanished. I no longer had the sense of anyone there with the chair or otherwise, which was a bit of a relief. I didn't want spirits cluttering up the place with wheelchairs!

The consultation itself was a productive one and my client left feeling fairly certain where her life was heading. I couldn't, however, shake this overwhelming feeling of terrible sadness. My client knew this but as neither of us could explain it, I guess we pushed it to the side. I said goodbye to the client, presuming that the emotions I continued to feel would leave me before long.

In the meantime, the client went home. She'd been home only a few minutes when the phone rang. It was the nursing home. As I've already said, her mother wasn't in the best of health, but when the client last saw her, she was fine. Now the nurse in charge was ringing to say there was bad news. Her mother had taken a turn for the worse. Could my client just pop round?

When she arrived, it turned out that the charge nurse had wanted to spare her. Her mother had, in fact, died earlier, before the phone call was made. It was all very sudden but the old lady had gone peacefully, sitting up tranquilly and almost happily, in the chair she had asked to be wheeled to the bed.

The Hero Ghost

Are people who commit suicide allowed to meet with their loved ones? I used to believe this wasn't the case, that these poor, tormented souls were to stay in outer darkness, being denied this vital joy. I don't know where I got that belief from – it stems back many years. However, I no longer hold that view. I have had too much evidence that the spirit can communicate and be reunited with loved ones, no matter what the cause of death – natural, after great ill health or suicide. I am certain, too, that one particular spirit didn't want his beloved wife to join him until the time was absolutely right. Selflessly, he realized that the time wasn't right for them to be together and that he would have to wait.

Mrs Greville had been devastated by the death of her husband. He had died suddenly at the age of 60, having been perfectly fit and healthy. When she first visited me, she was in a state of deep shock. How could this have happened? How could he have been fine one moment and gone the next? Sadly, these were questions I felt ill-equipped to answer. His death was so recent – only six weeks had passed – it was no wonder she was in such a state. So much so, I found it impossible to tune in to her. I was being blocked by the sheer, overwhelming grief she was suffering. I suggested she come back to see me in a few months, allowing time for both spirit and bereaved to come to terms with their separation.

Mrs Greville did come back. Only by that time she was even more distressed. Nothing in her life had any meaning. Her thoughts were consumed with what she had lost. The only difference between now and six months previously – and a very worrying difference it was too – was that on this occasion I could see her husband. In his hand was a calendar, a large one, with the dates displayed in prominent black. November 16th was the one he wanted me to see. Then he pointed to his wife's hands. In one hand she held a glass of water – her other hand was cupped but I could clearly see she was holding a pill bottle! It was obvious he was warning me. She intended taking her own life and there was nothing anyone could do to prevent it. No one, that is, except him.

I told Mrs Greville exactly what I was seeing. I felt so strongly, and for reasons I didn't fully understand, that no matter what she was contemplating, this was something he didn't want her to do. I told her if she did end her life, she might not see her husband again. I said that, unsure if it was true or not. It just seemed that he so wanted her to live. He had left her suddenly. Her death would only increase his sense of misery and that of their family.

I did not mention dates, simply that I believed her to be in danger. I knew that a great deal of what I said went in one ear and out the other. However, in December of that year, Mrs Greville telephoned me. My immediate feeling was one of relief. I thought, 'At least she's still alive.'

She told me she had been very low, so low she had seriously considered taking her own life. She had it all worked out. She met with her lawyer, putting all her affairs in order. She wrote individual letters for each of the family, and had even left a letter detailing her funeral wishes. She then filled a glass with water and poured out a handful of pills.

Thankfully, right at the last minute, she had remembered my words, 'If you do this, you will not see your husband again.'

As she continued to speak, I could sense she had turned a corner. She would never stop missing him and the pain she felt after he died would be with her always. However, I could tell that she seemed to know her life had to go on. Maybe she knew there was some reason she had to wait, something else perhaps, that was still to happen in her life.

These next words are ones I shall never forget.

I asked her, 'Out of curiosity, when was this exactly? Can you remember?' Her reply was, 'It was a few weeks ago. In November. November 16th to be precise.'

The Tidy Ghost

I'm actually quite fond of this story. In fact, I only wish there were more spirits like this one about. Even as I write it, I see shades of old fairy tales, where certain castles had a friendly brownie or elf, and we all know what we can sometimes win Brownie points for, don't we? Yes, tidying up. Only in this instance the lady concerned didn't have a brownie in her house. She had her husband. In spirit form of course.

Long after her appointment time, Mrs Ball finally arrived – in a state of utter harrassment. She reminded me a bit of myself in that it was clear she never had a minute to herself. 'Bustle bustle' was all around her, and almost as soon as she sat down I could sense two things. One, she had been busy doing housework right up until she left home to attend her appointment. And two, she had not arrived entirely alone. I sensed she had brought someone with her, someone who couldn't be seen.

I felt quite sure she was a widow and the spirit she had brought with her was that of her deceased husband. It seemed to me he was the most likely candidate, although I had no idea of the circumstances of his death, or indeed, at this stage, if he was in fact deceased. I knew only that this presence was male. However, the more I described him, the clearer it seemed to me that this was her husband.

My client seemed a little sceptical, perhaps afraid to believe he was there. She clearly required proof – a fairly common reaction in some readings. So I tried to delve a little deeper to see if he could give me something so concrete that his poor, bereft wife would know for sure her beloved husband was near to her.

'Were you ironing before you came out today?' I asked, finding my question comical.

'Yes,' she said. 'That's why I was late.'

'Were you ironing a white duvet cover?' I asked, amused at what I was hearing.

'Goodness, how do you know that?' By now she was becoming quite astonished. In all honesty, I was a little astonished myself.

When you're dealing with the spirit world you think the messages that come over will be earth-shattering. In fact, that is very seldom the case. And there was such 'ordinary domesticity' about this one.

I explained to her that I was hearing everything from her husband. Her face went several shades of pale as I continued. 'You didn't finish what you were doing,' I said, quite clearly seeing, in my mind's eye, a pile of neatly folded ironing lying atop the ironing board.

I then told her that when she got home she would find the white duvet cover in her bedroom. I laughed as I told her not to expect the cover to be on the duvet, but that she would find it lying on her bed.

'That's impossible,' she told me. To be honest, I also felt a little unsure of what I was saying.

'Your husband's going to put it there,' I told her, feeling less confident than I sounded. 'It's his way of letting you know he is with you.'

After discussing many other things, my client left, promising to phone me if what I had said about the duvet cover was true.

Later that night the phone rang. I recognized the voice immediately. It was Mrs Ball. 'I just wanted to tell you,' she said. 'I went home and it was all exactly as you said. The cover was on the corner of the bed – not made up – but lying there, ironed and folded the way I had left it. I know for a fact that I left the cover on the ironing board!'

Mrs Ball now had clear evidence her husband wasn't far from her – something she so desperately needed to know. And, in heaven, as he had been on earth, he was such a meticulously tidy soul.

Sweet Caroline

Caroline immediately admitted that she had never consulted a paranormal expert before so would I forgive her if she seemed nervous? She told me that, quite frankly, she was terrified. I talked calmly to her, telling her there was nothing to worry about. I would be gentle with her!

Minutes into the consultation, I became aware of a spirit. I knew this spirit was anxious, too, as its body language was uncomfortable. It quickly became clear to me that the spirit was that of a young male. His cause of death initially seemed a bit of a mystery, but as I slowly began to relay his words to Caroline, it became increasingly obvious.

First he spoke of his 'beloved' motorbike (I immediately felt Caroline's tension at the mention of *that* word). Gary's name was mentioned and again I told Caroline that. She merely nodded, looking grief-stricken. 'Gary's body is whole again, Caroline,' I tentatively told her. 'What is not whole is his conscience. He seems devastated by his death.'

At this point I thought that of course he would be devastated. Here was a handsome young man, his life in front of him – a whole life tragically cut short in a horrifying way. 'Gary says you must stop fretting and regretting that you didn't view his body. This was his wish. Although you were broken-hearted at his sudden death, I know more sadness followed when you changed your mind about seeing his body but were refused permission. Gary would not have wanted you to see him like that. The only person to see Gary in his coffin was his brother, and that was purely for

23

identification purposes. No one got to see him, not you, nor any of his close friends and none of his family. He was in a dreadful mess physically.'

I can only describe Caroline's face by saying it was chalk white. She gave a tiny sob and I begged her not to hold back the tears. I told her crying was a hugely important part of mourning and that she was doing herself no favours by holding her feelings in. Everyone was worried for her. Gary was worried for her!

'I love him, Katie, I truly loved him!' I remember Caroline's broken words to this day. Oh, how they tug on my heartstrings. All I wanted to do was go over to Caroline, put my arms around her and take her very severe, almost tangible pain away from her.

However, I continued to relay what Gary was saying. 'Did Karen make it?' he asked. He seemed to have no way of knowing whether Karen was alive or dead.

'He seems worried about Karen. He's asking if she made it? What does he mean by that?'

It turned out Karen was his pillion passenger – a friend from his early childhood. Caroline just nodded. I passed the vague message back to Gary, assuring him that Karen had made it.

'I told him not to buy that motorbike,' Caroline almost spat the words. She seemed angry now, angry that her loved one had been taken. I still wasn't 100 per cent sure what the exact cause of death was, although I was fitting the pieces together. At this point I heard the screeching of tyres, then a sudden bang, several different types of screams and breaking glass. The sound of metal hitting metal made me cringe.

Then everything went silent. I knew for sure now that Gary had been on his motorbike and had fatally crashed.

I then heard him ask about the van. As soon as he mentioned the van, two pictures came into my mind. I saw a small, red, rusty-looking van. I also saw a little girl wearing a turquoise dress and hat. She couldn't have been more than four or five.

'Did Gary hit a van?' Caroline nodded. 'Was there a little girl in the van wearing a turquoise dress?' Again, Caroline nodded. 'Do you know where they are now, Caroline?' Caroline looked up, tears streaming down her pained face and spoke in a childlike voice, 'The little girl escaped with only cuts and bruises.'

'And her father?' I blurted out, not knowing who was in the van with the little girl.

'He broke a few bones but he's alive.'

'Is Gary in any pain?' Caroline asked. I heard him reply that he was free of pain. He proceeded to tell me that he knew very little at the end – it had all happened so quickly. All he remembers was seeing the little girl as the van swerved into his path. He didn't see the driver, and after that he only vaguely remembers lying at the side of the road, obviously very injured but feeling extremely calm and happy. 'My gran was there at the accident,' Gary told me. I passed this on to Caroline, who told me that Gary had been devastated by the death of his beloved gran a matter of only months before his own death.

I explained to Caroline that Gary did not have to make the journey to heaven alone, that his gran had come to take him personally.

As Gary began to fade, I heard Neil Diamond singing 'Sweet Caroline'. But, I didn't know whether to tell Caroline this for fear it was gimmicky – it was an obvious song for a girl named Caroline. However, I did decide to tell her, and she said that it wasn't corny at all. She could relate to it entirely as Gary had sung that song many times since they met. It was his favourite karaoke song (even before meeting Caroline), and he sang it to her less than a week before he died.

So 'Sweet Caroline' did indeed have significant meaning for my client.

Dearly Loved David

Mother and daughter sat opposite me, both crying sorely for the son and brother they had lost. David had been murdered, his life cut short before he had even reached the age of 20.

The first time these two clients came to see me, I couldn't get David at all but I did manage to make contact with another young boy who relayed messages of David's arrival and how he was in the throes of his healing process. This explained why David himself couldn't come through. At this point, I was unsure if my clients felt any comfort.

A few months later, however, they came back. This time David was as large as life (pardon the irony). I knew someone was there because I was met with the very strong aroma of men's aftershave. This wasn't just any old after-shave either – it was much stronger than your everyday aftershave. I asked the significance of this and was informed that David wore cologne imported from the Far East. And the two agreed that it was indeed very potent and powerful stuff!

I then began to relay various messages from David. He told me about the bike race, which my clients watched him compete in a matter of weeks before his untimely death. I almost laughed when David told me about his dental appointment and how he had gone to great lengths to avoid it!

This cryptic message was explained when David's mum told me that David had a dental appointment, the first in over 10 years, on the very day of his funeral – the appointment was scheduled for 2pm. What did happen instead that day – and at exactly 2pm – was that David's body was lowered into the ground. No matter how poignant that sounds, David's mum and sister managed to smile at the thought. They told me how terrified David had been of the dentist and how he had agreed to go purely because one tooth had given up the fight. It had been neglected for so long that it had to be extracted.

I then began to see an image of a motorbike. Standing in front of the bike was a tall guy, not unlike David facially. He was older than David but there was a definite strong resemblance. I could see the man's face quite clearly – he was speaking into a mobile phone and, for some reason, I just felt that the conversation he was having related in some way to the motorbike.

I then heard David speak again. This time he told me, 'Colin has sold his motorbike.' Again, I relayed this to my clients, but they shook their heads, telling me Colin, David's best friend, wouldn't sell his motorbike – he loved it. However, I was convinced and stuck to my guns. Colin had sold, or was in the process of selling, the bike. My clients were still unconvinced.

They telephoned me that same evening to tell me that Colin *had* sold his motorbike – that very afternoon in fact! Apparently, some of his friends were going on a biking holiday and Colin couldn't go as his bike wasn't fit for the long journey.

The buyer had begged Colin to sell his bike to him. When Colin refused, the guy was so desperate, he offered nearly double the bike's value. And who could refuse such an offer?

The Not-so-holy Nun

One thing that never ceases to amaze me is how forgiving some people can be. I'd like to think I am the forgiving type, but as a Leo, I must admit I find it hard more often than not. However, I am often humbled by stories of forgiveness I read and hear, as well as by some of my direct experiences in my work. One such story has stuck in my mind for years. I remember this one vividly, as if it were only yesterday.

To protect her identity, I shall call my client Jane. I immediately felt Jane was sincere and genuinely nice. She was relaxed and easy to talk to. I felt instantly comfortable with her. And yet her eyes were sad, distant-looking. I suspected she was hiding a gruesome memory, probably from her childhood.

We talked a great deal about where Jane's life should be going and which moves were necessary to ensure she stood a chance of finding the correct path fate intended for her. A number of spirits became clear and I duly passed on the messages they gave. Nothing startling – a great-grandmother who described herself and the circumstances around her death; an old friend from school saying she was happy, and so on.

Throughout all this, however, I was extremely interested in another spirit who was reluctant, I felt, to make his or her presence known. All I could hear at first were their footsteps – as they walked, one foot came down heavier than the other. And, for some reason, I felt this spirit not only had a bad leg but also wore a strange-looking boot. The boot seemed an important piece of the jigsaw but when I heard why, I was utterly horrified.

As the consultation drew near its end, I sensed the spirit was much closer. I was then met with an image of a nun's habit, beneath which came into view the boot I'd been hearing. The nun began to cry – quite uncontrollably. I began to pass all of this on to Jane. The nun interrupted, repeatedly saying how sorry she was, and could Jane ever forgive her. 'Please forgive me,' were words spoken with real feeling.

When I put all of this to Jane, she too had tears in her eyes. In my naivety, I could not fathom why a nun would have any cause to plead for forgiveness. Nuns were good people, weren't they? As it turned out, this particular nun had been anything but a good person while alive. She had, in fact, been a very cruel woman.

I asked Jane the significance of the foot and whether she knew of a nun or of someone with a club foot. She told me that she had been raised in an orphanage run by nuns. One nun in particular – this spirit – did have a club foot. In fact, it was by using her club foot to kick or hold the children down that she administered her punishment.

I expressed my dismay. Surely children didn't deserve such a cruel punishment? Jane readily agreed but she also told me – and it is the way she said this which has stuck so firmly in my mind – that she didn't resent the nun. She wasn't angry with the nun because she believes she knew no other kind of life. She was raised in the same way and therefore knew no alternative. Yes, she was strict and yes, she was cruel, but Jane forgave her.

I found this one particularly sad because it was clear that it wasn't until this nun reached heaven that she realized her cruel and severe ways were wrong. She was obviously remorseful but I wonder just how many children she affected as badly, and how many didn't grow up with Jane's marvellous forgiving nature.

Jane is now a mother herself and, as you can imagine, is a wonderful, caring and patient parent.

The Elephant Man

I have to say that I find difficulty in using this subheading for the following story. My more sensitive side feels it's cruel. However, as you read on you will see why I have decided to use it.

Linda Millar came to see me in July of 1999. The minute she walked in, I knew she had experienced a great loss. Her eyes were dark pools of sadness. I was instantly drawn into a feeling of immense grief, pain and loss. Linda had clearly lost someone she loved deeply. But there was more – at this point I didn't know what, but somehow I knew I was about to find out.

After the usual brief small talk, I suddenly blurted out, seemingly from nowhere, 'Tommy is here and at last you can have your questions answered.' Tommy was clearly the person Linda had lost – the one she was in mourning for.

From the very outset, I felt left out of this consultation. I say this because Tommy so desperately wanted to pass on crucial messages to Linda, and Linda even more desperately wanted to hear his messages.

I heard Tommy speak clearly, 'I *really* looked like the Elephant Man! I didn't want you to see me looking like that.' I remember being intrigued by the way he emphasized that he 'really looked like the Elephant Man'.

I passed this on to Linda who began to cry uncontrollably. Then Tommy said, 'I remember nothing. I felt no pain. In fact, I slept through the whole thing!' After passing that on to Linda, she seemed calmer. She looked relieved. I must surely have looked perplexed!

It was my turn to ask for some answers. 'What does all this mean?' Linda went on to tell me that her beloved husband of only two years had died in a house fire – in their beautiful new marital home in fact. She had been at work and received a call halfway through her shift advising her of the tragedy. She raced to the hospital, terrified, fearing the worst. The worst was confirmed minutes after she arrived. Her darling husband had died in the fire. He was dead before they got to him.

The consultant at the hospital refused to let her see Tommy, a decision backed by other senior staff, police and members of her family. Linda admitted to me that she was just as devastated by that as she was by her husband's death. She could not get over the fact that she never got to say goodbye and then was denied the right to see him in his coffin. They'd told her he was just too badly burned and that it was deemed entirely for her own good that she did not view his body.

When she asked if he had suffered, the consultant merely shook his head, admitting that they had no way of knowing. Poor Linda had visions several times a day of her beloved husband screaming, terrified, knowing he was locked in a blazing house with no way out. She had nightmares of him trying to escape but failing to do so. She imagined the fear, the pain, the awfulness of it all.

But now, on the day of her consultation, without prompting and without me actually having a clue about what was going on, Linda was finally told the truth about what happened that fateful night.

I asked Linda if she thought it a bit cruel of Tommy to say he looked like the Elephant Man – surely he couldn't have been *that* bad. But Linda merely laughed and told me that Tommy had been a vain man, and as he had bushy hair, he spent a long time fixing it. He would joke in the morning, when his hair was all over the place, that he looked like the Elephant Man. Apparently, one side in particularly was very bushy and stuck out much more than the other side. So Linda reassured me that Tommy wasn't being hard on himself, that he did in fact use the term jokingly.

I wonder just how badly marked Tommy was. It must have been bad if the medics refused to allow Linda to see him. At least she now knows he didn't suffer, that he didn't even know about the fire until after he died.

What comfort Linda must have felt that day. And thank goodness there *is* life after death, otherwise Linda would have gone on for years enduring the most horrendous nightmares and day visions, wrongly assuming that her husband had suffered a torturous death when, in fact, he had simply stayed asleep, quite oblivious to the blaze about to take his life.

Jim, My Gay Spirit

Messages from spirits come in all shapes and sizes – all styles and all sorts of different, unimaginable formats. One, which caused me and my client great hilarity, sticks in my mind. I still smile about it today, some four years after it occurred.

Jim from Glasgow arrived for his scheduled appointment. Without wishing to sound demeaning, he was 'obviously' gay. In fact, Jim took this as a compliment. To say that Jim was camp would be an understatement. He was clearly a colour freak, as I counted at least six different bold, bright colours on the clothes he was wearing. And his nature was equally colourful.

Jim was a delightful man but a sad man. He put on a brave face for the world but underneath his gaiety (pardon the pun) lay a very unhappy and lonely man.

Jim had lost his lifelong partner, also named Jim, just a few years earlier. My client wasn't a young man. In fact, he was well over 60. In his words, being gay in those days wasn't as easy as it is today. He had only ever known one partner and vowed he would end his days alone, as no one could ever replace his Jim. I believed him.

Jim told me his reason for visiting was that he so desperately needed to have proof that his partner was near him. I instantly told him that of course he was because I firmly believe the dead are so very near us. But Jim told me he desperately needed proof, real proof. He had visited many other psychics, clairvoyants and the like, but no one had given him anything of substance. 'What makes him think I can', I wondered. However, I knew I would try very hard because it was clear to me that this colourful, amusing chap in front of me was aching for some sign that his lover was nearby.

I didn't have to wait long, for within a split second, the loudest, most gregarious, most delightful spirit joined us. In an acutely feminine voice, I heard words to the effect of 'Why did you do that to the lounge? What possessed you? And those curtains, tuh! Those curtains.' I could all but see this spirit's hands rise in disbelief. 'And get that bloody awful wheelchair out of our bedroom – I hated it when I was in it, so don't make me have to look at it every minute of the day!'

Jim burst out laughing. This indeed sounded like his lifetime partner. He admitted that Jim was bossy, loud and brash, liked his own way and more, but he was so, so thrilled that he had come over.

Jim had kept his lover's wheelchair – not for any sinister reason but because he felt it was such a part of him. Clearly the other Jim did not want it to be a part of him. My client told me it would be removed as soon as he got home – to his newly decorated lounge.

Spirit Jim had much more traditional taste. Although client Jim admitted he really hadn't minded, their home was largely decorated to spirit Jim's taste. After his death, Jim redecorated and completely changed the look of their home. It was evident that his dead lover did not approve, yet everything he said, albeit in a somewhat imperious manner, was really quite light-hearted. I somehow knew to take no offence from the spirit's words, and clearly so did my client.

My client was by now much happier and the entire consultation was taken up by the spirit giving orders, making affectionate comments, then giving more orders. Clearly the two had loved one another deeply. We laughed a lot, and when Jim left, I thankfully saw that not only were his clothes colourful but his face, his eyes and undoubtedly his heart and soul also had a great deal more colour than when he'd arrived.

If you're reading this, Jim, I hope you are coping with Jim's orders, even now, beyond the grave.

Wartime Sweethearts

A lot of people wrongly assume that my kind of work is sought only by 'women of a certain age'. This is certainly not the case. My clients are of all ages and come from many different walks of life. I have teenage boys, old men, professionals and manual workers among my clientele. So why am I telling you this? Read on …

Bertie came to me at a ripe old age. He was an agile man for his age, although arthritis had made him smaller as the years went by. The lines on his face defied his age but his heart was worn out, both physically and emotionally. His eyes were sad. In fact, I'd say his eyes were pretty dead. Gone was the sparkle I immediately saw when I imagined him as a much younger man.

Bertie came into my office and sat down. I was about to close the door behind him when I stopped as I felt the presence of another. I waited and unseeingly allowed the other person to follow us in. As they did so, I was engulfed by a smell I couldn't name but which reminded me, for some reason, of my childhood.

This 'other person' floated past me. I heard her say, 'Hello dear, I'm Elsie' as clearly as Bertie had said, 'Hi Katie, I'm Bertie'. But no, I didn't go as far as to pull up another chair!

Naturally, I described everything I was seeing to my client, and to my surprise he told me he already knew. He told me Elsie had been his wife for most of his adult life. Together they had survived a war, the raising of seven children and many other hardships life had thrown at them. But they were strong and as much in love more than 60 years later as they had been the day they met.

Visions crossed my mind, many going back to when they were young. I simply sat and narrated to Bertie everything I was seeing. I saw their children, now grown, as little people playing in a park (this particular scene flashed before me many times and clearly I was seeing them over many years as the children were bigger each time). Bertie smiled at this as he remembered well the park I was seeing. He told me that the park no longer existed and that it had been turned into a housing estate.

One very profound scene involved Bertie as a handsome young man, dressed in war uniform. The couple looked sad, which was to be expected, but there was something about Elsie's eyes that made me more inquisitive. I asked Bertie why I felt extremely sad, apart from the fact that he was going to war. My query was answered when Bertie told me that the day he left to go to war was the same day Elsie buried her mother.

If this story serves to teach me anything, it is that death needn't be final. Bertie believes he has lost his wife – at least he's lost her body – but he firmly believes her soul and everything she was inside is with him every waking moment. He still misses her, even though he is comforted by the presence of her spirit.

Sisters

Caroline had been troubled for some time. This was by someone or something that seemed to be following her everywhere. She had never believed in the spirit world. To her it was nonsense dreamed up by people with vivid imaginations who wanted to believe that their loved ones hadn't left them. That was why she was so surprised when she first sensed that the shadow flitting round herself didn't seem to belong to anything. This was just the start.

Caroline found herself haunted by someone who picked up pieces of jewellery from places where she had left them and put them down elsewhere, by a shadow which went into rooms ahead of her and put on the television – a ghost which seemed to know exactly what she was thinking. Caroline was terrified.

When she first came to me I was a little sceptical. Caroline lived alone and I thought she might be suffering from an over-exuberant imagination – one that saw ghosts in every corner. But then I became convinced. As the reading progressed, it seemed to me Caroline did have a spirit round her, and this was someone she should have known well, because it was a sister.

The trouble was, Caroline said she didn't have a sister. She was, she said, 'an only one'. This didn't seem possible. The girl I was seeing was exactly like Caroline. In looks, in height, in weight, they might have been twins. I was amazed she could say there was no one in her family like this, that her parents had never had another child. What was more, it was coming across clearly to me that this sister had chosen to look out for Caroline since she moved away from home.

'But you must have had a sister,' I could only gasp. Like most of us, I hate being wrong, and in this instance Caroline's insistence made me feel like a complete fool. Here I was, having actually set out not believing her story, now saying it was true and a non-existent sister was looking out for her.

I was very glad when Caroline left my office. This was one phantom that didn't exist, a real 'phantom phantom', so to speak. I wanted to go and lie down in a darkened room and forget about ever doing a reading again!

I didn't though. The next day I was back at it, with several new clients. I'd even managed to put Caroline out my mind when the phone rang and there she was. 'You won't believe this,' she said. I confess I actually thought, 'What is it now? More doings of the phantom sister?' – quite uncharacteristically, I must add!

'I expect this won't much surprise you, but I do have a sister. I asked Mum.'

It turned out that Caroline was not an 'only one' after all. There had been a 'first born', a girl who, if she had lived, would have been two years older than Caroline. But she didn't live. She died roughly a day after she was born. Caroline's parents had been devastated. Then Caroline came along. With a typical 'stiff upper lip' they never again discussed the little girl they had lost, throwing all their energies into raising Caroline. And after a while there seemed very little point in mentioning it to her, until Caroline asked.

Yet her sister was very clearly with her. In fact, she had probably always been but was waiting for her moment, for the time when she felt she was needed. That was when she decided to make her presence known and do what every big sister does – look after the little one. It was as if she had decided that even death wasn't going to stop her.

'You must go back for Alison … she needs you'

When Kirsten first came to me, she'd no idea who this phantom Alison was. But she was very disturbed by the thought of her and by what had happened only a month before. So disturbed, she felt she had to seek help, at least to get it off her chest. The experience was so profound, she didn't know where to turn. Although she knew that the people, or rather the spirits of the people, involved were her own dearly loved parents, the confusion was such, she was left wondering if she had imagined it all. I was convinced, however, that she wasn't. When one of the things they said to her came about, what other proof was needed? When you hear this story, I'm sure you'll agree, to quote the bard, 'there are more things in heaven and earth …'.

Kirsten's story begins on Christmas Eve. She had been allowed home from hospital just for the festive season to spend some time with her husband and children. Kirsten had been very ill. So ill that, at one point, staff had feared she would die. Kirsten didn't die, however, but held on bravely. As Christmas approached, she begged to be allowed to go home. All the other members of her family – her beloved parents and grandparents – were dead, so she was especially desperate to be home with those she was devoted to. The hospital staff agreed, and at five o'clock that evening, the taxi carrying her drew up at the door of her house.

She was delighted to be home but she had not been there long when she began to feel unwell. The excitement of the trip had been too much for her and she begged to be allowed to go upstairs and lie down. Her temperature shot up. She became delirious and, as she did, realized she had made a mistake in asking to come home. Downstairs she could hear her husband and children laughing as they set up the table for the next day. Suddenly she felt strongly it was a meal she was never going to see.

As she grew progressively weaker, the room seeming to fade away before her, she attempted to rise from the bed. But she was weak and toppled over. Instead of falling down, however, she was aware of a strange sensation, as if she was floating. Suddenly, she didn't care if she hurt herself. She was too weak to cry out for help. The feeling was wonderful – all her cares were draining away.

A mist grew up round her. As it did she saw that the room was swathed in layers and layers of white tulle – so beautiful, she gasped. Then she became aware of the figure coming towards her. It was her father, as clear as if he was still alive. Behind him, and looking exactly as she remembered him, was her beloved grandfather. Now Kirsten's eyes filled with tears – ones of happiness though. She tried to reach through the mist towards them in the hope of touching their hands, but though they both looked happy enough to see her, her father shook his head. Kirsten remembers clearly the words he said.

'You must go back. You will recover and you've much do to in your life before you can join us. You're to go back for Alison, she needs you.'

Only at that point did Kirsten feel that she was being robbed. 'But I don't know any Alison,' she said. 'Please let me come with you.'

Her father shook his head. Kirsten felt the image fading. Then she must have fallen asleep. She was woken by her husband bringing the children in to show her some of the decorations they had been making for Christmas Day.

Kirsten had no idea whether what she had seen was a dream or not, but for the first time she felt better. The next day passed wonderfully for her and she went back into hospital to be told she was on the mend. She came to me because she wasn't sure. There were things about what had happened she didn't understand. Most importantly, she'd no idea who Alison was. She needed to find out.

'Well, that's not a problem,' I told her. 'I'm surprised you don't know already. My vibes all tell me you're pregnant.'

This was, of course, a great shock to Kirsten. She already had three children and a fourth – well, that would make things difficult, she felt. Was I sure?

'I'm very sure!' I told her. 'What's more, it's a little girl.'

In this respect I was proved right. Kirsten did have a baby daughter, just under eight months later. Naturally, she called her Alison. Even then, as she remembered what had happened on that Christmas Eve, she still had cause to wonder about many things. Had she really been as close to death as all that? Was what she saw a vision of heaven? Did her parents and grandparents really watch over her?

Eventually, as Alison grew into a lovely little girl, there were no doubts. 'That's granddad,' she said one day, pointing out a picture of Kirsten's dad, one that had been taken three months before his death. 'He wasn't well then.'

'Yes,' Kirsten was amazed. 'But how do you know?'

The little girl smiled. 'Because I've met him.'

The Man who Went to his Own Funeral

Old John McFarlane was a very determined man – so determined, in fact, that he went to his own funeral and was seen there by no fewer than four people. I got to hear of it when one of them came to me for a reading.

Since she was his daughter, it seemed natural that Shona would be one of the first to notice the man in respectful black, standing at the fringes of the crowd. He was only there for a second or two but, to quote her own words, 'she knew her own father when she saw him'.

John McFarlane had been ill for some time and had died only a few days earlier. But it seemed he wanted to go to the funeral. Why? It was something I immediately wanted to know. Even before I had put the question, however, Shona told me. 'He wanted to see who was there,' she said. How did she know? Well, apparently, John came to her in a dream two days later and told her. He was a bit of a mischievous charmer. That much I certainly picked up on from the read-ing, where he came over to me and said there was no harm done, he hadn't intended to frighten anyone!

Shona came to see me because she was worried about her mum. Since the funeral, this lady's health had gone downhill – she had seen John that day but that was not the reason for her deterioration in health. With someone as strong-willed as John about, it seemed silly not to ask him. Clear as day, I heard him say, 'She just misses me!' He also kept using the word 'dream'. I believed he was communicating through this medium, using it to tell Shona to get in touch with him, through me, if there was anything worrying her at all.

My own vibes, incidentally, weren't bad. I could see many happy occasions for Shona's family in the future, all with her mum there. This suggested to me that whatever illness her mum had, it was temporary. In this I was proved correct.

The next time Shona contacted me, she was in a state. Her dad had come to her, again in a dream, and explained there was nothing seriously wrong with her mum and she wasn't to worry. But then he had told her he didn't know if he would be back, although he would always watch out for her. It was almost as if he'd got himself into bother by attending his own funeral. I had to admit it was quite daring of him really. In all my work with the paranormal, I'd not come across it very often.

When Shona came for another reading, this time there was no sign of John. He'd quite clearly said his goodbyes to her, several times really, if the appearance at the funeral and the dreams were anything to go by. And, in its way, although his actual appearance at the funeral had been unnerving, it was oddly comforting too.

It had said to Shona that her dad was with her always and that death was only a veil between them. Knowing that had helped her through a difficult time and allowed her to help her mum. In many ways John's appearances were a gift, one she had been grateful to receive.

'Peter Put the Kettle on'

We've all heard of Polly and her little friend Sukey's antics with the kettle, but this is the lesser-known tale of Peter who much pre-ferred 'teasmaids' when it came to boiling up a cup of tea. Peter was the husband of a client of mine. He had been dead for six

months when she came to see me. Although grieving, she had a
secret that made it easier for her to accept Peter's death. This was
the belief that he wasn't really gone. In fact, he'd never been gone.
From the first time she heard him turning over in bed to switch on
the machine for their morning cuppa, she knew.

The couple had always had a teasmaid, one of those little machines that makes the morning cup of tea. And they'd liked having one so much, they had one on each side of the bed. First of all, the radio alarm would go off; then Peter would reach over and put on both teasmaids and the teapots would start to churn. Regular as clockwork, every morning, he made this his first duty.

After Peter's death, both machines stopped working! Obviously, this wasn't normal and it greatly upset my client. That was why, having shed tears about it, she was so astonished a few days later when she heard the switch click on her own teasmaid and the chug chug of the mechanism as if it was brewing up a cuppa. She sat up but there was no one there. Her teasmaid was on – something she hadn't done and it couldn't have done itself.

At first my client thought she was dreaming. The next morning, however, she heard the ping of the switch, then the chug chug of the cuppa brewing itself. Again, she sat up and, as she did, she also heard footsteps going down the stairs. For a moment she froze. Was someone in the house? The sound was very like Peter. Then she heard the hall window being opened and she smiled. Peter had always done that when he was alive. Now she was certain. He hadn't really gone.

My client has continued from that day to this to hear Peter. There isn't a morning that goes by without the teasmaid clicking into action. His has still never worked, which makes it all the more strange that hers always switches itself on! After a few moments, she hears him going down the stairs.

On other occasions, too, when she has been unbearably lonely, she says, 'I have felt him snuggle into my back and put his arms protectively around me. I know some people will say this is wishful thinking, but it's not. I know he's there.'

I think it would take a particularly cold-hearted cynic to disagree. I can tell you now I've always believed her. Not just because of the business with the teasmaid but because of the amount of letters I've received about similar experiences – the presence of a loved one continuing to carry out all the little tasks they did in life.

In my opinion, this is ample evidence that our loved ones are still very near to us indeed.

The Persistent Papa

When Stephanie first came to see me, she brought someone along – her dad. As I've said before, there's nothing unusual in that and, yes, before you ask, he was dead. But what was unusual and caus-ing trouble was that Stephanie had no idea this was her dad. Her mother had been hiding a secret. Stephanie had always believed her dad's name was George, but the man with her, who wasted no time telling me who he was, was called Charlie.

Stephanie's mother had never been happily married and had known Charlie only briefly. But Stephanie had no idea of this. To be honest, neither had I. When I told Stephanie about Charlie, she didn't know who I was talking about. In fact, she even thought I was a fraud! We had a bit of a disagreement, which in many ways wasn't unnatural. I suppose I put my foot in it to some extent.

However, I could see Charlie so clearly. It was almost as if he was waiting for the opportunity to tell Stephanie how he felt about her. And that was proud. He hadn't always been able to be with her. He was honest about that much. But never having achieved that much himself, he was glad to know that Stephanie had worked hard and become a teacher. She had been one of the top students in her year and was well respected by her colleagues. Charlie was also proud of Stephanie's son who was nine. He knew she couldn't have more children and was therefore devoted to the boy. Like her mum, Stephanie's marriage wasn't especially happy or secure but she still put all she had into it, and he admired her for that.

These were all the things Charlie wanted me to tell Stephanie. But, to be truthful, she didn't want to hear them. Her parents had finally separated when she was 12, and the man she believed to be her dad had died eight months previously. When I first started to talk about 'her dad', she was delighted. But the moment I said his name, she lost interest. As things went on, I decided it might be better to stop talking about Charlie. I'm sure you can appreciate why. This was a delicate situation and I wasn't entirely clear about it myself.

When Stephanie left, I felt an immense sense of relief, but this was followed by a deep feeling of sadness. I could sense that Charlie was still with me and I felt he was saying, 'You've failed me. I thought this was my chance. I've waited years for this, watching that girl. She's mine you know.' And this upset me. I don't like to think I've let anyone down, especially those spirits who have come along to see me with a special purpose in mind. 'I'm sorry, Charlie,' I had to say in this instance, 'But you only gave me half a story.'

I don't know whether this reproach had anything to do with it but a week or so later I had a letter from Stephanie. She hadn't felt able to phone me. It would, she said, have been too traumatic. But she wanted to make another appointment because there were things she had to discuss.

Soon after, Stephanie came back to my office and I was fairly mesmerized. After she'd left me the first time, she had gone to see her mum and asked her outright who Charlie was. At first, her mum was unwilling to tell her, which was hardly surprising as it was still a painful subject for her. But later she told Stephanie everything, about her unhappy marriage and how she had met Charlie. It had been a brief affair. Charlie had wanted Stephanie's mum to leave her husband, but as she had a son of three – Stephanie's half-brother – she wouldn't leave.

It wasn't until after they parted that Stephanie's mum found out she was pregnant. There was nothing else she could do, she felt, but stay as she was. In those days, it didn't do to admit you had been having an affair.

Charlie had been killed in a road accident when Stephanie was a year old. But Stephanie's mum had never forgotten him. In many ways, her marriage ended then, but she kept things going till Stephanie was 12.

There were so many things Stephanie wanted to say to her mum. But she knew at this stage that she couldn't. She had no idea how she would get used to the idea of this other father, but somehow so many things from her childhood now made sense, including the fact that the man she thought of as her dad never had any real interest in her. 'I just thought he didn't love me. Now I see why,' she wrote.

I never heard from Charlie again, but I know with absolute certainty that his spirit would have been with us that day, listening and feeling proud of his daughter, and smiling with such fondness.

Not One but Two!

As you know by now, my office often plays host to a spirit during readings, but there have been occasions when more than one has come along. In fact, I can think of several instances, but the one I rather liked was the story of Elma and Elaine, two sisters, both dead, who liked to keep an eye on their niece. Her name was Sophie and she had come to me for a reading.

Elma and Elaine had obviously liked to party, but as that was during the 1920s, their idea of a dance was quite different from ours. But they were unabashed about doing it. Elma even showed me some of the steps of the charleston! They were delightful ladies and had had sad lives, but that didn't stop them looking out for their niece. What was more, she knew they did. When she came in for a consultation, she told me she'd probably brought visitors with her. And sure enough, within about five minutes, I was aware of the almost overwhelming presences of these ladies. 'They're supposed to be my old aunts,' Sophie said. 'But they don't behave very much like it!'

The strange thing was that although it was Sophie who had come for the reading – and she was perfectly open in talking about her aunts – they were the ones who wanted to speak to me. Elma in particular. She'd had an unhappy love affair, just after the First World War, and been forced into marriage with a much older man she didn't love, who was cruel to her. There had been a baby with her lover, whom she had also been forced to give up. It was something Sophie's mum didn't know because she had only been a small child at the time, and Elma had never spoken about it. She wanted Sophie to know this, however. She had never been able to be with her son or have other children, so that was why Sophie was so important to her and why she spent so much time hanging around her.

Sophie didn't dispute this story. She had always felt there was a secret unhappiness about her aunt Elma. Sophie shed quite a few tears at her story because she had always been fond of her. When Sophie was a little girl, Aunt Elma had been a 'great pal'. Her sense of fun was immense, and even as an old lady she had been young at heart.

Elaine, on the other hand, had never married, and she was honest about the fact that she was what at that time was known as 'simple'. Her life had been one of drudgery and she had looked after her mum. But she had adored Elma, and that was why she wanted only to be where her sister was. The pride she had in Sophie was clear – if for no other reason than that Sophie had done the things in her life Elaine would have liked to do. She had married and had children, then gone on to train at college. If only Elaine could have had these chances, but she hadn't.

But what she wanted Sophie to know was that, no matter how she had been viewed in life, she was entirely different now. In fact, she went as far as to say she had gone to college with Sophie and trained too!

'I can believe it!' said Sophie.

The ladies didn't stay. They understood Sophie's need to discuss some things that were private, and at that point they vanished. Sophie wasn't worried. She knew that when she arrived home they'd probably be waiting for her and that they'd make their presence felt by switching the kettle on for her when she got in.

I could believe this too. These were fascinating ladies, with the right modicum of respect for their charge. It's not always true of all spirits, but Elma and Elaine were certainly in a class of their own.

The Mum who Wanted to be Remembered

Let's face it, isn't that what most people want? To be remembered? To be known and appreciated by their loved ones? Well, spirits are no exception. Their longings are usually very much the same, only theirs have the added poignancy that they're gone, often leaving loved ones behind in terrible situations.

When Yvonne came to see me, I thought that such a spirit had to be connected with her. I instantly had a sense of the most beautiful young woman with her – a really refined girl, with naturally curly auburn hair and sparkling green eyes that seemed to shine. She had such a calm, quiet aura about her and was determined to follow Yvonne in.

Before I began the reading, I felt I just had to know who this woman was. Her presence was so clear to me, I actually thought Yvonne herself must be aware of it. But she wasn't. When I told her what I could see, she looked surprised. No, she hadn't lost her mum, or an aunt, or sister, or anyone that close to her. But as I described the lady, and how exceptionally pretty she was, Yvonne did become thoughtful. She opened her handbag and fished in it for a moment or so. Then she produced a photograph. It was of a very handsome young man. The hair was dark but the eyes were entirely the same as the woman's.

'That's Pete, my boyfriend,' Yvonne said. 'Does he look like the woman?'

It turned out that Pete's mum had died when he was only two and he had never really known her, but he had been told about how stunning she was to look at. He had always longed to know her and regretted never having the chance. His dad had remarried and he was close to his stepmum. It was just that he wished he had known more about his real mum, so I was glad of this opportunity to tell Yvonne some things about her.

In particular, she had been very musical. She also suffered from a circulatory problem which meant her hands were always cold, no matter how many clothes she heaped on. As

I relayed this to Yvonne, she smiled. This was one of the few things Pete knew about his mum.

'You know,' I said, 'She's come for another purpose. You're going to have a baby before the year is out and she wants you to know everything will be fine.' This was especially poignant because Pete's mum had died following complications when she was giving birth to Pete's sister.

Yvonne was surprised by this. I don't think she believed me, or wanted to at that stage! But Pete's mum was adamant. She went on to say that the baby would be a girl, and that she wanted Pete and Yvonne to get married, although she understood that Yvonne was waiting for a divorce.

As things turned out, Pete's mum was surprisingly accurate about these things. I hadn't even begun to read Yvonne's cards and didn't know that this was the situation. But Yvonne soon confessed that it was true.

After the reading, Yvonne got back in touch. It was to say that she had talked to Pete and, although at first he had been sceptical, the woman I had described was his mum. He was going to send me a copy of a photograph he had of her with her lovely auburn hair. And he did. In it she was exactly as she came over. And I still keep it to this day to remind me of that special session.

Yvonne did become pregnant and she and Pete had a little girl, who was later a bridesmaid at their wedding! So far as I know, they're still happy. Pete's mum certainly never said they wouldn't be. And her predictions were absolutely a hundred per cent correct. In some ways, though, I'm glad she's a spirit. She might put me out of business otherwise!

Picture the Scene: My Own Ghostly Encounters

This is my favourite chapter. Some would say that's because it involves talking about myself – and they are probably right. Here I describe experiences I have had personally. My diverse encounters range from seeing the ghosts of close family members to famous ghosts, such as Robert the Bruce, while at a haunted castle or while investigating a reported sighting. I try to convey these experiences vividly to you by describing what happened to me, what I saw and what I felt at the time.

The German Soldiers

A few years ago I made a trip to Neilston to visit my cousin and admire her new home. The house itself impressed me and, of course, she was as proud as Punch. We began walking towards the back garden, out through a large patio door. At first it was the size of the garden which struck me, but then, within a matter of seconds, another scene began to unfold in front of me.

I was amazed to see a whole troop of German soldiers. No one else could see them but they were so clear to me. To this day I cannot explain how I knew they were Germans – I simply knew they were. I also knew they were soldiers from the Second World War.

They seemed jovial and were happily chatting away with one another. I noticed they were busy making something, which looked quite intricate to me. I couldn't see what it was but I could see them as clearly as the 'real' folk around me.

I told my cousin about this – she knows what I'm like and is never sceptical or unsure of anything I say anymore. She told me she would go to the local library the following day and find out if there was any explanation for this. Why were there so many soldiers here, all looking pretty relaxed and far from confrontational?

So intrigued was I and so desperate for an answer that I mentioned it in my column in the *Sun* newspaper. I invited readers to write to me with any explanation, if there was one, for what I had seen.

A few days later, my postbag was full. Apparently, although not held as prisoners, several German soldiers were punished and removed from war duties and placed in a farm behind the Neilston mill – a hessian mill. The soldiers were treated very humanely and fairly and were given duties such as making hessian slippers. If any of them misbehaved, they were moved on to a much less informal destination where I believe they weren't treated with such privilege.

Most of them, however, were well behaved and caused the Neilston natives no concern at all. In fact, many became friends and some actually stayed on after the war and married local girls.

Indeed, one of the letters I received was from a reader in his 70s – a German. He had known many of the men serving in that area and was one of many who never returned to Germany.

I also received letters from locals who remembered the German soldiers, and a few letters from readers who were the children of local women and their German husbands.

I found out that most of the soldiers had now passed away but they must surely have remembered their war days and the town of Neilston with fondness. After all, it is Neilston they come back to, apparently preferring it to their own home towns.

Every time I visit my cousin, I make a point of going to the patio door and standing, just watching the German soldiers again. It never fails to amaze me each and every time.

My Captain

My own cottage is haunted by the spirit of the captain of a ship, which was once anchored out in the river Tay – the Mars Ship.

For many years, the familiar cry 'Behave yoursel' or ye'll get sent tae Mars' was the scourge of the male youth of Dundee. In this case, Mars was not a planet but a training ship that sat directly outside my house, docked on the river Tay. The ship was mainly used to house juvenile delinquents but I have subsequently found out it was also used for orphaned boys.

It has long since gone – many decades ago – but it is remembered still by the natives, its legend passing through the generations.

I'll talk some more about the ship, its captain and its occupants later, but at this point I want to describe the first time I saw him. I wasn't the first to see him – a couple of my clients saw him, months apart, and yet described where he was standing, what he was wearing and his physical appearance in the exact same words.

I had been eager to meet him but my first encounter was pretty scary. I'm fairly used to ghosts, as you can gather, but I have to be in the correct frame of mind, otherwise I jump out my skin just like everyone else. Well, the first time I saw him, that's exactly what I did – I nearly jumped the height of myself with fright!

My office is directly opposite my bedroom. As I often do, I had been burning the midnight oil in my office. When I'd finished for the night, I began to walk from my office across to my bedroom. The hallway was in darkness and the only light came from the third-floor landing. Through the huge bay windows up there, a little light shone from the outside sensor light. It was by no means bright and yet, as I looked up, I saw the captain in all his glory, down to the clothes he was wearing and even the pockmarks he had on his face.

My house has three floors, and at the top is an open-plan, converted attic. The view from there is stunning. Since moving here, I've pet-named this area the 'Mars attic'. The captain once owned my 300-year-old cottage, and legend has it that he had the huge bay window made especially so that he could sit and watch his boat – and, more importantly, those on board!

That night, I was not in a psychic frame of mind. I had been working on something entirely different in my office, so ghosts were the furthest thing from my mind. I blame this for my reaction, which was one of terror. I never made it as far as the bedroom for I turned on my heels back to my office. Once there, I found myself beginning to type frantically.

I wrote about what I had just seen, trying to conjure up the scene I had witnessed, and then sent it to my editor at the *Sun*. I just typed and typed and typed. I was acutely cold and, for some time, felt too afraid to leave my office.

I deliberately wasted no time sending the story to my editor as I felt it was important not to dwell on the experience and risk changing it. I wanted the readers to feel what I felt and to sense what I had sensed. Interfering with what I had written, after the event, would have spoiled this aim entirely.

The following Friday, the article duly appeared. It did make interesting reading and I received many phone calls about it. One of those phone calls was a little bit special, however. When I listened to what I was being told, even I had shivers down my spine.

The caller was a client whom I'd seen maybe twice or three times over the years. We'd had a meeting a few weeks prior to the article. The reason Isobel was calling was to tell me, almost hysterically, what had happened to her.

I use the Mars attic as a waiting area for my clients. It allows them the peaceful view of the river, and many admit it calms their nerves while waiting for their allocated appointment time.

Isobel was one such client. I was running approximately 30 minutes behind schedule that day and, as she waited, she sat gazing at the water. Her deep thoughts were disturbed by the footsteps of someone coming up the stairs. She automatically turned to look and was met by a man. The man sat down beside Isobel and they chatted for 10 minutes or so. They spoke mainly about the water, the weather, the view – general small talk. Isobel at this stage thought nothing of the situation she found herself in. The man was quiet but then Isobel was a talkative type.

Isobel knew I had an old friend, Bill, who stayed with us and looked after Athena (my little girl). She assumed Athena was having a nap and that Bill had come upstairs for some relaxation until she woke.

The only thing she found strange was the way he was dressed. She recalls he was very smartly dressed, way over the top for not only that time of day but also for the climate. However, she merely made small talk and, shortly afterwards, he took his leave.

Isobel read my article that morning and, in her own words, 'didn't know whether to laugh or cry' or whether to call me or not. She just didn't know what to do. But in the end, she decided to call my office. And I'm so glad she did.

The man, she told me, fitted the description of the captain in my article. He in no way resembled Bill. In retrospect, a lot of what she found strange about him now seemed to make sense – the way he was dressed, the way she did most of the talking while he gazed impassively out at the river. Although there was no 'disappearing into thin air', she also remembers thinking how quickly he descended the flight of stairs. As he took his leave, she turned to look the other way but looked back towards the stairs quickly – only to find he was gone.

Isobel thought so little of this at the time, assuming that the man she'd had a 10-minute conversation with was alive and well, that she never bothered to mention it to me. It was only after reading the article on the captain that she put two and two together.

Isobel has no doubts that she spoke to the spirit of the captain of the Mars ship that day. Nor do I. The captain is still here and makes his presence known from time to time. Since that night, however, I have never felt afraid of him.

The Iron Mask

A Radio Clyde programme led me to investigate the following sightings. The setting was the very picturesque village of Kirk O'Shotts, a tiny place just off the M8 motorway between Glasgow and Edinburgh.

One listener called the show to tell of a frightening experience she had just encountered while driving home along the Canthill Road near Shotts prison. This struck a chord with many listeners who phoned to say that they had also experienced something strange at that *exact* same spot.

The story I was told was vague. Apparently, 'something' had jumped out into the path of moving cars as if trying to commit suicide. This was so real that every motorist who experienced this stopped their car, terrified they had killed a pedestrian.

Each one checked their car, checked the road, looked behind walls and hedges – all to no avail. No one could find any explanation for what could possibly have caused the almighty thud. Some were afraid; some put it down to their imagination … until that phone call to Radio Clyde. Suspicion and curiosity increased and so I was called in to investigate.

Arriving at the scene, I was overwhelmed by the prettiness of the area and its stunning 15th-century kirk. Kirk O'Shotts is only minutes from both large cities, yet its beautiful setting could equally be 100 miles from anywhere. The kirk is rumoured to be one of the most famous in Scotland. Locals claim it was the very spot where a giant of a man, Bertram Shotts, fell to his death after an altercation with one William Muirhead.

Some people say they have seen a ghost here. They all tell the same story of a shadowy figure wearing a cape and a carriage hat. Many have their own opinions and beliefs on who this man was. When I visited the area, I found some very interesting goings-on indeed, none of which bore any resemblance to the other guesses made by those who had seen the ghost.

I met with my colleague Matt, and together we began to walk slowly around the kirk itself, and then onto the road where the incident repeatedly occurred. We also strolled around the graveyard and, very quickly, I began to see and feel things. Matt started scribbling down every word I uttered, and although at the time it didn't make any sense to either of us, he continued to write.

Somewhat cautiously, I began to voice the feelings I had and the words I was hearing. History was never one of my favourite subjects at school, so what was coming over to me made very little sense. My first impression was that the spirit *wasn't* wearing a hat as those who'd previously seen him had suggested. No, this was no hat. What I was clearly seeing was a mask, the kind worn by an executioner!

Other locals speculate that the ghost is a young man called William Smith, a covenanter who was run down by the Duke of Monmouth's horses before being stabbed to death. It is my belief, however, that the Canthill ghost is the duke himself, and he wants to beg pardon of 'oor Wullie', hence his ghastly act of chucking himself under cars.

I merely voiced names during the investigation – to be honest, hearing names such as Charles II and James II meant nothing to me. I hadn't a clue what the connection was. And as for the Duke of Monmouth, I'd never heard of him. However, such is my experience that I never hold back what I'm hearing or seeing. I blurt it out and then hope for the best. Everything is then pieced together by researchers.

I had a strong feeling the duke was angry with Charles II. In fact, I experienced hatred coming from the duke. I was so puzzled. It was as if the duke was doing his best to rebel against everything the king demanded. I stunned myself when I uttered the words, 'They are father and son!' This was not something I had expected, given the rivalry between them.

I was later to learn that the Duke of Monmouth was indeed the son of Charles II, but he was an illegitimate son who sought love and approval from his father. But this was not to be, so he rebelled. The fact was that Charles II, a staunch Catholic, was in constant battle with his Protestant son.

Very suddenly, I then had the most severe pain in my head and neck. I heard someone whisper the words 'One, two, three, four!' What on earth was I being told? Then I saw exactly what was happening. The duke was being beheaded.

The Duke of Monmouth won many battles and at one time was hugely popular. However, shortly after his father died, James II, brother of Charles, took over the crown. Formerly the Duke of York, James II detested his nephew. The duke was executed for treason against his uncle. His head was covered in a black mask. Legend has it that he was ordered to wear a mask so that James II would not see his nephew's face as he died.

My researchers also found that it took *five* blows to the duke's neck before he died. In fact, a second executioner was forced to take over after the fourth attempt failed. That explained why I could hear someone counting from one to four.

I believe that the Duke of Monmouth roams this particular area in search of his father. He won the battle of Bothwell Brig and I sense he is desperately sorry for going against his father who was, after all, king at the time. The spirit of the Duke of Monmouth is a sad and sorrowful one. It's no wonder he staggers around on that road. If you were forced to wear a mask, you'd stagger too!

So if you do happen to be on the Canthill Road in this rather spooky area, do take care. This is one jaywalker you don't want to look at too closely. But, if you do hit him, remember you can't kill him. He's already dead!

The Phantom Nanny of Airth Castle

The phantom nanny of Airth is interesting, which of course is something that could be said of any ghost. She is said to haunt one of the rooms in the castle, doing penance for her horrific neglect of two young children who perished in a fire there. Poor things! She was quite dreadful to them apparently. But the most fascinating thing about this particular phantom is that she's so 'phantom', she doesn't exist at all. Well, not in my opinion anyway.

I visited Airth Castle 'on a mission', after many reported sightings of what was believed to be a ghost. Much speculation led everyone to believe this spirit was that of a nanny who had perished along with her two charges.

I had been filled in on the whole story – who had seen her, what they had felt and what they concluded. However, what I found during my investigation was different – much different.

Airth is haunted alright, but it's not by her. The 'children' frolicking in and out of the kitchen and along the stone floors of the basement are happy children, the boys and girls of servants, and probably all died in their beds, or at least from natural causes. Nothing untoward there. Nor would I say the fire took place where claimed. The ghosts who haunt Airth, and the story of the fire, are different from what is claimed. At least in my book! So let's take a closer look and see what's what and who's who.

Airth Castle, which is now a hotel, is a fairly stunning place and so is its history, as I found out after my visit there. It has stood on the Forth at Falkirk for over 700 years.

William Wallace rescued his uncle from the keep after the English had imprisoned him there, and the family of that other Scottish figure to feature in the fight for independence – the Bruce himself – also lived there.

Edward Bruce and his wife Agnes were master and mistress, and it seemed to me that something wasn't quite right in their marriage. These feelings came to me literally within minutes of beginning my investigation. Edward certainly worried me, and my vibes all said he had an eye for the ladies.

My first stop was room nine, where many visitors claim to have seen a young woman. Several say she leaned over them as they slept. Others say she touched their face or put a hand on their shoulder. Everyone who saw, felt or smelled this young woman had one thing in common – they were all male. I believe this poor woman was desperately seeking affection.

I heard a child cry and then saw the sweetest looking little boy. His mother held him but, again, the scene in front of me didn't ring true. Something wasn't right. With every move I made, the scene before me would change.

Agnes was a deeply unhappy lady who would stand at the bedroom window day after day, awaiting the return of her husband. I had the feeling he regularly travelled to London – to Parliament if I wasn't mistaken. (It was later confirmed that Edward Bruce was a Member of Parliament and travelled regularly to London.) I felt such sorrow for Agnes. She was a fragile woman, alone and neglected by her husband, and her unhappy spirit haunts room nine to this day.

From that same bedroom window I could see a long, sweeping drive – or at least my 'psychic eye' could see the drive. There is no drive there today. All you can see from the window is grounds – grass-covered lawns. My researchers were later to discover that the entrance to the castle had indeed once been where I could see it.

Still in room nine, I again had the feeling the room was different now to how it had been. Walking back out into the long hallway, with a photographer and journalist in hot pursuit, I showed them where I believed the room was. By my reckoning, the room was once three times the size it is today.

Back in the room, I could also sense the presence of Edward, and this made me feel such sadness. I described an ache to my Matt, my colleague, who was taking notes of everything I said. I told him that I didn't much like Edward. I sensed he was far from a good or kind man and was a quite horrid husband.

I decided I wanted to move on to other parts of the castle. We entered a very dark room with the most grotesque furniture. A large four-poster bed dominated the room. It was ancient looking, almost black in colour, with obscenely large columns. The dressers were of the same design and the whole place filled me with dread. Apparently, this had been a maid's room during the era I was investigating. A small alcove led me into another room, this time tiny in size. I again heard and saw the same little boy playing there.

As I turned to go back into the main bedroom, Matt felt my arm grip his. He knew something was wrong and saw the worry on my face. I couldn't hear his anxious words for the scene which met me was of the master, lying in wait, with a sickening grin on his face. I began to feel sick and afraid, and I was clearly experiencing the exact same feelings the maid would have felt more than 500 years before. It was as though she had momentarily taken over my body and mind. I was shaking with fear for I knew what the master wanted.

'She's his "chosen one",' I told Matt. He began taking notes again as I continued. 'She is so like Agnes, her mistress. They both have the same pale complexion and the same red hair. She feels afraid!' I whispered. (I wasn't aware I was whispering – I was only told this after we left the castle.) 'He treats her so badly. He abuses her, rapes her and even beats her! She's terrified but knows she must go to him and do as he asks. And I'll tell you something else,' I continued, apparently in a much more aggressive tone, 'she gave birth to that child, not Agnes. Edward is the father and they raise the child as man and wife but the maid is the real mother! Very few people know this as Edward pretends he and Agnes are the parents but that's not true!' I was now quite incensed by it all, again feeling what the poor maid must surely have felt at losing her child to her employers. I doubt in those days there was much she could do to prevent it. She'd be too afraid.

The photographer took a few photos of me in that awful room. One, where I sat on the bed, clearly showed how pale I had become. The horror and fear in my eyes could be seen by everyone. Many people have commented on how different I look in that particular photograph.

I was relieved when we left that room and made our way to the laundry room. This is another room reputed to be haunted. Some have heard a female sigh heavily, while others describe the smell of cooking. Laughter is also heard in this room by some.

As I entered the room, I was overcome by the heat. I couldn't even stay inside the room but instead had to stand in the doorway. I asked my colleagues to go inside and see if they could feel the heat. They couldn't. 'This wasn't always a laundry room,' I said, a scene of huge stoves manifesting in front of me. Massive things they were, with huge metal plates. And there were several of them – so no wonder I felt such intense, almost burning heat. How the cooks could have stood such heat and still managed to work endless hours inside this room was a mystery to me. 'This was once the kitchen,' I told Matt as he scribbled down what I was saying. (Again, the researchers were later able to confirm this theory.)

And as for the famous fire? This was the only information I'd been given prior to my visit. The fire was indeed a documented fact. Alas, while inside the castle, I could feel nothing that would suggest there had been a fire, at least not during the era I was working in. There had undoubtedly been many changes, such as large bedrooms being split into two, kitchens relocated and so on, but none of these was because of a fire.

Finishing off our time in the castle, we left puzzled as to why I could not feel anything about the fire. We then headed for the ruin – once upon a time a grand church, which stands some 50 feet from the castle. Bingo! The moment I entered the ruin, I could smell smoke and see flames. 'The fire wasn't in the castle!' I told Matt, 'It was here in the church.'

We walked around the ruin, talking and taking notes. Then the most awful scene unfolded in front of me and the words tumbled from my lips almost uncontrollably. 'Although this was a church, I don't know that much religion was practised here. I may be going into a different era now!'

I warned Matt, 'but there is a sinister feeling here. This place was once used for ritual killings and I strongly feel someone was burned at the stake, right there!' I pointed to the area I was talking about.

My only hope was that the poor maid wasn't involved in any of this. I hoped, with all my heart, that her death was not as traumatic as her life had been.

And so, anguished ladies, terrified maids, laughing children, sighing cooks, not to mention the suggestion of a fire licking round its nearby walls – Airth Castle is a fascinating place but not for the fainthearted. If you ever stay there, just make sure you choose your room with care!

The Council Tenant

Castles and churches seem to have their fair share of spectres, with a long and often bloody history attached. However, spirits can also be tempted by more normal, fairly down-to-earth settings if they happen to know the resident. A local council flat was the scene of a haunting in the following instance.

Mark, a man in his 20s from Kirkcaldy in Fife, experienced strange goings-on in his council flat. For two years he put up with all kinds of things – ones that often went bump in the night, quite literally.

Mark often found himself pinned to the bed, quite incapable of doing anything. Sometimes, too, a ghostly shape could be seen wandering about the bedroom in the middle of the night. The kettle kept switching itself on and off.

But one of the most frightening incidents was when a baseball cap flew up and landed on his bed. I say 'flew' because that really seemed to be the only way it could have got there. It was lying on the floor where Mark put it – kept putting it actually because it repeatedly landed back up on the bed. Obviously this was a spirit who wanted to play. But who with, and what at, was another matter.

The apparitions had even driven Mark's girlfriend away. He could think of no reason for the hauntings. The house wasn't even that old. Mark contacted the *Sun,* who in turn called me to ask if I would investigate. I jumped at the chance – this was right up my street after all.

It seemed to me that Mark's spirits had nothing to do with the house at all. This was a case where one spirit had attached itself to a possession and another to Mark himself, largely because he knew Mark when he was alive. In fact, the spirit that had attached itself to Mark was his granddad – someone Mark had been very close to.

Even before entering Mark's house, this man wanted to make his presence known. He had died two years earlier, which was roughly the time Mark's problems began. He had been a very active man, one who loved mountain-biking and also fiddling with electrical appliances. This explained why Mark was having such problems with all his gadgets. But it didn't explain all of Mark's mysteries.

I had taken along a colleague, a journalist and a photographer. We all inspected the place but when we walked into the bedroom I asked to be left alone as I was picking up on something and I needed to have no interference.

I was very drawn to a cupboard just to my right but naturally, not being an intrusive person, didn't dare open it. I lingered a while longer and then called for everyone to come back in. I told them that I felt there were several explanations for the ghostly goings on – certainly two that I was picking up on.

The first thing was rather difficult to describe. I started by calling it a 'rather old-fashioned painting'. Then I changed my wording to 'one of these black velvet on board affairs, the ones with the metal wire/silver thread made into shapes'. I believe Mark had put this in a cupboard, possibly the one to my right to which only moments earlier I had felt drawn.

There was no doubt in my mind that his granddad wanted this object brought out of the cupboard. But part of that, in my opinion, was also down to something else – the presence of another spirit, also an old man.

Some months before, Mark had bought a mirror from an antique shop. Its previous owner was someone I could clearly see – an old man with a deformed leg. When I said this to Mark, he agreed. It was something he was told when he bought the mirror. This old man was harmless, as Mark's granddad was too. Only Mark's granddad liked to be 'top dog'.

'This is my grandson's house, so behave!' was something he said a lot. And just to make sure this happened, he would chuck the baseball cap. It seemed to me that the two old men were throwing the cap at each other!

Mark had often thought about having the flat exorcised, but when he heard it was his granddad doing the haunting, albeit with a companion, he changed his mind. He was used to his two lodgers, so long as they didn't fight. He just wasn't sure about asking his girlfriend round!

The Ghost who Never Was

Widower James McAvoy was a frightened man. For three years he had found his way down the stairs of his terraced house in Bellshill, Lanarkshire, with his eyes closed. He had stopped reading in bed, preferring instead to jump in with the lights off and keep the duvet up over his face so that he wouldn't hear, or worse still, see whatever was causing the sound.

The 'thing' caused his heart to pound every time it walked past the bedroom door. He feared it could bring on another heart attack, one which could prove fatal to the paper-thin walls inside his chest and force him into the spirit world, where he was convinced this thing came from.

He knew this much – it was a little girl in a white tunic.

James had no idea who she was. The first time he saw her, standing at the foot of his stairs, he thought one of the local children had wandered into his house by mistake or for a dare. Then he noticed the way she was dressed. All the local children wore the uniform of 'trackie' bottoms, tops and trainers. This girl was wearing a long tunic, a long white tunic. Then he noticed her face. It too was white but translucently so. That was when James realized the girl he was looking at didn't exist. Not in his world certainly. She wasn't a real person. She was a ghost.

James was terrified. He felt the stabbing pain start in his chest. Somehow he managed to get back into the bedroom and sat there for a while, willing the pain to go away. It did. But it seemed his little ghost friend refused to go away. That night, through the glass panel of the door, he saw the girl again. This time she was smiling at him. James didn't think she meant him any harm but who was she and what did she want?

By the time James contacted me, he was in a state. The girl had become a regular visitor to the house. Her haunting ground, so to speak, was the downstairs hall and the upstairs landing. It was clear that she wanted to be seen. She wanted to be seen by him. Every time he went down the stairs, she was standing at the foot of them, smiling. She was, he thought as time went on, a beautiful girl, perhaps aged 12 or 13, but the knowledge of *what* she was unnerved him.

So James asked me to come and see him, and when I did it was very clear to me who the girl was. She was his granddaughter. Only James didn't have one. Not one who had died at any rate. Not only did the girl he was seeing not exist in this world, she didn't exist in the spirit world either. She wasn't even a ghost. This was so extraordinary. Yet I was convinced.

I wondered then, almost in desperation, if either of James's daughters had ever had a miscarriage. It was an incredibly long shot. I was physically disappointed when he told me they hadn't. I left feeling a failure for being unable to solve James's problems.

That was then. A little later James contacted me. The story he had to tell was amazing. He had spoken to his daughters, almost as a last resort, explaining what I had said. When he did, the youngest's face turned white. 'But Dad,' she told him. 'I did have a miscarriage.' It was long ago and James had had so many other problems at the time, she had decided not to tell him.

'When was this?' I asked James.

'Thirteen years ago,' he replied sadly. 'If the baby had lived, he or she would have been twelve.'

But the baby hadn't lived and James was being haunted by a girl who never was. The granddaughter he didn't have. Yet it seemed she wanted him to know about her. Once the truth did come out, the hauntings stopped. The girl in white never came back.

If she had come back, James wouldn't have been afraid. He understood why she kept smiling at him and was glad of the opportunity of knowing her.

Sadly, James has now passed away and I dedicate this, his story, to his memory.

The Dancing Couple

A few years ago, I decided to embark upon an ambition I'd had for many years. I wanted to learn to play the piano. So, I found out the name of a local teacher and tentatively began my piano practice. I wasn't much good at it. I'm still no Liberace all these years later. However, I did look forward to Tuesday mornings and my piano lessons. One of these lessons has stuck in my mind for years. I shall never forget what I'm about to tell you – nor will my piano teacher!

We were sitting with our backs to the large, airy room when I heard a voice telling the time. I identified this as a talking key ring – a gadget I'd been given as a gift. This was strange in itself as the key ring was in my bag, and to hear the time you had to press a button. I looked around but immediately put the incident down to coincidence – the button had probably hit something in my bag. Then it happened again. Once more, I looked around, but this time the room was not empty.

My teacher was sitting to my right but she could not see what I was seeing. A happy, loving-looking couple danced beautifully in front of my eyes. I began to tell my teacher what I was seeing. I described the pair to her and continued a running commentary on what they were doing, what I was seeing and what I was feeling.

When I turned around again, my teacher had tears in her eyes. She told me that I had just described her beloved parents who had passed away recently, only months apart. They loved to dance, she told me, and then she rose, telling me she wanted me to see something. A few minutes later she reappeared carrying a photograph. She asked me again to describe what her father was wearing. I did so, down to the hat, which I could only describe as Australian-looking with its wide brim and everything but the corks dangling from its edges. She then showed me the picture and I was amazed to see the very same man, dressed in exactly the same outfit, staring out at me. There were no differences at all. The image was a carbon copy of the one I had just witnessed.

My teacher had taken her parents' death badly as not only were both deaths sudden, but they were also very close together. Her mourning was twofold. I know she gained great strength that day and was comforted by the fact that her parents were unmistakably together and very much around her.

The key ring never again set itself off, and I know it did so that day to attract my attention and cause me to turn around and witness the scenario set up for me. I know, too, that this was done by two very loving parents who couldn't bear to see their daughter in so much emotional pain. I think this particular message brought happiness and reassurance to spirits and living alike.

The Victoria Doll

'The Victoria doll moved! She moved!'
'Moved?'
'Her hands. They moved! I saw it! Put her away! Put her away! I'm frightened of her!'

When Gwen Symond's little girl told her this, she didn't doubt her for a second. After all, the 'Victoria doll' had been hers as a child, and her misgivings about putting it in her daughter's room and letting her play with it all centred round one thing. The doll *did* seem to move.

When she herself was a little girl, Gwen had seen it do the same thing and had been terrified by it. But she couldn't throw it out. The doll had been a Christmas present from her parents. One they had saved hard to get. A big, beautifully dressed thing with a straw hat and shoes that fastened with real buckles, which had broken the bank balance when times were much harder for people. 'Take her by the hand, and she really walks', the caption in the catalogue had said. 'Lean her forward and she says "Ma-ma"'.

Gwen's parents laughed at their daughter's utter excitement when handed the gift. Opening it with enthusiasm, her little face beamed. Then, however, the moment she saw the doll, its eyes wide open and gazing when they should have been closed, Gwen ran screaming from the room.

'It occurred to me she was an evil doll. I don't know why. She was lying on her back in the box, staring at me. Her eyes should have been closed but they weren't. I was five years old and she was as big as me. I was terrified. My parents were very upset. I hadn't liked their present. The one they'd saved so hard to get. But it wasn't that. This was about 1960 and my dad had no doubt been working overtime every night to make sure we had a nice Christmas. I wasn't taking what they'd spent for granted. I knew it had cost them. The doll was just something I didn't ever want to see again. Unfortunately, I did.'

'We'll call her Victoria,' her mum suggested gently, unsure of why her daughter was reacting in this way.

At that time Gwen shared a room with her parents, and the doll sat on a large basketwork chair in the corner. It was 'pride of place' but Gwen couldn't stand it. The coldness round that spot was something she's never forgotten, nor will she forget the way she used to wake up in the night, screaming that there was something black, something evil, on the chair. 'A mass,' she felt it was, rather than a manufactured doll with substance. For a time, believing the doll's eyes followed her everywhere, she covered them with a bandage.

Gwen loved her parents dearly and didn't want to offend them, so she attempted to play with the doll she had grown to loathe. But every time she did – taking the doll's hand, much as the caption suggested – it would fall over or poke her.

'Of course, I was very small and the doll was quite awkward, so there was probably nothing in it. But really, I used to hurt myself on her and I would cry. Once I whacked her in exasperation and got a telling-off from my mum. She said if I couldn't treat my toys better she would take them away, and I thought, "Please do." I really chucked the doll about after that. I wanted rid of her.' But that didn't happen, although eventually the doll was wrapped up in polythene and put in a cupboard.

Gwen grew up and married. When she did, the doll was transferred to her attic. Gwen still used to look at her and remember how terrified she had been but she decided it was all in the past, a figment of her imagination. Just the same, the doll stayed in the polythene. By now, Gwen was thinking an old thing like that might well become a collector's item one day. It was like new, after all. All that was missing was its straw hat.

More time passed. By now Gwen had children of her own and another house. This time the doll was put in an empty room, one that in the process of renovating the house and the attic was being used to store junk. When Gwen's younger daughter, Lizzie-Anne, saw it there, she was curious.

'She really wanted to know why I'd put this lovely doll – and it did have beautiful golden hair – in a bag in the corner.

She wanted the doll. A part of me was saying, "Remember how that doll upset you. Is this wise?" But Lizzie-Anne was so insistent. She went and got all these baby clothes that had been hers to dress her up in. She kept them all in a box and dressed the doll up every morning. She even found a little straw hat for her.'

Gwen didn't know if this restored Victoria to her former spirit, but that same night Lizzie-Anne began screaming. As she cowered under the duvet, her eyes glazed with tears, stuttering and stammering in fear, Gwen caught two words. 'She moved.' Gwen didn't hesitate. Grabbing the doll in anger, she left her daughter's room. She almost broke into a run until she reached the junk room. Once there, she opened the door and threw the doll inside. As far as Gwen was concerned, the Victoria doll was going out in the morning – to the bin.

But that wasn't the end of the story. Gwen remembered everything she had ever felt about the doll. But she said to herself, 'I am 42 years old. This is ridiculous. Toys are toys. They don't move and they don't possess spirits. This isn't Hollywood. That's not Chucky up there. Lizzie-Anne imagined it. I imagined it.' Just the same, she decided to throw this particular toy out to be 'on the safe side'.

However, an unexpected person came to the doll's rescue – Lizzie-Anne. Things must certainly have looked brighter in the morning because she confessed she had been reading a spooky story about a ventriloquist's doll and, naturally, it had upset her. She didn't ask for the doll back. But she didn't want it thrown out. So Gwen, still believing that toys are toys and glad to hear her daughter had an overactive imagination, let the doll stay.

Three weeks later and sufficiently recovered from her fright, Lizzie-Anne took the doll back. Now there were other things going on. Nightmares. Lizzie-Anne was waking up crying, saying someone was making a noise in her room at night.

It was then that Gwen, whom I'd known for a year or so, asked me if I would pop in for five minutes to see what I thought. She didn't mention the doll. She only told me that she thought they might have a ghost.

I walked around the house feeling nothing untoward – until I reached Lizzie-Anne's bedroom! I walked in and immediately felt my hackles rise. I stared directly at the doll. Its head was up as if it knew what I had come for, and I actually felt its eyes follow me round that room. Never before had I felt such fear from an inanimate object, let alone a little girl's dolly! She was sitting in among some other toys, mainly cuddly ones, but the scene was far from cute. I had to get out.

As I came down the stairs, I actually expected it to get up and follow me. There was no doubt in my mind that somehow, attached to what should have been a toy, was some kind of force – and it was far from playful!

'Tell me about the doll,' I said to Gwen. And when she did I was shocked. Not only because of what she said – that all seemed strange enough. But what was worse was when she interrupted me as I described how the doll was sitting in the middle of the other toys.

'But that couldn't possibly be, Katie,' she said. 'There's nobody else here. I was last in that room today and the doll was sitting in a little rocking chair!'

When Gwen went upstairs, she found the doll was back in the rocking chair. Even I was stunned. That seemed to convince her. She took the doll straight out to the bin for the rubbish collectors to remove the next morning.

Perhaps it was only imagination or perhaps it was because of what I'd said, but as Gwen lifted the doll she felt as if an invisible hand was trying to wrap itself round her throat. She was nonetheless determined to get the doll out of the house.

Imagination, or a real-life Chucky? I don't know. My feelings about the doll being a conductor for some kind of malign force were so pronounced I've always been glad Gwen didn't ask me to find out. This was one of the strangest cases I have ever come across in all my years of spiritualism and psychic intervention.

The Orphaned Imp

Lorraine and Raymond, clients of mine from way back who have since become firm friends, have agreed to my using their story, which happened in their house.

Lorraine and Raymond had invited me and some other friends around for dinner one Saturday. It was a miserable, cold and wet night, but the warm atmosphere of their new house soon made us feel relaxed, cosy and very much at home. I'm not much of a drinker, but as everyone else got stuck into the booze, I sat chatting away. Dinner was served and, as ever, eaten with huge appreciation. The whole evening was a wonderfully relaxed, close and warm time. In fact, a ball was had by all.

A few hours into the evening, I excused myself to go to the bathroom. We had already been given a guided tour of our friends' beautiful new farmhouse home. It was stunning, and the refurbishments they had made served only to make this already divine property even more divine.

Once inside the bathroom, I was met with the cutest little boy – curly hair, impish face, huge saucer eyes, the works. He was adorable. 'How did he get here?' I wondered to myself. I went towards him as if to pet him, but my hand went right through him! 'Okay, Katie, this is your field,' I told myself. 'Don't get alarmed. This little boy is not real. He is a ghost.' Normally ghosts are not a problem for me – I deal with this kind of experience daily, albeit when I'm in a 'tuned in' psychic state. He was as lucid as my friends downstairs. There was no sense of him being a mirage, no shadowy outline. There he stood, a bona fide, completely intact little boy. I knew he couldn't harm me. He was too tiny – golly, he was too gorgeous. So I calmly stood away from the child and asked him his name to which he replied, 'Toby Ramsay, miss.' 'Gorgeously impish and polite too,' I thought to myself.

'So, Toby Ramsay, what are you doing here? Are you look-ing for someone? Do you live here?' I told myself to slow down with the questions as the little guy clearly couldn't take them all in.

'I used to live in this house, well I think it was this house – it looks kinda different now. I don't think Mummy would have liked the kitchen – there's no wood in it!'

'Where is Mummy?' I asked very tentatively. (I was excited at having a conversation with a ghost – it does happen from time to time but not nearly often enough for my liking!)

'Daddy went to war. Mummy never told me where war was but I know it couldn't have been a nice place because Mummy cried all the time.'

Toby then went on to tell me, in perfect English, that a long time passed and then his Mummy took ill. She was taken to a hospital and he never saw her again. His auntie told him Mummy wasn't very well but he wasn't to be sad because she was in a good place now – and that she was with his Daddy. This seemed to bring Toby a great deal of comfort.

My interpretation of what he was saying may have been wrong but it sounded rather like his mother had died and that his father had died too, hence Toby being told his Mummy and Daddy were together.

Toby then told me his aunt and her horrid son Harry came to live in his house. Aunt Collins was her name but he didn't seem too struck on her! Toby then left the bathroom, using the door I have to add, and I never saw him again.

Knowing my line of work, my friends are always fascinated by the ghost stories I tell them so I had no qualms about telling them what had just happened. They sat listening intently. Despite being, shall we say, pretty 'tanked up' by now, they nevertheless offered no ridicule, nor did they make inappropriate comments of any sort.

My friends Lorraine and Raymond are firm believers in my kind of work, and they promised that night to look into the history of the house. They weren't one bit surprised by my tale because they had both seen this little boy, although not as clearly as I had. Nor had they ever spoken to him. He had appeared to them in a hazy manifestation on two occasions, and several other times they had heard his footsteps, and his little voice quietly singing a song.

A few days later a very excited Lorraine telephoned me. 'Katie,' she squealed, 'I've just had a phone call from an old lady who lives a couple of doors away.'

Lorraine proceeded to tell me that this old lady remembered her mother talking about the 'poor orphaned boy living at number 20'. Apparently, his father had been killed in action and the mother took ill, was admitted to hospital and, as far as she could remember, never came home. Lorraine's mother apparently attended the funeral.

The little boy's Aunt Collins and her family moved in to look after Toby. Her husband was also at war and, as far as the old lady could remember, she had a son slightly younger than Toby. They lived, the three of them, in the house for a few years before moving on. No one heard of them after that.

So the ghost in my friends' house is nothing to be scared of. Instead, it is that of a cute little boy who lost his parents, yet still seemed to find comfort in his early childhood home. Most probably because this was the only house he actually lived in with his parents. In any home afterwards he would, of course, have been an orphan.

I've tried to talk to Toby several times when visiting my friends but he never seems to be there. I only hope he has found his Mummy and Daddy now, and has at last been able to be part of a proper family.

My friends tell me they haven't seen or heard him around for some time, so maybe this cute little imp ghost is finally at peace.

What a Waste of a Life

One Saturday night a few years ago, I was driving into St Andrews with a crowd of friends for an evening out. As we approached the town, just before the Old Course Hotel, I saw something lying on the road. As I drove nearer, I began to see clearly that the person on the road was a pretty young blonde girl. She was covered in blood. No one else could see her, so that's when I knew I was seeing yet another ghost!

'She looks dead,' I told my friends. 'She is lying completely still, her body grotesquely contorted and there's blood everywhere!'

I heard a few gasps from some of my passengers. One of them, however, a born and bred local, told me something very interesting. Several years earlier, a young girl – a student he believed – stepped out of a car at that exact place and was hit by a car coming in the other direction. It had been forced to swerve as the car the girl emerged from had stopped at a most inappropriate spot. As he swerved in a bid to miss the stationary car, he instead hit the girl passenger as she got out. It all happened so quickly and the girl died instantly.

The scene I, and only I, had witnessed had left me feeling sad. The girl, despite all the blood and contortion of her body, had clearly been a beautiful young woman. What a waste of

85

a life. I found it difficult to erase the images from my mind. I had been privy, it would seem, to every gory detail, down to the very clothes she was wearing.

A few weeks later, I met up with someone who had known both the driver and the victim. He told me that they had had a row, and the girl had demanded her boyfriend stop the car as she wanted to get out. He knew very little of what happened to her boyfriend thereafter, but he does recall the shockwaves around the university when the news broke.

I can't explain why I saw what I saw – why I was supposed to see what I saw – but see it I did. And, the backup research did verify that I am still sane (thank goodness), and that in fact what I was seeing was a glimpse of the tragic accident at that very spot some 15 years earlier.

That Poor Plumber!

I just love sceptics. I shouldn't really say that, but it's true! What I love most is when people who don't believe in my work then change their mind. I have to say this happens much less now, as more often than not I'm able to blurt something out which stops them dead in their tracks – a sight to behold I can tell you!

One such time involved a workman I had in my home. Let me be brutally honest here – he was very sarcastic, rude and downright horrible. Although he had no right to, he took it upon himself to attempt a conversation about my work. Assuming initially that he was genuinely interested, I soon realized he was trying to ridicule me. He accused me and others of talking nonsense. In fact, it would be fair to say that this was as nice as he got. The rest of the conversation went downhill rapidly. I was pretty outraged and told him that as he was in my home on a professional matter, he had no right to become personal. And would he please stick to what he was being paid to do.

However, still he continued, saying all sorts of borderline nasties, progressing from 'hocus-pocus' to far more rude comments. I left the room after hearing quite enough but I was boiling inside. I couldn't concentrate on my work, so I went back down to the kitchen where 'Hagar the Horrible' was working (well, he looked like him!). I put the kettle on, deliberately and pettily not offering him a cup. And he started his baloney again! I was fizzing by now. So, with delicious tea in one hand, yummy cake in the other (which I could tell he would have died for … how cruel!), I stopped him in his tracks by telling him that his father was beside him. Each time he tried to interrupt, I just talked over him.

I told 'Hagar' everything I was seeing and hearing – how his father hadn't wanted him to become a plumber, how he had wanted so much more for him. He had brains (I doubted this but never mind!). His father was disappointed he hadn't finished university, that he had given up for the wrong reasons. I told him how his mum was also disappointed in him, although she had never said as much to her son. I just kept talking and talking.

Hagar was rooted to the spot! Within a matter of a few moments, this male chauvinistic, rude, intrusive man had turned into a whimpering child. By this time, me being me, I began to feel sorry for him. So much so I eventually poured him a cup of tea (you see, I'm not totally heartless!).

We sat for a while afterwards – Hagar suddenly enthralled by my work. Of course, I made no reference to his cruel and unfair words of only a few hours ago but instead listened to his tales of woe and of how he just knew he had let his father down.

Hagar has now finished with plumbing (and I now have a much less intrusive plumber) and is in his final year at university, studying the subject he had always shone in. So his future looks very bright. He comes for a consultation at least once a year now. In fact, Hagar the Horrible turned out to be pretty cool after all!

And all because of a message from his dead father.

The Polish Guest

I decided to take a weekend break with some friends so we trotted off west towards and beyond Glasgow. We stayed at a beautiful hotel complete with golf course, clay pigeon shooting and the all-important glorious food. The hotel was ancient and was once owned by a well-known family of ship builders.

Sitting in the lounge area on the second night, we felt comfortable and relaxed. A coal fire was burning, warming up the entire room. Midway through our conversation, I was startled to see a smallish man walk past us on his way to the dining room. No one else had seen him but I described him physically and guessed that he was foreign, most probably

Polish. I don't know what make me think that – perhaps his height, his clothing – I really don't know. What I did know, as I do so often, was that he was a ghost.

My friends, as ever, were intrigued and wanted to know why I had seen him when they hadn't. So, I advised them to keep watching the fire, because the flames had wafted when he passed the fire the first time. I told them to watch the flames and I'd turn my back and tell them when he passed again. It was some time before he did walk by again and, interrupting the conversation once more, I said, 'He's just about to leave the dining room now.' All eyes, apart from my own, were fixed firmly on the fire. All three of my friends saw the flames waft and, in fact, one of the logs fell deeper into the fire.

One of my friends, I'd say the least open-minded out of them all, turned to me and said, face chalk white, that he hadn't just seen the flames react, but that he had seen the man himself. He was shaking as he asked me if I had noticed how shiny his shoes were. Yes, I had noticed this, but I hadn't mentioned it when I first described the man. My friend had obviously seen the same man and agreed with me that he looked Polish. Again, he didn't have a substantial reason for this assumption. He just 'thought he looked Polish'.

Later that night, after a number of 'refreshments', we set about retiring for the night. As we walked through the lounge, the night porter was there. We got talking about things in general but then the subject of my work came up. I told him what I had seen and my friend backed this up. The other two had certainly witnessed the movement the fire made, as if someone was walking past causing a stirring of air. To our surprise, the night porter was very open to the idea. In fact, he recalled hearing something about a Polish family who had lived there, or had been guests of the then owners of the house, long before it was turned into a hotel.

The Ghost who Was Scared

One night a few years ago, I had a visit from a friend, a girl who lived nearby. This in itself was nothing unusual. But what she had to say was.

She asked if I would come back to her neighbour's house. She was looking after it while this lady was on holiday. There had been happenings. Too many for her to pass off as normal. The last straw had been when a cooker ring was put on. She knew she hadn't done it and the neighbour had been away for two weeks. If the house wasn't haunted, then someone real was going in and out, and if they were she would have to get the police.

Of course, I was fascinated by all of this. So much so, I fetched my coat straight away. Maybe the evening would end with my friend having to fetch the police because there were intruders, but somehow I didn't think so. My friend wasn't much interested in ghosts. In fact, she was another one who had always denied their presence. As we walked along to her neighbour's house, how-ever, she told me some of the things that had changed her mind.

To begin with, when she stepped into her neighbour's house for the first time, she had been appalled by the smell.

Not knowing the woman terribly well, she had thought that perhaps she was living next door to a murderer, someone who left the body lying in their living room, rotting for weeks on end. But then, strangely enough, the smell just vanished. This really was the oddest thing because every time she went into the house the smell met her somewhere, then, just as quickly, it disappeared. The previous evening, too, she had heard noises, ones that convinced her that her neighbour had come home early. She telephoned through but there was no answer, and after a time the noises stopped, yet no one had gone in or out. Or were in, come to that. She knew this because she'd telephoned more than once.

Things had come to a head that night though. As she stepped in the door, she felt herself being shoved out of the way. Someone had brushed past her but there was no one there. That was when, looking into the kitchen, she saw one of the cooker rings was on. The switch was off at the wall, yet the ring appeared to be blazing merrily away. My friend knew she hadn't touched it. She knew too that it hadn't been on the previous evening, or any of the others. She'd have noticed it if it had.

As we stepped into the hall, I have to say that we weren't met by anything. Whatever it was had obviously gone out for the evening! And in a great hurry, if the things my friend had said were anything to go by. Just the same I felt they had been there. I was absolutely certain that the spirit was that of the lady's husband, who had died a year or so before. What was more, it seemed to me that the lady knew perfectly well that he was there. She often chatted to him. He had been expecting her return and got the fright of his – well, I don't want to say 'life' – when my friend started coming in instead. I actually felt that he'd gone out to look for his wife.

'We better hope he comes back!' I joked. 'Your neighbour will miss him.'

Although my friend had now become a firm believer in ghosts, to some extent I felt she was a bit sceptical about her neighbour knowing.

'She definitely knows,' I said. 'She was probably in two minds about going but if she'd said anything to you, you'd have thought she was mad. Be honest now!'

Of course, this was the part I wanted to put to the test. When I arrived back home, I asked my friend simply to tell her neighbour about the cooker ring and see what she said. After all, if her husband hadn't put it on, there must be something badly wrong with it. She would be doing her a favour by saying so.

A few days later, my friend was back at the door. 'Well, you were right,' she said, and I'm sure you can guess the rest of this tale!

Margaret, my friend's neighbour, did have contact with her husband. The cooker ring was turned on every week and sometimes, yes, there was a smell. There were other things too. My friend listened, rather aghast I have to say, as Margaret reeled them off. The radio was something else her husband liked to fiddle with, and she often thought she heard him saying, 'Let's have a cup of tea, love.' It was his favourite beverage.

Margaret just hadn't wanted to say so. 'I thought I was imagining it,' she said to my friend. 'Oh I do hope he hasn't been scared away!'

As things turned out, he wasn't. He's back as far as I know. Although now, when Margaret goes on holiday, she leaves the house locked up for the duration, instead of asking anyone to keep an eye on it. With her late husband around, she reckons she doesn't have to!

Together Forever ... and Ever

In the room, the couple seemed very close, the man sitting in the chair, the lady bustling about. She was young and pretty, but something was terribly wrong.

I suppose you might say they weren't dressed properly. By that I don't mean they were in their underwear! Quite the contrary. Overdressed was the word I was looking for. And very old fashioned, the woman's dress sticking out in a stiff fashion, the man in a too-tight collar and cravat. This couple wasn't real, not any more any way. They were ghosts. But they were so obviously going about their daily business as if they were alive.

Whoever they were and whatever they had done in life, the habit was such they wanted to repeat it. As I looked at them I could tell they had been affluent, prosperous and clearly devoted, and not just to one another. The property had been their pride and joy. That was perhaps why they didn't want to leave it, although their appearances were causing problems to say the least. When Gwen Ritchie opened the door to her bathroom to be confronted by half a spirit wafting about the floor, she was convinced she was losing her mind. That was when I became involved.

The first thing I was able to tell her was that the house itself had been converted into flats. It seemed to me that the part Gwen was staying in had been the main part of the house but ceilings had been removed and floors added, which explained why sometimes she could see half an apparition. She had complained to me that she often saw a man and lady both wearing Victorian clothes. I believed this couple to be a Mr and Mrs Short who had owned the property when it was built.

They were young but the house had been a gift from Mr Short's father who was particularly well-off. He was also very interfering, and the couple seemed to spend a great deal of time discussing this. Mrs Short, unusually for her times, had a keen business sense. She appeared to me to be teeming with ideas. I doubted if she ever had the chance to put these into practice, although I certainly felt that she eventually did an excellent job of having the house converted into flats and selling them off, netting herself a tidy sum.

While I was saying all this, Gwen was nodding frantically. I don't think she was taking in what I was saying. She was just glad that someone else could see what she could, but she was jotting some of my findings down.

I continued my observations, saying that Mr Short, on the other hand, was very much a silent partner. 'He always sits in the chair,' said Gwen. 'He's obviously a bit lazy.' I didn't thing so. I was picking up on the fact that his health was poor and that he might have had some kind of heart condition. Certainly he hadn't lived long. I could actually sense that he must have died about 1910.

'They were only married 10 years,' I concluded. Anyway, it would be possible to check. I advised Gwen to ask her solicitor for her title deeds. There would be something in them, I felt, about the Shorts. Whoever they were, they certainly seemed to me to be a harmless couple, who weren't aware that they had passed on … or should have.

It was some weeks later when I heard from Gwen. By this time, she had contacted her solicitor who had brought the title deeds out of mothballs for her to look at. So many things were right, there was no denying the spirits did belong to the Shorts – the name for a start, but also the references to the house being divided.

It had apparently happened much as I'd suggested. Mrs Short had sold the remaining flats, but although she died in 1970 at the ripe old age of 90, she clearly hadn't left the premises and neither had her husband.

A little more digging turned up their marriage certificate. The date? 1900. His death? 1911, January 1911. All fascinating stuff. As far as I know, Gwen still sees them from time to time. In fact, she sees them so often she almost regards them as family members. How they regard her, or indeed whether they regard her at all, I've no idea.

Living or dead, it's seldom that I've come across a couple quite so wrapped up in themselves as the Shorts.

The Phantom Bandstand

I get lots of letters every day, and this particular morning was no different. No two letters are the same but they often contain similar themes. People ask for my help in finding solutions to their problems. Which career should they choose? Are they making the right decision? Many people want a sign from their deceased loved one.

One of the first letters I opened contained a beautiful photograph. It was of a splendid bandstand, domed in gold. I could imagine the Edwardian ladies with their picture hats and hourglass waists, wafting past on a summer's afternoon, arm in arm with the man in their lives. The bandstand had huge wrought ironwork, trellises and scrolled pillars pointing up to the sky, like a giant confection.

As my imagination subsided and reality hit, I saw someone else in the picture. Someone who was not in my imagination. Was it an Edwardian lady? No, this figure was too small and thin. Not quite the right height or looks, or standard of cleanliness come to that. No, this figure was an male urchin, very reminiscent of something out of *Oliver Twist*, except that would be the wrong vintage.

I studied him for a while. It was wonderful to see an old photograph like that. But then I looked again. This was in colour. They didn't have colour in those days, not in photographs anyway. A reproduction then? Maybe one of those fun photographs taken at some amusement park? Not wanting to spend too much time gazing at it, I put it aside.

That was in the morning. In the afternoon I decided to look at it again. It had been sent in to my letters page so I thought I would have another peek and perhaps even try to tune in to it and answer the reader's questions. Since I was already drawn to the photograph, I didn't think it would take long. The only trouble was I couldn't find it.

On my desk was a great clutter of objects, a mountain of paperwork on top of which the picture should have been sitting. Although I looked and looked, becoming steadily more frantic as time went on, I couldn't see it. 'Oh that's just great!' I remember thinking sarcastically. Imagine losing someone's picture! And not just any old picture – not that any of them ever are, mind – but it was a repro, a 'special', which had probably cost the person who sent it a great deal of money. I felt dreadful. Yet I hadn't moved from the desk all morning, so how could the photograph have disappeared?

I had put it on top of a pile of letters. There *was* a photograph there now. I could see it but it wasn't the one of the bandstand. This was of a plain, open, grassy area. Only the sky was the same. And the size of the picture. Now, although I still looked, my eyes kept coming back to it. The more I stared at it, the more I had to ask myself, 'Why would anyone send me a photograph of a plain piece of parkland? Was there something on it they wanted me to see?'

I turned my attention to the note pinned to the back of the snap. 'Dear Katie,' it began, 'I would be grateful if you could tell me what you see in the picture.' 'So,' I thought, 'I'm not the only one to see things!'

There was a telephone number attached. My heart was beginning to beat rather fast, and not just with the exertion of turning the office upside down! I lifted the phone and dialled. A moment or so later, I was speaking to the woman who had sent the snap.

'Well,' I told her flatly, 'I see the bandstand.'

'The bandstand?' she sounded puzzled. 'I've never seen that. But I do see the boy – on the right of the picture. He's very dirty looking.'

'An urchin?' I asked her, quizzically.

'Yes, like an urchin,' came the reply. 'I thought I was going mad. That's why I sent it.'

'Why did you take it?' I asked, sceptical of why someone would photograph an area of empty grass.

'It was an accident. I pressed the button in error. But when I got the film developed, I immediately saw the little boy, although I don't remember seeing him on the day I took the photograph. And he's the kind of sight you're not likely to forget. I see the boy every time I look at the photo.'

I explained how I hadn't been able to find the photograph and how this had infuriated me. I knew where I'd put it but when I went to get it, it wasn't there. I'd spent the last hour looking for it. We then chatted about the picture for a few minutes.

As the day progressed, I moved on to other work and forgot about the photograph. That night, I cleared my desk, tidying as I was going. All that remained on my desk was my diary. Nothing else.

When I came back to my desk in the morning, I was stunned to see the photograph sitting dead centre of my desk – right in front of where I sit. It was placed there, in my opinion, so that it would be the first thing I'd see.

However, although I looked at it again and again during the course of the next few days, I never saw the boy or the bandstand. Perhaps I wasn't meant to. I don't know. I can't explain it. But the boy had been very real, a reminder of a time that is past. He had peered out at me as if he wanted to be remembered. And my reader had seen him too!

The photograph has long since been returned to its owner and I've heard no more about it. But I know what I saw that day. And both the reader and I agreed, word for word, when we described the little urchin boy.

The Noble Nurse

A few years ago, while staying at a hotel in the Borders, I had a wonderful experience with a ghost whose eyes were possibly the kindest I've ever seen. The ghost I'm referring to wore an old-fashioned nursing uniform – the kind I had only ever seen in films about the First World War.

My vibes were instant and very strong. I remember feeling amazed that this lady had actually served at the front line, nursing the poor, wounded youth of the nation – a youth cursed by that particular conflict. As I looked at her, I could almost hear the screams of the poor boys she had nursed, the torment of those lying horribly wounded, knowing they would never go home again.

The first time I saw her, she actually put a finger to her lips, as if to shush me. I understood I was to say nothing. So I didn't at that point. I returned to the hotel for another short break three months later because I love the area. I didn't know if I'd see the lady or not. But my question was very quickly answered. As I went downstairs that first evening, I heard a faint step behind me and turned to see her, coming down after me. On this occasion she didn't look at me but hurried on towards the front door where she abruptly vanished.

The next night, I saw her again. She was standing at the dining room window, looking out. Her expression on this occasion seemed incredibly wistful. I still didn't know if I should say anything. Like all good guests, I didn't want to rock the boat! And so the situation continued for a while.

I must have seen the spirit of the nurse at least a dozen times before deciding to say anything to the owner of the hotel. By now I felt it was time to stop being secretive about her. It seemed to me she was troubled by something, and someone must know who she was. Although the First World War was many years ago, I believed there would be those who might even remember a story about her so that I could discover why she still hung about the house, generally with this sad aura.

The moment I mentioned her to the owner, I could detect she wasn't that surprised. What was more, she knew immediately who she was – her elderly mother's twin! Apparently, her mum, who had died several years before, had a twin sister. By all accounts she was a very caring girl who worked as a nurse in France during the First World War.

The experience of war had unnerved her, and when she came home she was apparently never the same. In fact, within a year or so of returning from war, she became desperately ill herself. In the early 1920s, she passed away, leaving her sister devastated. She had never been forgotten, though. The lady who owned the hotel said her mother often spoke of her. She brought out a photograph – and there was my nurse!

As I looked at her, I confess I was surprised. I had seen this lady so often and now here she was, looking so much younger and prettier, smiling and looking proud in her uniform, unaware of the horrors she was about to see. 'If only I could have told her,' I remember thinking. Yet I doubted if it would have made any difference. I could see the determination to go out and help in her eyes.

There are many other reported sightings of this young nurse, and I feel privileged to be just one of many.

The Woman in White

Most spirits when encountered tend to be white. My own experience suggests this is because they appear more as fuzzy lights than white-gowned entities. Many people live in a house for years with no apparent problems until one day, for no apparent reason, they become aware of a spectral figure crossing their path. I remember several clients in this category but one in particular, a lady in Glasgow who, for no obvious reason, suddenly found herself being 'visited'.

It happened out of the blue, some 14 years after moving into the house. During those years, there was never any evidence of ghostly goings-on. Then, all of a sudden and for no apparent reason, doors started to slam – so forcefully on occasions that the house shook. Objects moved from where they had been left. One evening, most frighteningly of all, a face appeared at the window. This really did terrify the owner. She began to think seriously about selling the house and moving elsewhere.

A few days later, she encountered a presence in her garden. She stopped dead in her tracks as she saw a white figure standing at the end of the path, gazing up at the house. Her fright was such she initially thought of phoning the local police. But she didn't. Something stopped her. When she sat down and thought it all through she realized the figure she had seen had been transparent – almost. That was when she was convinced she was being haunted and contacted me.

When I received her letter, I was fascinated, and not just because this was another letter about the paranormal. This one was different and caused a tingle up my spine – a common reaction for most people when reading this kind of thing, but a very unusual one for me. I then began to feel afraid and was enveloped by a very sinister feeling. I felt the person she was seeing had been murdered.

I believed the dead girl's father had been involved, that he had lost his temper and abused her. The reasons why she was appearing now were more straightforward. That, I felt, was down to personal stress on the part of the woman who had seen her. I told her this when I wrote back and was gratified when she confirmed this by letter a few days later.

It appeared that her mind had been sharpened recently by a whole series of happenings, things she just hadn't expected. The moment I knew this, I knew too that the murdered girl had always been there, waiting to be discovered as it were. It had taken my client's stress levels to rise for it to happen but happen it had. I wondered if there was any way of confirming my theory on the murdered girl.

I had felt from the start that this incident had taken place some 40 years previously. In that case, perhaps newspapers from that time would give us some information. I suggested this to my client and waited. When she contacted me again some time later, she had found evidence about the murdered girl. She told me about the abusive parents and a girl who had been slapped so hard she had fallen backwards, fatally striking her head.

It seemed the house had indeed been occupied by a man who had literally beaten his daughter to death. The poor girl was only 12 at the time. Her mother had died, her father had turned to drink and the consequences were terrible for her by the sound of it. My client had a copy of the newspaper report before her. As she read from it, I could see an image of the poor tortured soul who had been troubling her. It seemed incredible. But there was no doubt.

For reasons unknown to me, the hauntings stopped. The murdered girl was never seen again. Perhaps her tortured soul had found peace simply in the knowledge that someone knew of her existence. And in doing so, maybe she had finally been able to find her way to the wonderful place I believe heaven to be.

'I Believe You Met My Mother'

This one happened many years ago, when I was a travelling 'psychic', so to speak – a term I don't like, although I have to admit it probably best summed up what I was doing in those days. I would be booked to visit someone's house for the evening and they would have their friends in so that I could do a reading for them all. You get the picture I'm sure!

On this particular evening I was visiting a house on the outskirts of Aberdeen. I had arrived early because I wasn't sure of the location, and this gave me time to kill. I sat in the car for a while outside the lady's door but she must have seen me because she came out and asked me to come inside.

The moment I stepped into the living room I felt a presence. It was so strong I had to say to the lady, 'Do you have any spirits?' I think she probably thought I meant the alcoholic kind and wondered what kind of person she had asked into her house, because she looked at me as if I had grown two heads!

'I mean of a lady,' I added quickly. 'I'm picking up on someone who was very bossy.' The lady looked amazed. 'You know,' she said, 'my husband has been on about that. Let me get him.'

Her husband, like many other poor souls in that category, had been put out of the room and was sitting in the kitchen while the readings went on! When he heard what I'd said, though, he came willingly. It transpired that the couple had lived in the house for 18 months and during that time he had often felt someone was watching him. This was most often in the living room. In fact, he felt it so strongly he didn't like being in there on his own. Initially, he hadn't wanted to tell his wife, although eventually he had felt obliged to confess.

'Well,' I said, 'there's someone here all right. She's tall and very authoritative. I think she probably raised her family single-handedly.'

At that point the doorbell rang. The couple's friends were starting to arrive. But although I began to read for them, I couldn't get the presence out of my head. I just felt she wasn't very taken with what was going on, although of course she wouldn't say so. It was no longer her house. That was the problem. So she just stood, looking very grimly at me for the next hour or so, before vanishing altogether.

When the readings had finished, I was glad to go. I felt drained, largely because of the presence of 'my friend'. I advised the couple to find out who she was. I didn't think she'd died that long ago – probably in the 1980s. Despite her grim exterior, she wasn't harmful, just accustomed to having things her way. Her life had been difficult I felt. She'd possibly been widowed and left with several children to bring up. 'You know, I don't think you'll have trouble finding her if you ask round,' I said, but more just for something to say.

I certainly wasn't expecting a follow-up, which is why I was so surprised when the phone rang two days later. 'Hello, it's Anne,' said the voice. 'You were at my house two nights ago. I've something to tell you.'

It transpired that after I'd left for home, Anne had mentioned the lady to her group of friends. In an amazing twist of fate, one of them was a neighbour of a woman who had lived in the house. 'I'm going to ask her about this,' she said and she did.

That was why Anne was back on the phone. What I had said had turned out to be true. In the 1960s, the house had been owned by a couple who'd had five children. The father had died suddenly of a heart attack and the woman had been left to bring the children up herself. Of necessity, she had been firm, a bit of a 'tadger' by all accounts, but very fair and hardworking. She had only died at the end of the 1980s.

'Goodness,' I said. 'Well, I'm glad I was correct. Have you spoken to her daughter yet?' 'Of course,' Anne replied. 'In fact, there's someone here I want you to talk to. Just confirm everything you saw.' There was a shuffling at the other end as the receiver was handed to someone else.

'Hello,' said a pleasant, well-spoken voice, 'I believe you just met my mother ...'

The Modern Haunt

Can a modern house be haunted – one in which the first occupants still live, where there's never been a death? Well, the answer is yes. Although the house is modern, the land it has been built on has been there for centuries. As this story reveals, sometimes more than one modern house can be haunted, like those that were built on the site of an old factory.

Within no time at all, the residents were experiencing problems which suggested they weren't the only occupants! When they contacted me, I asked each of them to write down what they had seen and felt and send it to me. In the meantime I would look at the photographs they had sent and make some notes myself.

The first thing I picked up on was that these noises were mechanical. I could hear voices and even horns blaring, but in the main I was hearing machines, as if the site had once been an old factory. The smell and smoke suggested that it was possibly a tannery. Certainly it was stifling, and I would have been surprised if the residents in the new houses hadn't noticed even a trace of it. It was so overpowering. It also seemed to me that the hustle and bustle of factory life was more pronounced than usual. This convinced me that the time period I was looking at was the Second World War.

The workers' matter-of-fact manner was quite amazing, since it seemed to me that many of them would have died during the war. There was no sadness however. They were all very busy, too busy perhaps to have time. While I was saying it was a tannery, there was also no doubt in my mind that other things were produced there at one stage, and that this had to do with the war effort.

When the war finished, the factory closed, although it wasn't demolished immediately. For a few years it was used as a storage facility. Ultimately, however, that too was closed but it still wasn't demolished. Instead the junk piled up and the debris gathered as it gradually fell apart. Then this fascinating place was completely demolished and the ground was cleared to make room for new houses.

Having sensed all this from the photographs, I was eagerly awaiting the letters that came in from the three sets of residents. When they did, I was so pleased. Each of them mentioned the same thing – the noise that sounded like machinery, the faint sound of a horn going off at periodic intervals, and the voices. One had clearly heard someone calling 'Margaret'. Another often heard doors opening and closing. One had noticed the smell but put it down to something in the drains!

On the whole I found this so interesting that I contacted the resident who had written to me first and asked her to make some enquiries with the council about what had been on the site previously. The council weren't much help there but the local library was – and yes, it was a tannery! The Second World War had been the time when production was in full force, but it had been closed a year after the war finished.

Closed, I hasten to add, but still very much open for business in the ghost stakes, as many other places are too! There's no doubt in my mind, from the many letters I receive on cases like this one, that we all leave something behind us, although for a factory to leave so much is quite something.

At least the residents realized they weren't imagining things! That in itself was comforting. Now, if they could only do something about the smell …

The Haunted Dog

In other parts of this book I've written about places being haunted by an animal, and about people being haunted by other people. But this is a special story. It's about an animal being haunted by a spirit, in this case a previous owner. That may sound a little far-fetched but just keep reading!

The animal in question was a dog, and dogs are generally quite receptive to spirits. In fact, I've heard many stories of dogs who refuse to go somewhere, obviously afraid of something no one else can see. But usually this is because they are picking up on something that's already there. It's certainly rare for a dog to find itself as haunted as a human can be. So, believe me, when this letter first came in I was as sceptical as you probably are.

'Dear Katie, I began reading your page on its launch,' the letter began, 'and have been interested in your "ghostly" stories ever since.' The start of this letter sounded like many others that come in during the course of a week. But as I read on, I could see this one was different. The person knew their house was haunted and had accepted it. But their dog, which had been accustomed to a fair amount of goings-on, had recently started to behave very strangely. Often it leapt up excitedly for no reason, as if someone was there, and started going through its 'let's go for a walk' ritual.

There was never anyone there – at least no one the dog's owners could see. The hall was empty, although there was the dog standing with its ears up, barking at something. At other times, too, the dog leapt up yelping, as if someone was standing on its tail.

I looked at the photograph of the hallway sent by my reader and straightaway had the feeling that the spirit was not connected with the house. It was connected with the *dog*! It was clear to me that the dog had been owned by someone else, and that my reader had taken possession of the dog after its owner's health had deteriorated so badly that she could no longer care for it.

I could clearly hear her name – Daisy. And equally clearly, I could picture an old lady, no longer in robust health. Indeed, it seemed to me that she was very frail, and the reason the dog kept yelping as if someone had stood on its tail was because someone had. It was Daisy and she was blind.

At this stage I decided to lift the phone and ask one or two questions. This isn't something I often do, but I was intrigued. I just sensed that Daisy must have died and had returned to see her dog. That explained why it kept leaping up whenever it sensed she was there, as if it was expecting her to take it for a walk. I believed Daisy had adored it when she had been fit and able to look after it. But then she had become so frail she had to find a new owner for the dog. The poor dog certainly recognized her, even if she did keep standing on its tail!

When my call was answered, I didn't know what to expect. It's always a bit like taking a cold plunge. I say to myself, 'Will this be the one time I'm totally wrong?' After I'd introduced myself and explained why I was phoning, I felt better, especially when Elizabeth, the dog's owner, confirmed that they had got the dog from its previous owner.

I began to tell Elizabeth what I was sensing – about the old lady and how her health had deteriorated so badly she'd had no option but to allow someone else to care for the dog.

'Yes Katie,' Elizabeth confirmed with slight excitement in her voice. 'We got him from an old lady, a sweet woman who cried when she handed the dog over to us. The poor soul had gone blind and she wasn't able to take him for walks anymore or look after him. She was my friend's neighbour. Her name was Daisy!'

'Well, I think I've found your spirit!'

I think we were both amazed by that possibility. I asked Elizabeth to try to find out if Daisy had died at about the time the dog started behaving strangely. It was some weeks before I heard again. When she did eventually call, she confirmed all I had suspected. Daisy had died in a nursing home. She had largely been alone and the dog had been her greatest friend.

She never forgot him, apparently, often telling the staff about him. 'I just wish I could take him for a walk. He loved his walks,' she'd say to staff members.

Clearly, Daisy missed her dog terribly while in the nursing home. But it wasn't until after she died that she was finally able to see him and spend time with him, just as before!

So in this case, it wasn't an animal spirit coming to comfort its owner, it was the owner coming to comfort her animal!

The Mum who Came to Say Goodbye

Jennifer Lilburn was ashamed. She had done something she regarded as very silly. Yet it's something that probably 95 per cent of us would have done in the same situation. She had driven past her best friend's mother, Gloria. Is that so unusual, you're probably asking. In this case, it was pretty unusual because Gloria had been dead for six months!

Jennifer hadn't known what to make of it but she was convinced it was Gloria she had seen. She felt panic begin to rise, which in many ways is the normal reaction of someone who sees something they know they shouldn't. Then she drove on, nearly hitting a lamppost in the process I'm told! And who can blame her?

Gloria was apparently standing there, bold as brass and clear as day. There was no mistaking her. She even had the little handbag she always carried on her arm. And she was wearing her usual blue, knee-length coat.

Jennifer was stunned. She was just leaving Gloria's daughter's house at the time, pulling out of the driveway and turning onto the road. That's when she saw her in, dare I add it, 'all her glory'.

Jennifer drove on. What else could she do? Gloria was staring up at her daughter's house so wistfully, straining her eyes, hoping for a glimpse of someone. 'It can't be!' poor Jennifer said over and over. Then she thought, 'Yes it is!' And then she immediately stopped the car, reversed it and went back. She drove along the same road, passing her friend's house. She was hoping now to repeat the sighting. But Gloria was gone. The road was empty. 'Is my mind playing tricks with me?' Jennifer wrote to me. Personally, I didn't think so.

Jennifer seemed a level-headed lady and not one for fanciful ideas. She and Gloria had been friends for many years. There was no way Jennifer was mistaken. Then she asked me why Gloria came back after her death and why she was standing outside her own home. My answer to this was a gut feeling I had. 'I believe Gloria didn't get the chance to say goodbye to her beloved family, and this is why she stands outside the house, just hoping for a glimpse of one of them.' Jennifer was able to confirm this theory when she explained the cause of Gloria's death.

Jennifer felt such guilt at not stopping when she first saw Gloria. If only she had stopped. If only she had gone back sooner, she felt she could have helped the clearly distressed spirit. But it seemed to me that Jennifer's reaction was a normal one. Let's be honest – how many of us would stop in a similar situation? Perhaps not even as many as the five per cent I predicted at the start of this story. Probably most of us would have driven on and not come back, the provisional dust flying from our bumpers as we went!

Perhaps Gloria was glad her friend had driven off, choosing instead simply to be alone and wait and watch for the slightest glimpse of the family she had loved and from whom she'd been taken eternally.

I assured Jennifer that the stronger Gloria got, after being healed emotionally and physically in the place I call my 'heaven hospital', the more able she would be to make her presence felt so strongly that her family would have no doubt she was very near to them.

The Ghost who Wanted to Go Upstairs

Carla Johnston was haunted by a strange thing, the ghost of a man who, for whatever reason, wanted to go upstairs in her house. She had no idea who he was or why he felt this way. He was, however, clearly disturbed by his failure, and so was she. When she contacted me, she was at her wit's end. By that stage, not only Carla but also several members of her family could see this man.

Every time they did, he was a little closer to the top. But it was only by a step or so. Sometimes only by an inch! The man was old. He never looked at them. It was clear that he was struggling and they suspected that he meant no harm. Just the same, Carla wanted to know about him.

The first thing I picked up on when I stepped into Carla's house was the coldness in the hall, or rather the 'cold spots'.

It wasn't an unpleasant feeling as these things can sometimes be, but it was quite pronounced. There was definitely a great deal of 'activity' on the stairs. As I removed my jewellery – which is something I always have to do so as not to let it interfere with my actual 'work' – I felt we weren't alone. I sensed the old man rather than saw him on the stairs. The picture I had was of something quite different.

It was a beach, but not the kind you lie on in the summer, contemplating your next exotic cocktail. This beach was dreadful, a scene of unbelievable carnage. Overhead shells were flying instead of birds. The ratatat of gunfire strafed the water, and that itself wasn't blue. It was red, turned so by the blood that was seeping from the bodies of the men who were in it. I shuddered. I knew I was seeing something no one should be asked to watch, or for that matter, asked to be part of. But these people weren't asked. They were soldiers caught up in a conflict that defies description, the carnage known as the Second World War. These were the Normandy landings and I was privileged to be allowed to watch.

The old man had been part of that group. He had managed to jump from the landing craft into the water but there a shell had exploded, ripping his leg in half. Amazingly, he was pulled from the water alive. Even more amazingly, he survived. But he never walked properly again.

This explained why he couldn't manage to climb the stairs but it still didn't answer the question as to why he wanted to so badly. Clearly, he had lived in the house. Now it seemed that all kinds of things were coming to me. I saw that he had been lonely. Despite how badly he had suffered, he had lived for many years, not dying till the 1970s. In that time, his family had all grown up. His wife had died. His disability made going out awkward and his latter years were sad. The stairs were things he had never managed but before she died, his wife had been in one of the rooms above him. I could hear her calling out his name. She had wanted him to come and help her. He had tried and failed.

All these touching things were suddenly apparent to me as I stood there in the hallway. I also felt that this man still wanted to climb these stairs. It was something he had to do before he could join his beloved family. That was why he was struggling so, always being seen at a different point, always a little higher but never quite there.

I sensed that what he needed was encouragement. 'You can do it,'I whispered.'You know you can. Anyone who came through that terrible day when you were wounded and lost so much can do this.'

At that point I felt a great lightness. I don't know how else to describe it. To say it was a 'thank you' would be wrong. It seemed to me that the old man must have walked up six steps at that point! Anyway, he certainly reached the top. He was never seen again.

Carla waited and waited. Eventually, she had to admit the old man was gone. But sometimes, as she passes the upstairs sitting room, she has the feeling there's a crowd in there and a party is going on!

The Maid from Broughty Ferry

A house within a stone's throw of the railway line in Broughty Ferry is haunted by the ghost of a maid who worked there. The street itself is a quiet little cul-de-sac, which looks the last place in the world to be the scene of psychic happenings.

Behind the lace curtains, however, a little spectre lurks. Not a very friendly spirit if some of the reports are anything to go by, but certainly one who likes to make her presence felt.

'I was terrified,' said Linda, a woman who visited the house as a child. 'To this day I can still remember the insistent tapping noise she was making, as if she wanted me to know she was there. I just ran!'

As a little girl, Linda was playing with her friend who lived in the house and another little girl. 'We were playing in one of the attic rooms. I didn't like it up there. There was a kind of atmosphere about it. The stairs were painted red which didn't help. But when you got to the top of them there was a coldness that always came off one of the rooms at the top. Not the one we were playing in. I always felt someone was waiting.'

On the day in question, the two other girls had gone back downstairs. 'Please don't ask me why I didn't go with them. To this day, I can't answer that. But I do remember being enthralled by a dolls' house and wanting to play a little longer. I told my friends I'd come down in a minute. Then I heard a noise. Someone was drumming against the woodwork. I assumed the noises were being made by my friends.'

Even then, the fact it was anyone other than her two friends playing tricks didn't cross the girl's mind. That was until she heard someone calling up to her from outside. She went to the window, looked down and saw that everyone, including her family and her two friends, were in the back garden.

'That was when I asked myself – and I was all of seven at the time – if everyone was down there sunning themselves and calling for me to join them, then who was in the other room, tapping on the wall? My flesh just crawled. I almost flew down the stairs! The tapping followed me. I wasn't imagining it.

'When I got to the bottom of the stairs, I bolted into the garden. I remember my mum saying I looked pale, like I'd "just seen a ghost". I was so afraid and so out of breath that I said nothing.'

As children do, she forgot about her frightening experience. A few months later, she went back to the house to play with her friend. This time the events that took place were to be etched on her mind forever. It was a visit marred by a fainting spell and a complete blackout. She told me she felt she was 'floating' and that she was not herself, and she described the footsteps that followed her everywhere, every time she was alone.

'I had to get home,' she recalled. 'So I got my friend's parents to send for my mum. The moment I was away from the house I was fine. But I was never able to go back. While I was there, I actually felt as if something was trying to "enter" me. There were times when I was standing there but I wasn't me. Then I would come to and find I'd dropped a whole milk bottle or something. It was as if I was in a trance. I was terrified by it. I thought I had some ghastly disease. When I wasn't in the house I was fine, though. That was the strange thing. Nothing like that had ever happened to me before, and nothing's happened since then. Even now I couldn't even go back there.'

Intrigued by the woman's story, I went with her to the house. We went to visit, mainly to ask if there was anything odd about the house. The answer was quite amazing. Although the people who had owned the house when the woman was a girl had long gone, the present owners had also had bother. There had been noises in the glass-floored room and footsteps coming up to their bedroom door, although there was never anyone there. They had called in a psychic consultant who told them quite clearly that there had been an accident involving the glass floor.

A child of the house had at one stage fallen through the first layer of the floor. He had been rescued but the maid had been blamed for letting the little boy up to her quarters in the first place. There was even a suggestion that the maid's nature was such that she might have been happy to see the boy fall. She had been sacked, although plainly she hadn't quite departed! Unable to find another job, the woman began to drink, died in poverty and then returned to the house in spirit.

The psychic consultant suggested that the couple arrange for the house to be blessed, just as a matter of course, and since then there haven't been any further reports of disturbances. That still won't make the woman who had the terrifying experiences there change her mind. And given how much the maid seemed to take to her, perhaps that's just as well!

THREE

Over to You: Ghost Stories from My Readers

This chapter contains letters I have received from the public, regaling their experiences of the spirit world. Wading through the mountain of correspondence was great fun but it was so difficult to choose which letters to use in the book, as they were all so fascinating. I used my own vibes when choosing the encounters to include. Thank you all for entrusting me with your experiences. The hard work was done by my readers as this chapter is about what they saw and felt during their encounters with their dearly departed loved ones and, at times, with strangers – ghosts of people they'd never known but who had, for whatever reason, chosen to 'haunt' their environment.

The Friendly Ghost

It's not just that old children's favourite, 'Caspar', who's friendly to everyone. This is another story from one of my clients who was, not surprisingly, amazed when she learned she had been talking to a ghost – a very friendly old lady who still liked to wander round old 'haunts' that were hers when she was alive, chatting to anyone who would listen.

Clare met her when she went to visit her mum, who had only just moved into the area. As she stepped out of the car, she was greeted by a very friendly, smiling face. The lady was very small and dressed for going out. She said her name was Mrs Reid and asked Clare who she was. Clare, a little bemused by the tiny old lady's friendliness, decided to humour her by spending 10 minutes talking to her. After all, her mum was new to the neighbourhood, and Clare felt it wouldn't do any harm to get to know some of the folk who lived there. If they were all as friendly as Mrs Reid, Clare felt sure her mum would settle in quickly.

Mrs Reid told Clare that she had lived there for many years and was most specific about how nice the neighbours were. Clare's mum would be very happy, the old lady assured her. Ending their conversation, Mrs Reid asked Clare to say 'hello and welcome' to her mother on her behalf.

Clare, still feeling very bemused by it all, agreed. Mrs Reid went on her way. 'To the shops,' she said, something she liked to do every morning. She even told Clare how far they were and how to get there, as well as dropping in one or two other pieces of friendly gossip about Mrs Brown, who sometimes went with her, and Mrs Macdonald, whose husband tuned pianos.

Clare went into her mum's house. When Clare got inside, she saw another lady sitting chatting warmly to her mother. She too was a neighbour, the very Mrs Brown who had been mentioned, and Clare was by now delighted that everyone was so friendly. Her mum was lonely and this seemed an ideal situation.

She sat down on one of the chairs and waited for an opportunity to enter the conversation. When that opportunity came, Clare relayed the conversation she had just had with old Mrs Reid. 'She was such a sweet lady and asked me to pass on her best wishes to you.' Clare's mum looked pleased. Mrs Brown looked puzzled!

'Not Etta Reid?' Mrs Brown asked, turning pale as she spoke.

'Yes, I believe she said her first name was Etta. She mentioned you too, Mrs Brown, telling me you and she normally walk to the shops together.' Clare was a little surprised by Mrs Brown's sudden change in tone. 'Is there something wrong?' she asked. 'Well, yes. I used to go to the shops with Etta every day. But I haven't done for years. You see, Etta's dead.'

'Dead?'

'Yes. Five years ago.'

Clare was stunned to think the lady she had seen so clearly and spoken to for at least 10 minutes didn't exist. Everything Etta Reid had said to her, from the location of the shops to the names of the neighbours and their various occupations, was the truth. No wonder Mrs Brown had turned pale!

Stranger than fiction? Well, the truth always is!

The Mystery of the Trophy Room

This is a letter I received not long after I started working as a psychic columnist. And it stood out among the other 'problem' letters, as far as I was concerned, because it was a genuine paranormal letter. My mailbag sometimes bulges with the more ordinary – people wondering when they will sell their house, or if their partner is being faithful. This one, however, seemed a genuine ghost story, if you like. So I had no hesitation about choosing it for my page, which meant I could then answer it.

'Dear Katie

'For over a year now, my mum has been saying some strange things. At first, we – her children – thought it was just her vivid imagination. She speaks of how our dad comes to her at night and how he asks after each of us by name. She also tells us she can hear him moving about downstairs, especially in what we call the "trophy room".

'The trophy room is a small cupboard where my brother and I keep our trophies. Mine are for swimming and my brother's are for football. When we moved out of our child-hood home to be married, we decided to let mum keep the trophies. She was so proud of us, as was dad.

'Three weeks ago, as I was switching out the lights in my lounge, something caught my eye. It was the last trophy I ever won. I picked it up and wondered how it got there. Then I simply put it down and went to bed.

'The next morning, the first thing on my mind was the trophy. I went into the lounge but the trophy was gone. Now Katie, there is no way in the world I imagined that trophy was on the sofa. Mum didn't notice it was missing but I am still convinced some paranormal incident took place here. I am not a believer in the paranormal, although I have been astounded at times by your replies. What other explanation can there be, though, on this occasion?'

What did I see? Well, there was just no doubt that the lady who wrote it had been giving her poor old mum a hard time.

For over a year since her partner's death, this old lady had taken great comfort from the fact that he wasn't really gone, that he came to her every night and chatted away about the family he still loved. Now here was her daughter doing everything to tell her it wasn't so, that these things didn't happen.

The main bone of contention appeared to be the trophy room. As it was the focus of the old lady's pride, she was convinced it was only natural her husband should be in there, admiring the trophies, reading over their inscriptions. Perhaps he would even polish them every other week, as he had in life. How could her daughter not believe? Where was her faith?

The crunch time came after a particular visit when the daughter was just too impatient with her mum. Dad decided enough was enough. He lifted one of the trophies and placed it in his daughter's house. There is no other explanation. The woman had never seen it there before. The next morning it was gone. Yet she wasn't dreaming when she read the inscription and realized it was the last trophy she'd won.

A visit from the grave? I think so. From then on, let's just say that when the subject of dad was mentioned, his daughter always treated it with the utmost respect!

The Patient Ghost

To some extent we all treasure the image of ghosts as beautiful, lovelorn girls. This isn't always the case, as most of the stories in this book attest. However, the ghost in the following story was a beautiful girl, the kind to step right off the silver screen at that time, during the Second World War.

The letter was from a couple who had seen the ghost in their house. She was tall, with a hint of melancholy about her face. They had often seen her gazing out of the window and wondered if she might be looking for her husband. At first, I thought that might be the case too. But then, as I looked at the photographs of the house, it became clearer to me that whoever was haunting it was a very lonely presence, a girl who had never married. I could see that she had been misunderstood and that she may well have lost her lover, which would explain her presence at the window.

It seemed to me that this girl was called Margaret. I contacted the letter writer to ask if she could perhaps find out who had lived in the house before. I was about to suggest a street directory but the lady who had written said that she could check the title deeds first. She and her husband had actually lived there for nearly 30 years and had been convinced it was haunted since day one.

When she telephoned me again she was excited. They had bought the house from a couple who had also lived there for a good few years. The previous owner had been called Margaret, and she appeared to have inherited the house from her father. But it was obvious she hadn't lived long afterwards. By 1948 she was dead.

'Well,' I said. 'I think you've found your ghost. I have very definite feelings that this is her.'

I sensed that Margaret had died in a room in the house, and proceeded to describe one that was full of windows, almost like a turret. I hadn't seen this on the photographs, so I was surprised when my client took a sharp breath.

'There's a bit like that on the dining room, downstairs,' she said. 'A sort of large, round alcove, with windows in it, facing onto the garden.'

My client had never seen Margaret in the alcove but she had often felt strangely wistful when she stood there, almost as if she wanted to cry. The garden was lovely to look at, but not that lovely she should feel like bursting into tears.

I explained that I thought Margaret had died in her late 20s of some kind of disease. I felt that life had passed her by but that she had almost been happy to die because so many people she had known and cherished had passed before her. This was a 'stiff upper lip' generation who never complained. Margaret's lip had been stiff for so long, she was almost glad to relax it in death. At the same time, I felt terribly for her wasted life.

I was never able to pick up on whether or not Margaret had a lover. Was there ever a handsome soldier in her life? I would like to think so, and that this is the reason she stands so patiently at the window, waiting. Perhaps he's still alive. Who knows? If she should stop for any reason, then I feel that would be answer enough.

Our Soldier

A house in Kirk Road, Newport-On-Tay, is haunted by the spirit of a boy killed in the trenches in the First World War. 'I never believed in such things,' the owner of the house stated, 'until I came to live here.'

Down the years it seems there's been no other explanation. 'Tommy', as the family calls him, first made his presence known when they moved in. 'I was putting some ornaments on the shelf when someone tapped my arm several times,' the lady of the house explained. 'I thought it was my little girl. In fact, I was so certain I tapped her back and told her to give me a minute. When I looked round, there was no one there. My hair stood on end. I went to the sitting room door and shouted to my daughter. "Hello?" She answered from upstairs, "What is it Mummy?"

'"My God, what was that?" I thought, because my daughter could not have got upstairs in that space of time. There was just no way.'

Over the weeks that followed, more strange things happened. First of all there was the feeling, overwhelming at first, that the family just wasn't welcome in the house. Then there was the spate of things going missing. This ranged from valuable photographic negatives to pieces of jewellery, some of which have never been found.

'We're now at the stage where we don't put anything down,' joked the owner, 'unless we want to spend the next three weeks looking for it!'

Missing items generally turn up after a while but usually in a different place to where they were left. The owner added, 'We almost feel he doesn't mean to take them but it can be deeply upsetting too, especially if it's something of value or sentiment.'

I'm told that over the years electricity has been fiddled with, and lights switched on and off. They've had curtains draw by themselves. A plant mysteriously perched itself on top of the piano. These incidents are nothing out of the ordinary. But the real crunch came when an upper area of the house was renovated and the youngest member of the family started to complain about the noises in her bedroom.

'She was in hysterics because she insisted she could hear footsteps, as if someone was walking up and down the hall outside her bedroom. So I went and sat with her. Sure enough, I heard it too, although of course I didn't tell my daughter for fear of alarming her. Apart from us, the house was empty at the time.'

Of course, this could all be dismissed as make-believe, but it just so happened that a few days after this, the owner of the house spoke to the person they had bought it from. 'How are you liking having the extra attic space?' she asked, and the owner felt obliged to tell her about the noise. That's when the truth came out. The house was haunted. The previous owner had even seen the ghost in his splendid soldier's uniform and asked neighbours about him. She just didn't think the house would be sold if she'd told the truth.

So the current owner just decided to live with 'Tommy'. 'He's almost one of the family,' she says. 'After all, what's the point of having it otherwise? He doesn't mean us any harm. In fact, he's been very good at throwing the odd plant pot or lamp at those he feels do. So though that's required a bit of explaining and clearing up, I don't think it's much of a price to pay. At nights he knocks on the bedroom doors. And it's so real that initially you rise to answer the knock. But on the whole my attitude's been that I can live with him if he can live with me. I've never actually seen him and maybe that's a good thing. I do have to live here after all!'

The Supermarket Ghost

Gossamerish, yes – that's what people expect ghosts to be like – translucent, pale and ever so fragile. But gossipy? Now that's another matter. So is looking just like any other man, woman or child in the street. Or a friend's dad.

Yet this is exactly what happened to a young woman called Fiona Kellor when she returned to her home town after an absence of four years. She didn't realize that some people she knew had died in the meantime. Living away in Jersey meant she didn't always keep as closely in touch as she would have liked. And that was why she was so pleased when, on her first trip out to the local supermarket, she met her friend Avril's father.

'Aren't you looking well!' she said, thrilled to see a familiar face. 'I was planning on phoning Avril later today.' It was great to see the old man again. What was more, he obviously thought it was great to see her, to catch up on – and he was very clear about this – a little gossip. He asked how her family were doing and she returned the question. 'They're all doing well at the moment,' he smiled.

Fiona remembered he had always been a great family man. A doting father and husband was how people best knew him.

After chatting for several more minutes, the two parted with promises of keeping in touch and arranging a get-together in the near future. 'I'll tell Avril you are home and get her to call you.'

The next few days passed in a blur for Fiona – they always do when you're busy. But Fiona was a bit disappointed that she hadn't heard from Avril. Maybe her dad hadn't passed on the message … but why wouldn't he?

Several more days passed without a call from Avril and Fiona decided the old man had most probably not mentioned their meeting. Whatever the reason, she wasn't about to let anything spoil an old friendship, so she decided to call her friend.

Avril was delighted to hear from her – she hadn't known Fiona was back in town and was thrilled. The two arranged to meet for lunch and, of course, a good old catch-up.

The following day Fiona met Avril in a local pub. It was years since they'd seen each other, and before long the photographs and anecdotes were flying back and forth across the table. Just then, Avril's face became sad. 'Of course you won't have heard about dad,' she said. 'That's my one piece of bad news.'

'What is?' asked Fiona, remembering how well he'd looked and wondering what could possibly have happened in the few days since she'd seen him.

'He died a year ago.' As she heard this, Fiona felt the hackles rising on the back of her neck. It just didn't seem possible that she had been speaking to a ghost. But if it wasn't Avril's father, who could it have been in the shop that day?

'Is something wrong?' asked Avril.

'Well – well, I…' Fiona took a sip of wine then some water from the carafe on the table, which she poured into the spare glass.

'But he can't be, Avril,' she said eventually. Avril explained how her father had taken ill suddenly and died shortly after.

'But I saw him! I spoke to him! In the supermarket! A few days ago!' Fiona stuttered the words out.

'You couldn't have.' But Fiona knew she had seen him – they'd spoken for several minutes. Others shoppers would have seen him too. The shop had been busy.

Avril listened as Fiona went through every detail of their conversation, all he had said. Although Avril was absolutely incredulous, there seemed very little doubt. She knew her friend wouldn't make up something so bizarre.

But what finally convinced Avril that her friend was telling the truth was her father's clothes. Down to the last detail, Fiona described all that Avril's father had been wearing.

The very same clothes he had worn on the day he died!

Bride Beth

Sometimes spirits can really push the boat out for a big occasion involving a loved one. And these stories are so frequent I just can't put them all down to wishful thinking, or the desire to believe there is 'something'. I am personally very drawn to the particular 'happening' described here, largely because it seems to me there is proof this wasn't just in the mind of the person concerned. They say dead men don't walk, or women for that matter, but this is the story of one who did.

Beth was getting married and, like many other brides, was looking forward to sharing the day with family and friends. But her happiness was marred by the absence of one very special person to whom she owed so much: her mum.

They had been very close and had begun the preparations with great excitement. Neither could hide their enthusiasm and talked endlessly about the 'big day'.

That Beth's mum could laugh quite as much as she did was a source of constant amazement to Beth, because her mum's life had been very hard. This was a lady who suffered constant trials, for whom very little ever seemed to 'go right'. When she died six months before Beth's 'big day', it seemed ironic in many ways. She was even being denied her rightful place at her daughter's wedding. Beth was devastated.

Beth's mum didn't have much to leave behind. She had always thought of everyone before herself. The only thing of material value she owned was a particularly good coat, one she had literally burst the bank to buy in the first place so she could wear it on special occasions. Beth didn't want to part with it. It was rather stunning anyway, so she had it cleaned and hung it in the wardrobe. Beth thought she might even wear it herself at some point, if time and circumstance were right.

Beth's wedding day dawned. Everything was going as planned, except for that one thing we never have any control over – the weather. It was pouring with rain and, as she stepped from the car to the church steps, Beth's gown was splattered with mud. Still, Beth was determined. A little mud wasn't going to ruin the day. 'If only Mum was here to see me,' was all she could think as the organ began to play the

Bridal march. That, rather than the mud and the rain, was the only thing spoiling her happiness.

The vows said, the rings exchanged, Beth and her new husband stepped into the vestry to sign the register with the other witnesses. The usual photographs were taken, congratulations and kisses given, and Beth stepped out again to begin the walk back down the aisle to the door.

That was when she saw her, the lady in the beautiful coat, sitting right at the back of the church. The small woman, with no hat, beaming with pride and happiness. Mum. Beth turned to her husband to point her out. When she turned back, the lady had got up. 'She simply walked out of the church like any other guest at that point,' said Beth, who thought she had imagined it. 'By the time I got outside, she was gone.'

All right, so at this point it is possible to think that Beth was only imagining something she so wanted to see. Her mum at her wedding, there to share her happy day with her. Maybe it had been her imagination. But suddenly Beth had a great notion to see that coat. Suddenly, too, that coat seemed the ideal thing to have with her when she left for her honeymoon, given the way the rain was still pouring down. If she went home after the reception, she would be able to pick the coat up.

How Beth managed to get through the reception was something of a miracle because by then all kinds of thoughts were racing through her head. Had her mum really been there? Was she just imagining it? Well, the answers to her questions were soon answered.

As soon as she could, Beth raced back to her house and up the stairs to the wardrobe. The coat was there, exactly as Beth had left it. Still on its wooden hanger, still in its packaging from the dry cleaners. There was only one difference.

The hem was spattered with mud!

The Melancholy Motorcyclist

A house in the Bearsden district of Glasgow is haunted by the spirit of a young man who was killed while out pursuing his favourite pastime – biking. It happened some years ago, long before the present owners moved in. Diane and Stuart had been married for years and were thrilled with their new home.

When they bought the house, they knew something of its his-tory, including the young man's unfortunate death. Nothing, however, could quite prepare them for his frequent and almost stunning appearances, complete with biker boots, clumping up and down the landing at all hours of the day and night.

The first time she heard it, Diane thought there was an intruder. Only she couldn't understand why he was making so much noise. Did he want to be caught? Then she thought it was perhaps her son, but why would he make so much noise either? She opened the bedroom door to give him what she politely called 'what for', but to her surprise there was no one there. This was so alarming and puzzling, she decided she had been dreaming. But the 'dreams' continued the next night and the one after.

Eventually, she remembered the sad story connected to the house. She recalled being told the young man had a motorbike. The footsteps *were* heavy, as if someone was wearing heavy biker boots. Even then, however, she didn't quite believe the house had a ghost.

After a night or two, as suddenly as they had come, the sounds stopped. The owners were very relieved about this, putting the whole thing down to bad plumbing, noises in the pipes, shrinking floorboards – anything other than a ghostly motorcyclist.

Just as they were drifting off to sleep, they heard another noise. It was a slightly more familiar one – that of their own son wailing.

'There was a man sitting on my bed, trying to take his boots off!' their son announced as they ran to his room.

Of course, there were no prizes for guessing who he was. A quick phone call to the previous owners established that the room had been their son's. So the present owners decided to switch their son's room, to see if it made a difference. The noises stopped. The appearances didn't.

The family no longer uses this room, not just because of its inexplicable coldness but also because two of their son's friends have reported seeing 'something' sitting on the bed – the tall figure of a man, dressed in a black jacket and trousers. They both described how sad he looked. Rather than being afraid, they actually felt more sorry for him. 'His head was in his hands and he seemed to have tears on his face,' they both said.

The phantom motorcyclist? I would think so. He seems to have come home at last but everything around him has changed. No wonder he's sad. He was a young man, his whole life ahead of him, but because of a tragic accident, his life was over.

I feel sorry for him too and I just hope he can find his way to a happier existence.

Mum's the Word, or a Warning in Time!

Thelma was sure she was awake, though she wouldn't have minded in the slightest if she was only dreaming. Why? Because she was seeing her mum who had died some years before.

Thelma missed her terribly. There wasn't a day went by when Thelma didn't think of her mum, or wish they could have a little chat. Sometimes, too, Thelma wished she could dream about her. That was why she was so pleased when this finally appeared to have happened. To be awake, as she now realized she was, was even better.

There was just so much she wanted to say. In particular, she wanted to ask, 'Mum, what are you doing here? How have you managed to come?' Then she wanted to sit her down, to tell her all the things that had happened in the family. Her mum, however, waved her away. 'Don't be silly. I don't have time for that now,' she said. Thelma wasn't actually too surprised or hurt by that. Her mum had always been a busy woman, with never a moment to spare. It was what her mum said next that alarmed her.

'Get Rhona,' Mum said, 'on the phone. Tell her she's going into labour.'

Thelma froze. Rhona was her daughter. She was pregnant but the baby wasn't due for another eight weeks. 'Don't be silly,' she said, now convinced it was all a dream. 'Anyway,

Rhona won't thank me for phoning at this time. It's three o'clock in the morning.' 'You're the one who's being silly,' said Mum. 'Get Rhona right away. The baby will be early but she'll survive if Rhona gets to the hospital now.'

'She? You mean it's a girl?'

'It won't be anything at all if you don't hurry. Go on.'

Now very alarmed, Thelma lifted the telephone and dialled Rhona's number. Of course, Rhona was less than pleased about being woken up at three in the morning. With eight weeks to go till the birth, she was sleeping badly and was snatching all she could when the phone rang. She was even angrier when she heard why. 'Gran' appearing indeed! What a load of rubbish! Had Thelma lost her marbles? This was so stupid it wasn't real. Did Thelma know she was having a baby in eight weeks? Well, it didn't look like it or she wouldn't be ringing with stupid stories at this time of night.

Banging the phone down she went back to bed. But not for long. As she lay down again, she had a pain across her lower back. Within an hour her waters had broken. She was rushed to hospital where the baby was born. With eight weeks still to go, the signs weren't great, but everything was fine, largely due it seemed to 'Gran's' warning. Almost as soon as Thelma passed it on, this lady had disappeared never to be seen again. She was, however, looking out for her family. Rhona and the baby soon recovered.

And the baby's sex? Oh, it was a girl, of course!

Just When You Thought it Was Safe
to Go Back in the Garden!

Terry's dad had died. Of course, when these things happen, they always seem sudden, whether they are expected or not. What made it worse in Terry's case was the fact that he had no belief in life after death. He didn't believe in the spirit world or any of these things. As far as he was concerned, when you died, you died. That was it. His Dad wasn't any place.

So given all this, Terry was surprised one day to find, when he looked out of the bedroom window, that his dad was some place after all. Terry's back garden. He was standing there, looking up at Terry and he had a handkerchief in his hand.

Terry was amazed. In fact, to say he was amazed is an understatement. He missed his dad terribly and, although he was an unbeliever, he was prepared to be converted. 'Show me the proof,' he always said. And now, it seemed that here was something to convince him. 'Dad! Dad!' Terry opened the window and shouted down. Terry's dad smiled.

Terry remembered that he couldn't get enough of the sight. He shouted again and this time his dad beckoned him to come down. Terry hardly needed telling twice. He couldn't believe his dad was really there, exactly as he'd last seen him. What did the old man want? Why did he have the ridiculous handkerchief? Was he upset with Terry because he didn't believe? Was that the reason he kept holding it to his face? Well, Terry would believe now. If only his dad were there when he got downstairs, he'd believe anything.

These were the thoughts in Terry's mind as he ran into the garden. When he got there the path was empty. His dad had gone. Terry felt an absolute fool. Had he imagined the whole thing?

But there was one thing lying on the path where his dad had been standing. A white handkerchief. It was the proof Terry needed.

'He's Sitting There!'

Mary's husband had died. It was all very sudden and Mary was shocked. Not because she was grief-stricken as such. Guilt-ridden might have been a more apt description for the way she was feeling because the couple had never got along. They had married in 1922, at a time when jobs and money were short for a great many people. There were times when they were lucky to keep a roof over their head.

To begin with, Mary was thrilled to be married while many of her contemporaries had found themselves well and truly 'shelved', due to the shortage of men caused by the Great War. But the dream soon faded. She was a lively woman. A flirt. There had been romances but she had returned because, for her husband, she was the 'only' one. He was a quiet man, crippled due to an accident when he was young, but very steady and loyal.

When he died Mary was lonely. Suddenly there was no one to fight with. No one to walk ahead of in the street or leave behind at the bus stop, while she waved at him from the bus. She had a daughter, Eleanor, who visited faithfully. But occasionally there were problems between them because Eleanor had always been devoted to her dad, although she was great 'pals' with Mary.

For a while, Eleanor visited three or four times a week, despite having many commitments herself. She soon began to get concerned about her mother's behaviour. Every time Eleanor tried to go into the living room to take her coat off and put her bag down, Mary would bar the way.

'No, you can't go in there,' she'd say. 'He's sitting there.'

By 'he', Eleanor assumed Mary meant 'your dad'. And she was right. Soon 'he' was being taken his dinner and cups of tea. Eleanor was alarmed. One day she told Mary not to be so silly. 'Dad's dead!' she said. 'No, he's not,' said Mary. 'He's in there where he always sat. I'm looking after him.'

The truth was, as Mary was too proud to add, she was also a little afraid of him. He had come back to haunt her, she said, and she was worried about going into the living room. Instead, she had begun to live in the kitchen.

One day, however, Eleanor had had enough. As she went into the house and Mary started her usual fuss about the living room, Eleanor pushed past. 'This has to stop,' she said and she opened the door.

The room, of course, was empty, the same as always, but for one thing. Tucked down the side of what had been her dad's chair was an empty paper bag. It was the kind you bought peanuts in at that time, something that had been her dad's favourite treat. There was also a faint whiff of peppermints in the air – again, something he was fond of.

It was doubtful that Mary had put either of these things there. For the first time, Eleanor wondered if Mary had been seeing something. She understood why Mary didn't want to use the living room.

Not long after this, Mary moved house. Although she never said her husband visited her there, she lived in the kitchen – just in case!

'Oh Yes, We Do Have a Ghost. I've Seen Him'

A flat in the centre of Dundee is the haunt of a little old man who appears as a grey shape, usually when Elizabeth, the female owner, is alone. 'He's quite ugly,' she says, 'and he's wearing what appears to be a shroud.' But fortunately he doesn't seem to be harmful, despite his less-than-pleasing appearance. Sometimes he doesn't materialize at all but his shadow flits across doorways instead.

The first time it happened, Elizabeth was alone. Her husband had gone out and she thought he'd come back. When she got up to look, there was nothing. At least nothing that she could see. The ghost, however, obviously saw her because he kept flitting backwards and forwards across the doorway for the rest of the evening. When Elizabeth's husband did come home, he found her rooted to the sofa. Naturally, he thought she was making it up – a tall tale to keep him out of the local pub!

Elizabeth was quite serious however. About a week after this incident, she noticed there were cold spots in the hall where she had seen the shadows. She also started to find that things were being moved about the kitchen. Not by her and not by her husband either. The flat had originally been part of a hotel, and Elizabeth wondered if whoever it was had been connected with it. But then one day she stepped into her dining room and changed her mind.

'There was a grey shape sort of hanging there. Just for a second but it was enough to see. The shape appeared to be wearing a shroud. That was enough for me!' she said.

The flats are built on a burial ground. The skeletons of plague victims have been found in the vicinity and it has occurred to Elizabeth that her ghost may be one of them. 'Very ugly and old looking,' is how she describes him, and 'active', especially when she's on her own. She has, however, never thought of getting rid of him. He's not a malicious presence, although he does cause rows with her husband. That's because he's never seen him. Evidently this is a ghost who likes keeping Elizabeth all to himself!

Was this a Ghost or Not?

'Mrs Fraser?'
'Yes?'
'You don't know me. My name is Mrs Cuthbert. I hope you don't mind me phoning you. It's about your mum.'

Jacqueline Fraser felt cold. And this was no wonder. For a moment she thought about hanging up. In fact, her hand reached towards the receiver hook. But then she stopped. 'Mum?' she asked.

'Yes,' said the woman on the other end of the line. 'I just wanted you to know that I put her on a bus for home. I was a bit worried about her getting there. So I thought I'd phone and tell you she is on her way. Maybe you could contact her and see she's alright.'

'I would have a job doing that,' said Jacqueline, who had lost patience. 'My mum's been dead for a year now. Is this some kind of game? How did you get my number?'

The woman at the other end seemed to freeze and this was not surprising. 'I got it from her,' she said. 'The woman I met.'

Mrs Cuthbert began to explain what had happened and what had been said. She told Jacqueline that her mum had seemed very confused – something Jacqueline tells me her mum never was when alive. She was as sharp as a needle right to the very end. The old lady also told Mrs Cuthbert that she had just been to her brother's funeral and was on her way home to her husband, a man who couldn't be left long because he was housebound. She told her that she lived a few miles away in a small village out of town. She proudly spoke of her beautiful garden and how she and her husband loved it. 'We've had a pond built and a lovely ornamental fence around the whole garden.' Mrs Cuthbert told Jacqueline how her mother smiled when she mentioned the garden and how proud she seemed of their recent additions.

Mrs Cuthbert asked the old lady if she could phone someone to come and get her. 'I have two daughters, Jacqueline and Claire. Jacqueline married the Fraser boy and is expecting a baby in a few months time.' Mrs Cuthbert smiled at the news and at the way the old lady assumed she knew who the

'Fraser boy' was. 'Claire,' she continued, 'is married but never has any time. She's run off her feet with the twins and she has no transport, so please don't phone her.'

Assuring Mrs Cuthbert she would be fine, she walked off in what looked like the direction of a bus stop. So Mrs Cuthbert began her journey home in the opposite direction. She couldn't stop the niggling feeling she had inside though, and that's why she decided to phone Jacqueline.

Jacqueline didn't know what to say. Everything Mrs Cuthbert told her was true. Her dad, who was also dead, had been housebound. Her mum did have a brother in the area but he was still alive. Her parents had lived in another small village a little bit away, and a couple of years before her parents died, they did have a pond and fence built, exactly as the caller said. Jacqueline felt shocked, as did her sister Claire, when she heard.

To this day, neither knows what to make of it. Did the person Mrs Cuthbert meet really exist? Did Mrs Cuthbert really exist? Was she the one who was confused? Had she at one stage known the family and, in her confusion, thought she belonged to it? That would explain why she knew so much.

Who this woman was has never been clear. Jacqueline is a little sceptical about it but she admits she shivers every time she thinks about it, and she spent the whole of that week feeling as if an icy hand had touched her. Her beloved and adored mum had been dead a year and Jacqueline was at the stage where she longed for some kind of sign from her mum. But was this the sign?

Chillingly, there's always one other possibility. That this *was* a demonstration of the afterlife.

My vibes on this one were that Mrs Cuthbert was indeed who she said she was, and I fully believe she did meet Jacqueline and Claire's mum that day.

The Bakery

A flat in a small Angus village is the haunt of a woman who possibly worked there when the house itself was used as a bakery. The disturbances started when the lower cellar of the house was being cleared, almost as if whoever it is was waiting for the moment when they could pop out again and make their presence felt. Or maybe they just didn't like the place being so clear all of a sudden. Or perhaps they did, and they decided to have the whole house changed.

Whatever the reason, the owners were suddenly and dramatically alerted to the spirit's presence one evening when all the pictures fell off their sitting room wall. The woman reckoned it couldn't all be down to bad workmanship on the part of her husband – or frayed strings! Anyway, the strange thing was that the strings weren't broken and the hooks were still in the wall. That evening, the husband had an altercation with the neighbours. The couple sensed they were being warned to expect a turbulent time. In many ways, this was the start.

Not long afterwards, the couple had visitors and the conversation came round, as it often does, to the subject of ghosts. One of the women, Fiona, said she simply didn't believe. Two minutes later, the pictures came down off the wall again, one after the other, as if an invisible force was lifting them and throwing them on the floor. Again, the strings were all intact, the hooks in their places.

'I don't know if you should have said that,' the owners told Fiona, who by this time was a little less sceptical. On the way home that evening, a heavy mist came down and Fiona got badly lost, ending up miles off her route.

Eventually, she was forced to pull into the side of the road and wait until things cleared sufficiently. In the meantime, her husband had telephoned several times looking for her. Again, the pictures falling down was almost a warning of things going amiss.

Now, deciding that the pictures weren't such a good idea, the owners left them down. Instead, a cupboard door in the hall started to defy all attempts to keep it closed. In fact, the handle would swing down and the door creak open. This happened so many times that the couple decided to take the door off. Perhaps it was even what the spirit wanted. Their idea of interior design?

At any rate, the next set of disturbances was in the cellar. Waking up early one morning the couple heard what sounded like wooden trays being moved about, except there were no wooden trays. They went down the stairs, thinking someone had broken in, but the place was empty. Well, not quite…

'I sensed there was someone there. I never saw them but I felt they were female. And quite stoutish. I had a strong feeling she wasn't a happy soul and that life hadn't gone her way.'

After this incident the couple did a little digging, which perhaps isn't the best word to use in connection with spirits!

They found out that the place had originally been a bakery, and that a woman who worked there many years before had been quite besotted with the owner. She wasn't the prettiest or the youngest of girls, so he didn't bother with her. Her name was Margaret.

Whether this part is true or not, Margaret has certainly remained with the couple and has continued to warn them of small incidents. She's not harmful. They often speak to her by name. She never replies of course. Probably too busy redesigning their flat!

The Haunted School

This is the story of a school that was haunted by the ghost of a previous rector. Perhaps that was why he continued to walk the corridors. The story concerns a woman called Lesley, whose job in the school was her first.

Lesley had no idea about the haunting. On her first day at the school, however, she was terrified. This wasn't because of any ghost or tales of spooky corridors. Lesley's fears were caused by something much more tangible – the prospect of teaching gangs of awkward teenagers. It was enough to make her heart pound and her hands sweat. But somehow, with a great deal of mental tough talk, she managed to do it.

The first few days passed in something of a daze. But as her worries about whether she was up to the task receded, she began to relax into the role. It was what she'd always wanted to do, after all. And the staff were friendly. The rector, in particular, seemed to be keeping an eye on her, just to see that everything was going well. At least that seemed to her to be the reason why he was always walking past her door. Even after the first few days, Lesley could hear him when she stayed behind to prepare work and catch up on marking. It was comforting to know he was also the type who couldn't leave his work alone and took it so seriously he was prepared to put in all these extra hours.

At the end of the first week, when the rector popped his head round the door to ask how she was settling in, Lesley took the opportunity to thank him and to comment on the way he walked the corridors. 'What do you mean?' he said. 'I haven't left the office till now.'

This didn't worry Lesley unduly. She assumed it must have been another member of staff, and left it at that. The rector left, Lesley gathered up her things and locked her desk. As she did so, she again heard the footsteps in the corridor and looked out. There was a man there. She couldn't see his face but he was wearing a distinctive rust-coloured jacket and had quite long hair. This was at the back. It was actually quite thin on top. Lesley called out but the man didn't answer. He walked down the corridor and seemed to disappear into thin air at the end of it.

Lesley assumed the man was a member of staff. After all, it was a large school and she hadn't met everyone.

The next time Lesley saw the rector, simply for the sake of something to say, she remarked, 'Problem solved,' and went on to tell him about the man and how industrious he obviously was. Stunned, the rector told her that the description

147

she had just given matched that of the last rector, who had died suddenly at the age of 49, several years before.

Although Lesley went on to meet all the staff, none of them resembled the man in the rust-coloured jacket. What was more, many of them related similar experiences to hers. They never liked to talk of it, though, in case it caused problems for the school. After that Lesley started taking her work home instead of finishing it in the class. It wasn't that she thought the foot-steps were malign. It was just that she didn't want to hear them, and she was worried that if she looked out the door, she might see the man in the rust-coloured jacket, the devoted teacher who liked his job so much, he had returned to stalk the school corridors.

'The House is Empty Now Where Once They Played on Days of Gold Gone by...'

A house in Lothian is haunted by three particularly tragic spirits, in this case those of three young children who perished there in a fire many years ago.

When Stella, the lady who lives in the house, first moved there, she thought she was imagining things when she glanced at the stairs one day to see three small children coming down them. Then she thought she was mad. So did her friends. 'The children were everywhere – in the kitchen, all of the downstairs rooms and the upstairs bedrooms. The wee souls were always together and always looked as if they were going somewhere – out to play, or on an errand for their mum.'

Then, one day, one of Stella's friends called in. 'I see you've got some children round,' she said, clearly mystified because Stella had none. The friend pointed to a space in the garden where the children were sitting, threading a daisy chain together. 'Oh,' said Stella. 'They're not real.'

The friend was shocked. She thought Stella was having her on. These children were so real their shadows even fanned out across the grass. But they didn't exist. Stella sat her friend down and explained. For her, it was a real breakthrough to know she wasn't alone in what she could see.

From then on, other visitors noticed the children. They never made themselves invisible or sought in any way to frighten those who saw them. The only thing that was unusual was their dress. It was clearly from the late 1960s. So were the haircuts. Obviously, the children had been alive then and something terrible had happened to them. Stella was distressed at the thought. The children were so young. For the three of them to be dead seemed too horrible to contemplate but she did. Then she did more than just contemplate. She decided to find out. What was the secret of the house and these children?

Stella was expecting something terrible and she was right. A fire had broken out in the house many years before. It was during the 1960s, so there was very little trace of it now. In fact, the house had been more or less rebuilt. Apart from the scorch marks on the attic wall, where the fire had reached, and a blackened floorboard, there were no other signs that this had been a major emergency and a terrible calamity. Although neighbours and firemen had done their best to help out, the children all died trapped behind a wall of flame and smoke. At least their little bodies did. Their spirits, as Stella, her family and friends all testified to, lived on.

Spirit children feature prominently in ghost stories – always as some kind of malign force that threatens the adults whose homes they invade. In Stella's case, however, the children were anything but sinister. Just three lost souls, looking to re-create a time when they played happily without a care.

The Haunted Office

An office in the centre of Glasgow is haunted by the ghost of a very determined worker, a man, somewhere in his 40s, who comes complete with pince-nez – those elegant little spectacles which sit on the end of the nose – and an ancient briefcase.

'He has no hair,' says one lady who works there, 'and he wears a pinstripe suit. The first time I saw him, I thought I was imagining it. It was a bright, sunny day and I looked up and he was just standing there in the sun's glare. I was sure I had simply hurt my eyesight in some way. But then later, it was as if I had crossed a boundary. Gone somewhere I just shouldn't go.'

What convinces her of this is that, until then, there were never any disturbances. Since then, they've been continual. One of the most annoying is the way everything on the lady's desk gets moved. It seems the spirit was quite a meticulous person and doesn't like clutter of any kind. At first, the lady thought she was imagining that too, then she blamed the office cleaner. She complained to her eventually, asking her to leave things alone because several invoices had been tidied away out of sequence. 'I don't know what you mean,' was the cleaner's response. 'I never touched your desk. It was too much of a clutter.' Obviously ghostly hands were at work!

The amount of things that appear and disappear is a little too much for comfort. 'Just about every day it's something. You can set a file down, or get something out of your bag, then spend the next hour looking for it.' This isn't anything to do with the clutter, apparently. Often things turn up in the waste bin – clearly a favourite spot for this spirit – or on a shelf. Certainly, they're never where they were set down, and the havoc it causes is evidently considerable.

Once a cup of coffee seemed to fly off the desk. It was as if 'Henry' – the lady's pet name for the spirit – didn't like slacking either.

The lady kept her concerns about what was happening to herself for a number of months. But then 'Henry' was witnessed by one of the temps. Apparently she saw him going into the lady's office. She herself had some things to take in and waited, not wanting to interrupt. She waited a long time, however. He didn't come out again. So eventually she knocked and went in. There was no sign, certainly not of Henry anyway. She described him as 'tall and wearing the kind of suit that went out with the ark. It actually had a fusty smell off it'.

Maybe not off the clothes, eh?

Henry has also been heard running the water in the gent's cloakroom. He doesn't use the loo. Of course, one would hope not! But often taps are left on and can be heard being turned off and on. Maybe he's hoping to get rid of the fusty smell on his clothes and turn himself into the sort of dapper Dan who would impress the ladies and have them swooning at his feet? Who knows? If he carries on making appearances he just might, but it would be for the wrong reasons!

Henry has his name from an office manager who worked for the firm 50 years earlier. The workers aren't sure if it's him or not, but they decided to christen him this, just in case. In real life, Henry was a bit of a stickler and devoted his life to the job, causing his wife to leave him when she got fed up of waiting for him to come home. This caused Henry to crumble somewhat, and he died in quite miserable circumstances about five years later. But it now seems he's returned to where he was happiest and the place that meant the most. But perhaps his wife still waits for him in another part of Glasgow!

The Phantom Fisherman

A house in quiet Inverbervie is haunted by the ghost of an old fisherman. He evidently likes to carry his catch around with him, judging by the smell that occasionally permeates the hallway.

The first time the present occupants smelt it, they thought it was bad drains. 'In fact,' said owner Heather, 'we even brought a company in. Of course, by the time they arrived, the smell had gone. That made us feel silly.' But the smell came back, on and off. Eventually, the couple noticed it was always prominent at certain points in the month, and never noticeable at others, and it was a fleeting thing, almost as if someone was walking past them. The first time Heather realized this, she wondered if there was a ghost. The house was certainly old enough and had apparently been a fisherman's cottage originally. Of course, lots of houses have 'presences' and auras of the past round them. But what made this one different was that Heather's son, then aged four, began to claim he had seen 'the man'.

'My son said the man's name was Dougal and that he was an old man. He even described what he was wearing as what sounded like old-fashioned fisherman's gear. My son wasn't in any way frightened. I don't even think he realized what he had seen. The way he came out with it, it was as if Dougal was a person. He just said he'd come to the garden gate and asked him what he was doing there. My son told him he was playing. He asked Dougal about the fish and Dougal said he was going to take them into the house. My son thought he was going to give them to me. At lunchtime that day, he asked where they were. He said he had seen Dougal walk up the path to the side door. Of course, there weren't any fish. Dougal never got there.'

For a time, Heather thought her son was making the story up. But he was so persistent. She then wondered if there were any local fishermen who were perhaps selling their catch door-to-door. Even as she asked some people, she knew what the answer would be. By this time, she was tying her son's story in with the smell in the house, which was always near the side door into the hall. The one her son saw the fisherman go to. On more than one occasion, Heather has heard footsteps in the passageway from that door to the dining room. There isn't anyone there. But Heather can feel the boards vibrating, as if there is.

Once, too, one of the chairs felt slightly damp as if someone had been sitting in it in a wet coat. No one had been in the dining room all that week. Heather had only gone in to dust. She suspects the room may have been Dougal's bedroom. Because Heather is so convinced that they're not alone in the house and that what her son saw was for real, she has searched the title deeds of the cottage and found the following name among the previous owners – James Dougal Anderson.

He's listed as 'the late' in 1910. But despite this, and given all that Heather has to say, he's not as 'late' as all that!

ER Was Never Like This…

Alright, so many of us find hospital dramas addictive! Well, this is the story of a nurse who was clearly so addicted to her actual work that she couldn't leave. Or perhaps she just felt needed in some way. Or drawn to helping someone who really wasn't very well.

Let's call the invalid Jill and just say that she was so terribly ill she thought she was going to die. The staff all thought the same. In fact, it was something of a miracle that she pulled through. Whether that was down to the extra-special care she received isn't clear, but she did recover. It took a bit of time. Eight weeks in total. And when she did she couldn't help thinking about all the staff, the people who had helped her. They had done a marvellous job, always having time and attention for her, seeing to all her needs. But one in particular stood out. This was a lady in her 40s – a little older than some of the other nurses, it was true, and very dedicated.

Generally, she worked nights, which was great since that was when Jill was at her lowest ebb. It was never too much trouble for this lady to prop up a pillow, or bring a glass of water, or simply sit and talk. In the early days when Jill was very ill, she often sat by the bed. Her presence was so calming, so naturally caring, that Jill just felt she was going to recover. And it was good of this lady, when she had other patients, to give Jill this kind of time. Jill almost believed this lady was willing her back to health. Jill wanted to make the effort – for her.

It was good to know that someone could care for others in this way, over and above the call of duty. Jill thought she was tremendous, an inspiration to all around her.

When she was in hospital, Jill thought of this lady as part of the team. She didn't really talk about her. Why should she? It would, she felt, be wrong to single her out for praise to other members of staff. When she got home, however, it was a different matter. Although Jill had warm feelings for everyone she had met and all they had done for her, she wanted in particular to thank her friend. Chocolates would be appropriate she thought, or a nice bunch of flowers. Then she thought, why not just go the whole hog and send both? So she reached for the phone and contacted a service that would do just that for her, giving the nurse's name and the ward number.

The parcel never arrived. Well it did. What I mean is that the nurse never received it. Instead it was intercepted by the ward sister. Imagine Jill's surprise when she received a telephone call from this lady, telling her 'her' nurse was dead. That in itself was terrible. Jill was deeply upset. All the time she had been close to death her nurse had helped her through, and now her friend was gone and she hadn't been able to help.

But then came the real shock. Her friend had died nine years ago. Calmly, the sister explained. Jill's friend had been the most caring, the most wonderful nurse, but sadly this hadn't stopped her becoming ill herself. It had been a huge loss to everyone – her family most of all, but the hospital too. She had been dedicated to her patients, always giving her all. The flowers and chocolates arriving had been a shock. Could Jill have mixed her name up with someone else's? So Jill described her. And as she did there seemed no doubt.

Jill had been nursed by a ghost. A lady who had lost her hold on life but was nonetheless determined that Jill would keep hers. Jill has never forgotten her or ceased to believe that it was her kindness which brought her here today.

The Haunted Motorbike

There are so many stories of houses being haunted – and castles, hotels, schools, hospitals and so on – it's always good to come up with a story of an item that is haunted. Perhaps it would be better to say 'unusual'. When that item's a motorbike, you can bet the story associated with it is anything but happy.

That was the case with a young man called Angus and his bike – his pride and joy – which he soon found out had quite a history attached. It's certainly a story worth telling, largely because it shows that spirits can stick around. Whether you want to worry too much about it or what they say is a different matter.

Angus had just bought a new bike. This was something he'd always wanted and he had saved hard. Fortunately, the bike wasn't as expensive as he'd originally thought. When he first saw it in the garage forecourt, he thought it would cost an arm and a leg. It certainly was a fantastic bike. For days he sweated up the courage to go in and ask how much. When he did, he was amazed. It was only three-quarters of what he'd expected. This in itself might have told Angus something. But he was too happy to heed any warning bells. Anyway, how could there be warning bells associated with such a lovely bike? He could hardly wait till he rode it home and got a proper look at it. When he did he saw that everything lived up to his expectations.

Of course, bikes are bikes, boys are boys, and one of the great things about having a bike is the fun that can be had taking it apart, tinkering with it, stripping it down and putting it back together again. Angus was no exception in this regard. Soon he was spending many happy hours working away.

One evening, Angus was very busy. There was a bit of a problem with the fuel tank and he wanted to check it. As he had all the parts spread on the ground, he became aware of a noise behind him. He looked round and got a shock. He had been working so hard he hadn't realized a mist had come down. A beautiful girl was standing there. Then he realized the mist was only round her. The rest of the pavement and the roadway were clear.

'Hello,' she said. Angus was stunned. Her voice was so gentle and the way she smiled at him reminded him of an angel – except Angus hadn't ever known any angels.

'Hello,' he said or rather stuttered. She was so very young and lovely, he found he didn't know what to say.

'Be careful on the bike, won't you?' Then she vanished. Angus's hair stood on end. He'd no idea what to make of it. Had he imagined it? Or dreamt it? Or had he fallen over and hit his head? It was the only way to account for the strangeness of it all. The mist, the girl, what she had said to him. Or was it?

Angus reassembled the bike and drove to the garage. When he got there and asked the garage owner about the bike, he had another shock. There was a history attached and it wasn't ideal. The bike had been in an accident. There was very little damage, which was why it could be so easily repaired. Unfortunately, however, the accident had also been a tragedy. A girl had been killed.

'How old was she?' Angus asked, reeling now.

'About 18,' the garage owner replied.

There was no doubt in Angus's mind this was the girl he had seen. Angus was so shocked he worried whether her actual words were a warning. Then he decided on reflection that they weren't. There had been a wistfulness about her tone which suggested she just wanted him to take care.

So he did and the bike is still a treasured possession.

The Proud Mother?

Deirdre was feeling very nervous. For some time she had been under a great deal of pressure at work. There had been changes among the top personnel. While in some ways this was for the best – the firm needed a new image – it was causing apprehension.

In time-honoured fashion, heads were rolling down the line. Although hers wasn't on the block yet, Deirdre really feared it was only a matter of time. An important meeting and presentation were looming. She had to get it right or face the loss of everything she'd worked for.

The big week dawned and Deirdre tried her best not to be nervous. This proved impossible. She knew many of the people who were carrying out the assessments but the one she was to see was new to the firm. A difficult man by all accounts too. Deirdre didn't know his name, just his title.

The night before her presentation, Deirdre went over it meticulously. Every detail, every part, anything that could go wrong was worked on as she paced the floor, reciting her strategies, her answers, what she would do to expand her role in the firm in coming months. But behind the confident hand gestures, the rustling of the papers as she set them down to imaginary watchers, she recited a mantra. She didn't want to. The words weren't ones she wanted to think of now. 'I'm going to fail,' she said. 'I can't do this.' Then she would stop. 'Of course I can. I have to.'

Eventually, as the room darkened and Deirdre felt exhausted, she told herself that at least it wouldn't be for the want of trying. But just the same there were tears of frustration in her eyes. She didn't see why she should be put through this. Who was this man anyway? Why was it that he could do this to her?

Deirdre was just switching off the lights when the answering machine clicked on. This was strange in itself because the phone hadn't actually rung. She waited, listening to herself giving the usual message: 'I am not able to come to the phone at the moment, please leave your name and number.' Then she felt chilled as an unfamiliar voice began to speak.

'Steven's bark is worse than his bite,' it said. 'He's alright you know.'

Deirdre was stunned. All thoughts that the caller had the wrong number vanished with that first line.

'You're not to worry,' the voice continued. 'I know you're nervous. The interview will go well. Honestly it will. You've worked too hard and in many ways he's as nervous as you. It's not easy you know, coming into some place new. People always think the worst.'

Deirdre didn't know what to say. At that point she could hardly think anything. She listened fascinated till the caller finished speaking, then hung up. As the line went dead, she reached for the machine to play the message back. There was nothing. Yet she didn't think she was imagining it.

She had the strongest and the strangest feeling she had just been listening to Steven's mother. Who else, she felt, would know so much about him, and not be alive to tell the tale?

The next morning, as she entered the office and prepared her notes for presentation, she glanced at the name on the desk. She wasn't surprised to see it was Steven. As everyone had said, he was quite sharp and it was clear he didn't suffer fools gladly. But she wasn't intimidated. How could she be when someone had said to her, 'Steven's bark is worse than his bite'?

Needless to say, Steven found Deirdre's attitude refreshing, as if someone had thoroughly prepared her for the post. She went on to bigger things within the company and, as time passed, Deirdre realized that Steven's bark was indeed worse than his bite.

Steven and Deirdre have worked together for a few years now and become good friends. He often speaks of his mother who passed away a few years before. He clearly adored her and, from what he says, his mother adored her son. She obviously saw the real Steven and was therefore qualified to state that her son's bark was worse than his bite. Steven actually used these exact words one time, to which Deirdre merely smiled and agreed with her boss. She, of course, already knew this – in fact, she knew this before she'd even met her then new boss, but to this day she has never divulged to Steven who told her so.

'I Don't Know What it is, But This is the Only Place I See it'

Helen had never thought about it much before – the riddle of the white misty shape in the house. Whenever she saw it she just assumed it was the way the sunlight was hitting, or that she needed to dust – badly! It just seemed to appear from time to time, gliding like a mist before her eyes. Then it would vanish, leaving her to wonder if it had been anything at all.

The house was big and old. She had lived in it for a year but never thought of it as haunted, although the previous owner had made some jokes about it. It just never seemed unhappy in any way and Helen didn't think of herself as psychic. If she lost something or the electricity started playing up, that was down to herself or the age of the wiring.

But then one day something happened that changed that. A friend came to visit, nothing startling in itself. Only as they were sitting drinking coffee and chatting, the white mist seemed to pass across the room.

'What's that?' asked Helen's friend.

'I don't know,' Helen replied, 'but this house is the only place I see it. I think it's just the sunlight.'

Helen's friend shivered. 'But it's dark outside,' she said.

Helen had to agree about that. All of a sudden she felt very strange – light-headed, as if the coffee had been drugged, but she hadn't even touched it. She was oddly tired too. She had no doubt that her friend would think she was being rude. They saw very little of each other and had been looking forward to getting together for months. Now she couldn't stop yawning.

'I'm so sorry,' she said.

'No, I am,' said her friend, who tried to smile but broke into the most enormous yawn. 'I just feel very tired all of a sudden. I can't help it. Look, what is that white thing?'

'I just don't know,' Helen replied. 'I feel I'm talking strange.'

Helen tried to stand up at this point but found that she couldn't. She was terribly embarrassed. When she spoke it sounded to her as if she was speaking too fast and she didn't have a clue what she was saying. 'Please let me stop gibbering,' she thought. 'It must look like I've been drinking!' Her friend's speech sounded absolutely fine, which made matters worse. She did, however, look very uncomfortable – no doubt because of the way Helen was 'babbling'. But then her friend said, 'Look Helen, I'm so sorry. I don't feel well. Am I talking too fast? I sound like I'm talking too fast.'

Now Helen was very uneasy. Her friend didn't go away immediately. She stayed for another half hour. But the shape didn't go away either. It stayed for the entire time, and during that period Helen and her friend were so plainly uncomfortable in each other's company that Helen just longed for her friend to leave. This was mainly so she could lie down, but Helen also found she'd no idea what they were talking about. Her friend was plainly disturbed by the white shape, which seemed to hover in front of them, but neither of them could do anything about it. Also, her friend didn't know what to say, as Helen later found out. Eventually, though, apologizing profusely, Helen's friend left. The moment she did, Helen curled up on the sofa and fell asleep. When she woke up the shape had gone.

A week later, Helen's friend telephoned to say she'd been ill all week. Jokes about the coffee and the cakes followed, although nothing had been eaten or drunk that day. It had all still been sitting untouched when Helen cleared it away. Then the subject of the white mist came up. Helen's friend was convinced it was 'something', and by now Helen was too, although neither had any idea what it was. Both believed, however, that it wanted them to know it was there and to treat it with respect.

Helen's friend has since been back to Helen's house with no ill effects. The white shape has been seen many times by Helen. When it appears she gives it a wide berth. She believes they can both live in the house together and she's not afraid. Since that day she's never suffered any strange feelings. But perhaps that's because she quietly acknowledges it from the safest place – afar!

'And the Bride Wore …'

Brides make wonderful ghost fiction. If they're dressed in white, it's great for starters! About to be married against their will is even better. They're often found in genuine castle stories too – the bride of Lammermoor being one of the most famous. So it's interesting to find one in someone's ordinary semidetached in Renfrew.

It was a perfectly ordinary Saturday morning. Ordinary except for one thing – what Julie saw when she opened her eyes. Let's just say it gave her quite a fright. After all, she had gone to bed quite normally, not eating or drinking too much, or watching any scary movies. But she was scared now! It's not every day you open your eyes to find a stranger in your bedroom. Dressed as a bride at that. But that was the sight that confronted Julie that particular morning as she opened her eyes.

It was quite definitely a bride – the dress, the flowers, everything was there, and she was standing at the window looking out. Julie remembered that she looked radiant, so much so that Julie didn't think she was a ghost. Startled, thinking someone had got into the house by mistake or even – horror of horrors – she was in someone else's, Julie leapt up. But no –there was the bedside alarm in its usual place, the book Julie was reading, her clothes on the usual familiar chair. What was happening here?

When she looked up again, the figure had gone. Panic-stricken, Julie looked at the door. It was still closed. Julie couldn't explain it. Everything had been so real. Or had it? The bride's dress was a little old-fashioned. Now she came to think of it, it reminded her of photographs of her gran's wedding dress. And the girl had been very young, only 16 or 17. It didn't seem possible that anyone of that age locally would be getting married and come into Julie's house. Julie sat down on the bed and, catching sight of herself in the mirror opposite, realized her face was the colour of the bride's dress. She had just seen a ghost.

Julie had never really believed in such things, but her scepticism now took her to the local library. She wanted to find out who had lived at the house before – something that was generally possible through a street directory, except in this case there was no such thing.

Still, she wasn't put off. Through the deeds to the house it was possible to discover the names of the people who had lived there in the past. One couple in particular interested her because they had lived there just before the Second World War, and it seemed to Julie that the girl's clothes were from that period.

Julie then carried out a great deal of digging and asking around to uncover the fact that the couple had a daughter, a girl who was born about 1923. An old man who lived further down the street remembered her it seemed, although she was older than him by quite a few years, because he'd had a bit of a crush on her. Sadly, she had died just a few months earlier, he told Julie.

'But did she ever marry?' asked Julie. 'Do you know anything about her life?'

'Oh yes,' said the old man. She had married twice. The first time right from that very house, the one Julie was now living in. Julie held her breath while the old man went on to relate the story.

The woman's name was Rosemary and her first husband was a local man. The minute war broke out they decided to marry. They were very much in love, and the fact that dark clouds hung over the country gave their love an added poignancy and urgency.

Rosemary looked lovely that day as she came down the path. But her happiness was short. They could only have been married a few months. Her husband was called up, as they had obviously known he would be. She never saw him again. For this young couple, as for many of that generation, it was the ultimate sacrifice.

Rosemary was widowed. She was perhaps 19. Many years later she married again, but not before she had been through difficult times first. Her heart had been broken. Still, the old man remembered the look on her face as she stepped down the path in her bridal gown.

'There were so many weddings at that time, people in sailor's and air force uniforms. They were all so young. That day Rosemary wasn't wearing any kind of uniform. She was dressed in white but her face shone with pride. I suppose that was her uniform. She was beautiful. I still remember it. And her husband, he was proud too. But he never came back. That was just the kind of time it was.'

'When was it?' Julie asked. 'The marriage, I mean. Can you remember when it took place?'

'Oh, it was a long time ago now,' the man said. 'But I think I remember. It was March.'

When she heard this, Julie understood. More than 50 years later, in March, she had seen Rosemary standing at the window, probably waiting for her lost love to return.

The Love that Never Died

It was one of the saddest things. A young mum had died. It was at a time when women often had a large number of children and childbirth was much more dangerous than it is now. A little girl had been left to help bring up her baby sister and to look after her brothers. The father she loved and had always known as a kind, caring man had turned to drink. His moods were black and he was broken by his own loss and the responsibilities that had been thrust on him. For little Lydia, this was a hard time indeed.

What made it harder was the way her father treated her. Fathers were, she knew, supposed to love their children but for no reason she knew of, her father hit her. Not just hit. Often the beatings were so severe Lydia's body ached for days.

Lydia had the huge responsibility of looking after her brothers and her sister, of cooking for them and keeping the house clean. These tasks were frequently carried out with bruised fingers and swollen veins. Though she did everything to please him, there was just no humouring him when he was sitting in his chair with his glass of whisky beside him. A word or a glance was enough at these times to stir in his mind the memory of the woman he wanted to see and couldn't. Then Lydia would have to duck as the blows whipped against her stomach.

One morning, Lydia had a surprise. Well, it wasn't a surprise as such. But she was busy in the kitchen, putting out the plates for breakfast, when her little sister Marie came bounding into the room. Marie was at that time perhaps three or four, a lovely girl and she was certainly excited. Her hair had been done. It was very pretty, in a long ponytail, which spun and danced in the sunlight, quite as much as the little girl was doing herself. But it wasn't so much that the hair had been done, so Lydia didn't have to do it, or her sister's excitement, which grabbed Lydia's attention that morning. It was what Marie had to say: 'Mammy did it!' Her eyes shining, she reported, 'Mammy did it! She was here!'

It was an unfortunate thing to say. In an instant, Lydia's father leapt up. He had been lying in his chair, not paying much attention. That was until Marie said the word 'Mammy'. The mention of his dead wife, the suggestion she could have been in the bedroom that morning, brushing Marie's hair, was all too much for him.

The shouting began, word after word about how this could not be. A minute later the hitting started. Marie was unable to stand the pain as slap after slap fell on her little body. She began to scream. Lydia, who had already been the target of her father's rages on so many occasions, stepped forward. If Marie had been telling the truth, if Mammy had come, then this would be what she wanted Lydia to do. Even when she felt her knees start to buckle and her body thicken with hurt, she knew. Marie was only a baby. She must protect her.

A little later it seemed she was in her bedroom. The beating had stopped. She pulled herself up and crept to Marie's room. Almost instantly, when she saw her there, crouching on the bed, she forgot what she had suffered herself. She listened while Marie told her. Mammy had come. She had said her hair was beautiful. That was why she wanted to comb it. Marie had never seen Mammy before.

Then Lydia knew. She hadn't seen her mum since the day she died. But she had felt her there. Often in the mornings, just as she was stirring, she had thought she heard her calming voice speaking to her, telling her it would be alright.

That very evening, as Lydia lay in bed, her eyes closed so as to shut out the memory of the morning, she felt a hand on her shoulder. 'It's alright,' Mammy said quietly. 'He's a difficult man. You have to know that. But I'm here for you and I won't leave. I'll be with you always.' Then slowly she began to stroke Lydia's hair.

The Stirling Baby

The house was old and forbidding. Its secrets sealed in granite. Standing almost at the top of the hill, it cast an immediate spell over the couple who had come to view it. It looked so spooky they found themselves shivering. But the shivers were delicious, a sort of 'I can't wait' anticipation.

'Imagine living there!' they looked at each other and thought. Then they opened the gate. There was no doubt in either of their minds that they would buy the house. Then they would tell their friends. 'We've bought this unusual old place,' they would say. 'I bet it's haunted!' And their friends would laugh. Why not? They'd always been a pair who liked doing zany things. This was one more. Besides, they adored the house, even on that first visit. That was before they learned that 'spooky is as spooky appears'. Of course, they still adore the house but there is a story attached.

As in all good ghost stories, this one began about a week after the couple moved in. A baby was crying in an upper room. No one had told them they would have noisy neighbours like this. But hang on – the house was detached. How could they be hearing a neighbour's baby crying in one of the upstairs rooms? Unless there really was a baby.

Warily, the couple crept up the stairs to look in all the rooms. There was no one there. An acoustic trick? A noise coming from somewhere else perhaps? They didn't know. But they decided to think it was. After all, the alternative didn't bear thinking about, not after all the jokes they'd made.

Then some things started to go missing. This, too, is something that happens in all the best ghost stories. A letter here, a bill there. The bills, of course, were especially welcome to go missing, but it was disturbing. Carrie, one of the owners, became convinced she was losing her mind. She was certainly losing everything else – paintbrushes, her purse – all seemingly taken by an invisible hand.

Now she didn't laugh quite so much when friends said, 'How do you like the house?' Upstairs someone was pacing the floor. She could hear it. Often at nights the sound kept her awake, the creak, creak of the floorboards, which told her someone was up there. But it wasn't her or her husband. 'Should we sell up?' they asked themselves. But they loved their house. Sometimes they felt a sadness about it, a feeling that sat in the afternoon sun and touched everything, but never any kind of evil, as if something was lurking that they didn't like or believed they should fear. Besides, there was another reason they didn't want to move. Carrie was pregnant.

Perhaps because of this, they felt they had to know who was haunting their house. The joy of having their first child was tinged by the crying they had heard from that upstairs room the week they arrived. They wondered if it was some kind of warning.

That was why they had to go over the history of the house. This wasn't achieved in a day but took an age, with visits to the library and checks of old census records. It was, however, possible. What they found amazed them. In 1870, a woman had given birth to a baby in the house but both had died a year later from drinking contaminated water. A picture built up in the couple's minds. There seemed no doubt that this was 'their' lady, the person who walked the floor at nights, and the crying was that of her baby. The story seemed especially poignant given that Carrie was pregnant. It was as if the lady was looking after her in some way. Certainly the couple noticed that once they knew the history, the atmosphere in the house changed. The incidences of floor walking and items going missing stopped, and there was instead a feeling of tranquillity.

Carrie and her husband were never troubled by the crying of the ghostly baby again. And that was just as well, as shortly they had their own to care for! The feet walking the floor at night were their own, and they had the satisfaction of knowing that any sobbing was of the real human kind.

The Car that Moved

Of course all cars move, so if you're thinking 'that's not much of a title', you're right! But this was a strange case, part of an ongoing catalogue of events that led to the couple concerned becoming convinced they were being haunted by the wife's parents. Nor were they alone in this. The couple's children were equally convinced. In fact, it gave them the opportunity to get to know the grandparents they hardly knew – their granddad in particular. He had been a keen gardener, and they came to know him by his fresh earth smell.

The activities started shortly after Janice, my client, had buried her mother. The first sign took place when Janice came home from work. It was her first day back since her mother's death and she was naturally still feeling very sad. As she opened the door that evening, she felt a rush of air in the hall.

But there was no one. The hall was empty. Janice, I should add, is not the first client to describe such things. The following evening, the same thing happened. Janice, on this occasion, was stunned. Not just because she felt someone brush past her, but because she also heard someone call out her name. She could hear them clearly and she knew it was her mother's voice.

Janice was the sceptical kind. Her mother's death had hit her hard, and while she felt it would be wonderful to believe her mum was still with her, she thought that was too easy an option. Then she had a dream about her mother and in it she came to Janice and told her many things that would happen in her life. One of these wasn't the car moving, I hasten to add! But she did discuss, and if you like, predict, a number of events.

She said that Janice would soon be working at another job, that her niece was going to be married within six months – things that did come true. And as they did, Janice began to believe her mum was with her. In fact, she had the distinct impression that her mum's arms were often round her, hugging her.

For Janice, this was wonderful. It meant her mum hadn't left her. She only wished she could tell her family what was happening, but she was afraid she wouldn't be believed.

About six months after Janice's dream, however, her husband started behaving in a very strange way. He didn't tell Janice at first, but when he did, he described seeing the outline of a man in the kitchen – an old man, he said, dressed in gardener's clothes.

He had never known Janice's father, but the more they spoke of the old man, the more positive they became that it was him. At that point the couple had been planning a move but they jointly decided against that and decided to stay where they were.

Other incidents, which they both witnessed, also began to happen. Objects moved by themselves, things would go missing and then turn up in odd places. This more or less became a way of life for them. At Christmas, Janice distinctly heard low singing and was convinced it was her mum singing a favourite song.

The strangest thing to happen to Janice and her husband, however, was the day the car moved. It had been parked at the local supermarket. They were in no doubt as to where they'd parked the car because sitting next to it was a very old-style car, which both of them remarked on. The trolley park was also on the other side. When they came out of the supermarket, however, the car was gone. Not far, but it had been moved to another bay altogether.

Cynics might argue that this could have been a prankster, but Janice remains convinced, as do her husband and daughter who was also present. She believes her dad moved it, largely because the bay it was in was where he always parked! And they had their car keys with them at all times, so how *could* anyone else have moved it?

Janice no longer questions or doubts the possibility of life after death. If her parents can be with her in such a way, then the answer is obvious to her. They haven't really gone and she feels she is with them as much as ever.

Whoever says death is an end should talk to Janice!

The Phantom Letter

Enid was amazed. 'Dear Enid,' the letter began, 'I love and miss you. I know that perhaps that's not always the way it seemed at times but it's something I wanted you to know.'

The writer went on to talk about some private jokes, a special holiday they had shared, and how sorry the writer was for not being able to be with her now. It was signed by her husband George, and it was his writing. She couldn't mistake his writing. They had, after all, been married for 30 years. But there was no way on the face of this earth, so Enid believed, that he could have written it. The problem was the date. March 19th 1994. George had been dead since December 1993.

Had George written the letter in March the year before and made a mistake with the date? Enid glanced at the calendar, something she hadn't had much of an inclination to do since George died. It was just another day to her. March 20th, it said. This seemed to her too much of a coincidence. Besides, the letter was lying in a drawer she opened every day. No matter how bad she was feeling, she would have seen it. After all, it was addressed to her in George's handwriting.

Enid read the letter again. There was so much in it about their life together. But it was put in a certain way, the kind of way that someone might write about things if they were no longer part of that life. The nostalgia overwhelmed her. The parts about regrets, how he so wished he had told her how much he loved her, were not the kind of things that someone

175

who was alive would have written. This letter, she had no doubt, was from the spirit world. It had come to her from her husband.

For a time Enid could hardly believe it. The letter was her most cherished possession. She carried it everywhere and stopped at various moments of the day to read it. As she did, she felt so much better about everything. While she would always miss her husband and wish desperately that he was with her, it seemed that he was, in part, still there for her, that their love wasn't dead. This helped her immensely.

As that week went on, she felt for the first time that she was coping with life again, that she could smile a little at things on the television or in a book. Lifting the telephone, she made some arrangements to see friends. In the letter, George had made it clear she was to get on with her life. Now she started to feel like doing so. It had made all the difference to her to hear from him. Even her daughters noticed she was a changed woman. 'Mum's coming out of her depression,' they all agreed.

Eventually she decided to tell them why. It felt very natural all of a sudden. The letter was from their dad. Why shouldn't they be party to her secret and see why she had changed so much in the last few weeks? The letter was a special treasure, not to be hidden away as she had been doing. When they saw it, they would understand.

The next time they came to visit, Enid told them both, 'I've something to show you. I know you won't quite believe it. I didn't believe it myself to start with.' She went to her handbag where she always kept the letter, and the two girls watched mystified, wondering what on earth she was going to bring out. They watched as their mother searched. They exchanged glances. Enid was turning the bag upside down, emptying the contents out onto the table and raking through the lining in case it was torn. 'It can't be!' she kept exclaiming, but although she went through her bag thoroughly, she could not find the letter. She looked in a kitchen drawer. She even looked under her pillow as she remembers reading the letter one night in bed. No matter where she looked, though, the letter was gone.

Quite understandably, her daughters were concerned for their mum. They feared the worst – perhaps she was beginning to lose her mind. But Enid knew what they were thinking and decided to let the subject be dropped, never to be spoken of again. Secretly, though, she did wonder if she *had* in fact imagined the whole thing.

An entire week passed and Enid had still not found the letter. She admits she felt devastated that this could have been her mind playing tricks. But then, a few days later, she was lying in bed thinking about her husband when something on her dresser caught her eye. It was the letter!

Now she knew she hadn't imagined the whole thing. However, she decided to put the letter in a safe place and keep its reappearance a secret. The letter has never gone astray since, and every now and again Enid brings the letter out, reads it, gaining immense strength from its words, and then returns it to its safe hiding hole.

Coming to her as it did, at a time when she needed it most, she feels it bridged the gap between our world and the spirit world, allowing her to believe that her husband was still with her, in spite of death.

The Reassuring Spirit

So many people are afraid of ghosts. However, I have often found ghosts to be anything but frightening. Indeed, numerous stories centre on their desire to help. There are many stories, too, of how some don't even look like ghosts. They are as human and as real-looking as you or I. I've heard plenty of stories that involve someone speaking to a ghost without realizing they've just had a conversation with a dead person! Down the years I have received many letters regarding situations like this. I'm very fond of this one about 'Phantom Annie', which I received from a lady in Glasgow. It concerned her grandmother who, as you will see, was having a quite a time of it…

Bessie McCormick was worried, although she didn't really have time to be. At 25, she was having her first baby, but she was working – as was so often the case in those days – right up until her labour began.

Bessie was in service as a housemaid in a large house. The hours were long and crippling. No mod cons in those days! From early in the morning till late at night, Bessie was on the go, tending fires, blackening grates, fetching hot water, sweeping floors and so on. Her day was non-stop hard and heavy work.

In the middle of this, she felt her stomach muscles contract. Then, for a terrible moment as the gush of water ran down her legs, she thought she had wet herself. A complete novice at childbirth, poor Bessie was terrified. She had never felt pain like it. Gasping for breath, she managed to take a step along the hall. But as she did, another contraction hit her and she was doubled over by it. 'Oh dear God, help me!' she cried. That was when she felt a pair of arms go round her.

'Don't you worry now lass,' a voice said. 'We'll just get you to a seat. You'll be fine. The first one's always the worst.'

Bessie nodded grimly. She'd no idea how the woman opposite could know this was her first baby. But she didn't worry about it for long. By now she was in such pain, she felt she couldn't move. If the woman hadn't brought the chair over for her to sit in, she believed she would have fallen down on the floor. When she had sat for a moment, she felt better. The woman held her hand, stroking it, and Bessie, attempting to be polite despite her discomfort, asked her name.

'It's Annie,' she said. 'I work here too.'

'I've never seen you,' Bessie gasped. 'But I don't know everyone.'

'That's alright. I'm going to get help for you. I think your baby will be born here. But you'll be alright. Take a deep breath. Try to relax.'

Although she was only a young girl herself, Annie spoke gently and her entire manner was reassuring. After a while she left Bessie to get help. The mistress of the house appeared and Bessie looked for Annie among the crowd of faces that had suddenly gathered in the hall. She didn't see her. She supposed she must have been sent to carry out other duties.

Bessie's daughter was born within the hour and it was in the hallway, just as Annie had said. Everything went well. Bessie had nothing to worry about. She was delighted with the little girl and she wanted to tell Annie. She asked the mistress. Would it be possible to send for Annie and just let her see the baby before Bessie's husband arrived to take her home?

The mistress looked a little perplexed by this. But to her credit, her face didn't whiten.

'Annie?' she questioned her maid.

'Yes,' said Bessie. 'She was here with me at the start. She was so kind. She said the baby would be here soon. But she didn't panic.'

'That may well be,' said the mistress, 'but if you're meaning Annie, and there was only one Annie who ever worked here, you can't see her I'm afraid.'

'Has she gone home?' Bessie asked, thinking she'd gone off for the rest of the afternoon.

'You might say so,' the mistress's face was grim. 'You see Annie worked here before you. She's dead. She was having a baby and, well, things didn't work out for her as they did for you. She died minutes after her baby was born.'

Bessie was astounded. The funny thing was the mistress's lack of surprise. 'Oh,' she confided. 'I see her too. The first time it gave me quite a scare. But she's here alright. Don't worry about it.'

And, strangely enough, Bessie didn't feel at all worried by it. In fact, she felt as if she had found a very good friend in the dead lady. She knew for absolute certainty that if it hadn't been for Annie, her first labour would have been much, much worse.

She passed her lovely story on to her daughter and then her granddaughter. And that's how I came to hear about it. And now, in true story-telling tradition, I'm telling you.

FOUR

Famous Ghosts

This chapter looks at some well-known – and some less familiar – ghost stories. It was great fun to write because it enabled me to reinterpret some of these tales. When I started writing this chapter, I had heard some of the stories but many were unknown to me. When I researched, and often visited, these places, I was amazed to see and feel the overwhelming presence of spiritual activity each time. And the stories that unfolded were amazing.

The Glencorse Ghost

Lost loves, lonely woods, maidens wringing their hands in despair and, of course, leaping lovers… many such tales have been around from time immemorial. Some people meet with such violent and tragic ends that their spirit is left behind. For them, there is no such thing as peace. That seems to be the case with the Glencorse ghost.

It was towards the end of the Napoleonic wars that the handsome young Frenchman was imprisoned at Greenlaw house in Midlothian, later the site of the Glencorse Barracks. And it was in the glades of Frith Woods that he met the beautiful daughter of a local farmer.

Soon their friendship became more meaningful. She gave him food – apples smuggled from her father's house, bread and milk from the dairy. They were in love – something that had to be kept secret from everyone as they strolled through the wood hand in hand.

The girl was already engaged. She was to be married to a local man, a man she had been happy enough to have, till she set eyes on the Frenchman. Desperately they talked about running away together, about the life they might have when the war ended. Oh, if they could only be together. But this was never to be.

The girl's fiancé grew suspicious about the amount of time she was spending away from him. You can imagine how he followed her along the lonely paths, how furious he was when he found out what her secret was. He was devastated when he saw her in the arms of her lover.

The next night he went to the girl's father and told him what was going on, that not only was the girl seeing another man, but one who was an enemy of the country – a French traitor. The girl's father was naturally furious at the fool his daughter was making of him. He picked up a large stick. Together the men went into the wood where they found the girl and the Frenchman. She begged him to run but he wouldn't. He was an officer after all, and he believed he could defend himself.

Although rumour has it that he fought bravely, he was no match for the girl's father or her fiancé. After a long struggle, he was beaten to death in front of the poor girl who was then dragged home kicking and screaming. She was immediately locked in a room and left there to mourn her loss.

A storm then blew up as if the elements themselves were outraged by what had happened to the lovers. Later that night, the girl escaped. She climbed out of the window and fled from the house to the spot where her lover's body lay. What dread the poor girl must have been feeling. Perhaps she hoped to find that he was still alive and that she could help him. No one knows exactly what she was thinking.

When her father found she was gone, he started to search for her, as did her fiancé. But sadly their search was in vain. Eventually, the next day, when everyone had given up hope, the girl was found. Her body was lying at the foot of a gorge. She had thrown herself to her death at a spot which is still known as Lover's Leap.

Since then, there have been numerous sightings of a beautiful girl in the area of the barracks. Several people have been startled by a girl running towards the place where the Frenchman was killed. They tell me her hair is dishevelled and her eyes are wild. Many report the sound of someone weeping and see a girl standing under the trees at this spot. No one has ever reported seeing the Frenchman, so perhaps he is at peace. But the nature of the girl's death and the misery she suffered before it have clearly meant that peace isn't an option for her.

The Phantom Horseman

Always popular in traditional ghost tales, horsemen – occasionally headless – make regular appearances on many Scottish roads. This one actually has a head. His territory is in Penicuik, along

183

the Peebles Road near Eddleston. One eyewitness went to the police to report that she had seen a man on horseback leaping off the nearby quarry, to certain death. Naturally, no body was ever found. Maybe the ghost was trying to kill himself to end his torment. Who knows? What is known is this.

Young Thomas, the farm labourer, was in love. The object of his devotion was a rather grand young lady from the nearby farm. To impress her, he would borrow his master's horse in order to visit her. You'll notice the word 'borrow'. Perhaps that's the wrong word to use because his master didn't actually know anything about it. The young man would wait until his master wasn't around and then he'd take the horse.

This, of course, meant that he had to be back before the master could find out, so his time with his lady love was short. But it was also very precious.

One night, as he was riding along, he saw there had been an accident. A cart had toppled over, trapping the driver and horse. Young Thomas had no doubt heard the story of the Good Samaritan, but it had obviously had very little effect on him because he simply rode past. He knew he had very little time. His beloved was waiting and that was much more important than answering the driver's anguished cries of pain and pleas for help.

Thomas must have had a very nice time with her because it was late when he finally left for home. The cart was still on its side on the road, with the driver and horse trapped underneath. Once again, Thomas decided he couldn't stop to help, otherwise he would have to explain what he was doing out with his master's horse. However, the driver recognized him and he cursed him for leaving him trapped.

Thomas rode home, returned the horse and slipped into bed. The driver lay under the cart all night. By the time he was found by the quarrymen on their way to work the next morning, he was in a pretty bad way – so bad that he died shortly afterwards. Not, however, before he told the quarrymen about Thomas.

As soon as the word went round, Thomas hadn't a friend left. His master gave him his marching orders and, shocked by his heartlessness, his lover did the same. Thomas was in disgrace. With no job to go to and having no home, he turned to poaching and living rough on the land he'd once worked on.

Then, some months later, Thomas's body was found. No one was sure how he died. Was it an accident? Or suicide? Or had he been driven to it by something else – a ghostly hand? No one knew and no one actually cared. Feelings were so strong that the townspeople decided Thomas's body would not be buried in consecrated ground. Instead, a piece of wasteland was deemed good enough for his burial.

But things didn't end there because Thomas evidently decided to have his revenge on those who'd done this and has been haunting the area ever since. It is believed his ghost rides along the Peebles Road. It has also been seen falling over the edge of the Mount Lothian quarry. He has often terrified the lime-burners by chasing them home at dusk.

For Thomas, the torment doesn't seem to want to end, and all because he rode by on the other side of the road.

Flannan Isle

'For God's sake – what is it Dougie? Are any of them alive?'

'I don't know.' Dougie lifted the lantern he was carrying higher on the chain, so that the light made an orange pool in front of his face. But he still couldn't see and the boat was passing them now, the little huddle of men in its bows, silent and unmoving.

'Is anyone out there?' he called, the desperation in his voice increasing. 'Answer me! Do you need assistance?'

'They're dead men! Look!' Davie crossed himself. He pointed over the rail to where the boat was drifting. The moon had come out. It was peeping through the clouds so brightly they could both see.

In the boat the men sat side by side. Their hands were still clutching the oars and they were staring straight ahead. Dougie noticed the ghastly white appearance of their faces as they passed.

'My God! Poor devils. They must have died in the boat. Do you see their faces?' Davie cried. Dougie didn't answer. What lay ahead? Where would the boat drift to?

There was the lighthouse, two or three miles away perhaps, across the open sea. If the boat washed up there, the lighthouse keepers would get them – what was left of them anyway. The dead were never a pretty sight. Especially not when they'd lain in a boat for weeks.

Suddenly, the lantern slipped from Dougie's fingers. It fell on the deck. The grease spilt out and lay in a pool. Dougie looked at it. His hands were shaking.

'What is it, man? What did you do that for?' Davie turned on him.

'Their hands,' Dougie said. 'Their hands were moving.'

'Moving? How can they be moving? Dougie, for God's sake, they're dead!'

'No they aren't. Listen.'

It came across the black water, faintly at first but loud enough for them both to hear.

'What is it?' asked Davie.

'Oarlocks, going up and down. Listen. That boat is moving. They're alive.'

'But they almost ran us down! What's wrong with them? Can't they see where they're going?'

'What lies ahead? That light there, what is it?'

'The Eilean Mor, Dougie. Surely you know that?'

'Flannan Isle?' Dougie said.

Of course he knew it. Flannan Island. It was a haunted place.

Of course perhaps Dougie and Davie didn't really say these things that night. Perhaps there weren't men called Dougie and Davie at all. But the two sailors who saw the strange craft heading for Flannan Island on 15 December 1900 did exist, because they testified to the fact. They were on board the *Fairwind*, a brigantine, when its bow was cut by the said longboat of 'dead' sailors.

Shortly afterwards, a storm broke. Skippers in the vicinity were furious because, by this time, the lighthouse was dark and it was to remain so. The three lighthouse keepers were never seen again.

These are the final entries written by lighthouse keeper Thomas Marshall:

'**December 12**: Gale north by north-west. Sea lashed to fury. Never seen such a storm. Waves very high. Tearing at lighthouse. Cannot go out. Ships passing sounding foghorn. Donald McArthur crying.

'**December 13**: Storm continued through night. Wind shifted west by north. Me, Ducat and McArthur prayed.

'**December 15**: Storm ended, sea calm. Thank God it's all over.'

An enquiry was carried out into the loss of the lighthouse keepers. Investigators pored for days over the log book. Even at that stage they could see there was something very wrong with these entries. Descriptions such as 'waves very high', 'storm still raging', 'noon, grey daylight' were typical of the type of weather that was to be expected in these parts. The trouble was that the weather during that period had been calm.

There was no storm, no waves lashing the lighthouse, nothing until the night of 15 December, the night the men disappeared, or at least the light went dark.

What is clear is that on 26 December, the supply vessel *Hesperus* went to the island to investigate. It hove to and signalled. Receiving no reply, it sent out a small boat. They were expecting to be met by one of the keepers. But no one came.

The silence was something they spoke of at the inquiry. It was immortalized in a poem by W.W.Gibson:

And still too mazed to speak,
we landed; and made fast the boat:
And climb'd the track in single file.
Each wishing he was safe afloat,
On any sea however far,
So it be far from Flannan Isle.

Still, the men of the *Hesperus* did climb. They climbed and found the door open. They must have been worried about the sight that was going to meet their eyes. In his poem, Gibson also speaks about how all those who had kept the Flannan light had come to a sticky or a sudden end, and how three previous keepers had gone mad. But behind the open door, they found the table set for a meal. A chair was lying on the floor, as if it had been pushed back suddenly, but otherwise there were no signs of a struggle. The cupboards were well-stocked with food, the lamps trimmed and ready to light, the beds made. What they did not find were the men's oilskins or boots. This implied that they had left the building together.

So what exactly became of the Flannan men? Did one of them go mad and rush out into the storm so the other two had to rescue him? Well, the fact that he put his boots and coat on first rather does away with the idea of rushing anywhere, doesn't it? Did a boat run aground, so the men put their oilskins on and went to help? That's a nice theory, but that kind of thing would have been reported. Had a ship sunk or run aground off the island, there would have been debris, not to mention a search for a missing vessel. What about the reports in the log, which seemed to suggest the men were seeing things that weren't there?

Well, for centuries the Hebridean people had claimed that Flannan Island was haunted. The farmers only went there in daylight to check their sheep, otherwise you were asking for trouble, they said.

Which brings us back to Dougie and Davie, or whatever their names were. Did they really make the story up? Did the men from Flannan Island meet an ordinary fate, one for which there is a plausible explanation? Or were they visited that night by the strange, skeletal sailors Dougie and Davie claimed they saw?

Oh, I almost forgot! The investigators found something else, something very strange indeed. Inside the log book, there were some shreds of a kind of seaweed which had never been seen before.

Glamis Castle, Angus

While many castles have their tales of ghosts, Glamis certainly has the lion's share. Sometimes Glamis Castle is called the most haunted house in Scotland. Spooky happenings certainly abound and the legends go on and on. From human phantoms to phantom phantoms, Glamis has all kinds. There's the servant who was found sucking blood and promptly locked up somewhere in the walls, never to be seen again – at least not while still alive. And there's even a doggie phantom, which apparently greets visitors by breathing on their legs. If you're thinking of going, maybe you should invest in a good pair of trousers!

Where to start in Glamis is a real problem. You could try King Malcolm's room, where the floor was boarded over because no amount of scrubbing would remove his blood after he was murdered there in the 11th century. Or the hangman's chamber, which is haunted by a butler who hanged himself there. Was he driven insane, perhaps, by the ghostly goings-on? Who knows? But if you're looking for a culprit, there's certainly plenty to choose from.

Earl Beardie

Earl Beardie Crawford would certainly be one of my favourites for the position. He was, by all accounts, quite a gambler, and rather bad tempered too. At least it was his shocking temper which forced him to quarrel with Lord Glamis as they played cards in the tower one fateful day.

Something happened during that card game that made Lord Glamis throw Earl Beardie down the stone staircase. But this didn't deter him. He came back in, shouting that if no one would play with him, he'd play with the Devil. It seems he got his wish. A tall, dark man strode in. The two played. The stranger left without saying who he was, and Earl Beardie died shortly afterwards.

His eternity has been spent playing cards, if the sounds coming from the chamber in the tower are anything to go by. When he's not playing, Earl Beardie likes to walk about, sometimes bending over the ladies as they sleep, as well as passing through walls. It's only to be expected, after all. Forever is a long time, and the Devil must have other things to occupy himself with on occasion.

The Grey Lady

Reputed to be the ghost of Lady Janet Douglas, who was burned to death on Castle Hill in Edinburgh in 1537, the lady is often seen kneeling silently in prayer in the chapel. She is also known to flit mysteriously about the clock tower where the sun shines through her clothes in spectacular fashion.

Although Janet was burned as a witch, it seems unlikely that anyone who prays as often as she does could be anything as sinister. It is far more likely that the king ordered her death because of her disloyalty to him. Apparently, she was plotting to poison him.

The Occupant of the Locked Room

There are so many contenders for this post, I don't know where to start! Let's begin with the Ogilvys.

A few hundred years ago, the Ogilvys were having regular rows with their neighbours, the Lindsays. Having had enough, the Ogilvys decided to hide out in Glamis castle while things cooled down. The owner was a great friend of theirs. However, he was also a friend of the Lindsays – an even greater friend.

Pretending he was hiding the Ogilvys for their safety, he locked them in a cupboard. He left them there until they starved to death. A nice way to treat your guests, I must say! It's therefore no surprise that they continue to haunt Glamis. Secret locked rooms are, if you've ever been to Glamis, very much a feature of the place.

The Mad Earl

By far the most potent legend of Glamis Castle is the story of the Glamis 'monster' – the Mad Earl. He was so badly deformed he was shut up in a secret room for the duration of his almost un-naturally long life. 'It is fortunate you do not know it, for if you did, you would never be happy,' Andrew Ralston, the land agent to the Strathmores, once said of him. While the 12th Earl put it more succinctly: 'If you could only guess the nature of the secret, you would go down on your knees and thank God it was not yours.'

The suggestion is that the 'monster' was the son of the 11th Earl, Thomas, who did indeed have a baby boy who was born on either 18 or 21 October 1821. Guests often heard loud crashes and were disturbed by what they described as a 'giant' – things that, given the castle's reputation, could easily be passed off as spectral disturbances. But were they? It is thought that the spirit of the Mad Earl still haunts the castle.

The Grassmarket Ghost

Like any other capital city, Edinburgh certainly has its share of ghosts, as well as its share of strange characters. Everyone knows the strange tale of Dr Jekyll and Mr Hyde, as told by the famous Scottish writer, Robert Louis Stevenson. It was supposedly based on the tale of Deacon Brodie, a pillar of the church and community by day and a bit of a thief by night. But long before the Deacon felt the need to behave in this doubly confusing fashion, Edinburgh threw up another char-acter, who put him in the shade

– the infamous Major Weir. Thomas to all his friends – and there were quite a few. Not the kind you would necessarily want to meet yourself on a dark and stormy night …

Major Weir lived in a house in West Bow, Edinburgh in the mid-17th century. It was a place that certainly befitted his station as commander of the city's garrison. He never married but he shared the house with his sister, Grizel, a fine old lady and, like himself, a pillar of the community, one whose Presbyterian zeal was noted. At least that's how it looked on the surface.

Major Tom suddenly started making the most startling allegations. He was, he said, a servant of the Devil. His sister was too, and they had spent their lives engaged in 'most revolting practices'. The major begged to be arrested. Was he insane? The doctors of the day didn't think so, although Grizel was clearly very disturbed. She insisted that the major's walking stick was a special gift from the Devil, claiming it had been given in exchange for his soul.

Tom and Grizel were arrested and put on trial, which was, apparently, one of the sensations of the time, the front-page story of the day ('Walking stick was my familiar!'). Each day brought fresh revelations as people came forward to say there had been a variety of strange occurrences in West Bow, including the appearance of a 10-foot woman.

The pair also seemed to want to convict themselves out of their own mouths when they started raving about witchcraft and black magic. They were condemned to be strangled and burnt, as was the famous stick, which apparently took as long to dwindle into ashes as the major himself.

When it was Grizel's turn, she wowed the crowd by removing her clothes. This proved a bit much for the executioner, who tipped her prematurely off the ladder.

So were these unfortunate old siblings simply the victims of dementia and their time? Well, that's certainly possible, and there were those even then who seemed to think the major was simply insane. But who can explain the fact that no one could live in the house for a century afterwards, the fiendish laughter that could be heard within its walls, as well as the calf-like apparition that wandered about the bedrooms?

Today, West Bow is still standing but no one knows exactly where the house was, which shows it must have eventually been rented or sold without incident. Tom's ghost has been seen many times – a tall figure roaming around Grassmarket, tapping his stick. So those of you who have heard this sound now know the explanation behind it.

The Ardvreck Ghost

'I cannot live but that you do not love me. Whatever you have heard, it is as a dagger to me. And each wound it makes takes me a little nearer death.'

With her flowing black hair and clear, green eyes, Magdalen Jarron was the prettiest girl in the area of Loch Assynt. Of a strange family, it was whispered, but not so strange as the dowager Lady Agnes, who took a disliking to her. Magdalen had married a handsome local gentleman who was apparently used to his wife's gypsy-like ways and thought nothing of the fact that her family studied the occult.

'She's a whore,' the old lady told him quite bluntly. 'That child you have is naught but a bastard.'

The gentleman was so deeply in love with Magdalen, he didn't believe the old woman. But her words began to haunt him. A bastard wasn't something he particularly wanted in his house and, after all, the child didn't look like him. Magdalen was very beautiful. What if the old lady was right and she had been less than faithful? Before very long he had turned the poor girl out of the house and threatened to kill the baby if she ever brought it near him again.

Magdalen was desperate. For all his unkind treatment of her, she loved her husband. The old lady had – and people knew it well – a nasty, meddling tongue. When all Magdalen's pleas for her husband to love her fell on deaf ears, she knew she must get the old lady to admit she was telling lies. So she wrote to her two brothers, begging for their help.

'But of course,' they said. 'We'll see the matter sorted. You won't mind, therefore, if we bring one other?'

'Mind?' said poor Magdalen. 'I mind only that my lord no longer cares. I'd give all I have to have him back and be as we once were.'

On her part, that was perhaps a bit of a mistake. Anyway, the two brothers kept their part of the bargain and paid Magdalen's husband a visit. They asked him if he would come and see Agnes, who lived nearby, at Ardvreck Castle. Exactly what their methods of persuasion were isn't clear, but he agreed, no doubt after they'd hammered him about a little.

Agnes, too, was perfectly agreeable to them coming to visit. 'Of course, I've nothing to hide,' she told them. A big mistake, as it turned out.

Perhaps things would have ended there if Agnes had withdrawn her allegations, the husband had seen sense, or Magdalen had decided he just wasn't worth it. Only none of them did, so the younger brother drew a strange diagram on the floor and began to chant. He wasn't going to let the matter go either, and shortly afterwards the waters of the loch began to heave, the sky turned dark and, yes, a very strange man suddenly appeared in the corner of the room. This wasn't quite in a puff of smoke but it was very effective just the same. Everyone was terrified of him, except the two brothers. The stranger was tall and dark. I don't know if he was handsome but it seemed he was very intelligent. 'Put your question to him,' said the younger brother to Magdalen's startled husband. 'He can answer anything.' So he did.

'Has my wife ever been unfaithful to me?' he asked in a trembling voice.

'Never and you should know better than to ask it,' replied the stranger, without a second's hesitation. His voice was very loud and booming and quite aided in its dramatic effect by the windows crashing open and a chill wind blowing round the castle hall.

Magdalen's husband could see he had made a mistake. He did know better. But that was now. It was a pity he hadn't known before.

'Our guest will not leave us without payment,' said the older brother. 'He has answered your question. Who can you spare?'

'Oh!' sobbed the terrified Agnes, who was clearly expecting it to be her. 'Take that child there!' And she pointed at a small figure, an orphan serving girl who had run into the room.

'No,' the stranger replied in outrage. 'I daren't take an orphan. I'll ask you again. Who can you spare?'

'Well,' said Magdalen's husband, getting quite frightened by this time. 'How about the Lady Agnes? Wouldn't you like her?'

But the stranger didn't seem to like her. 'She is mine already, though her term has not quite run!' he boomed in that tremendous voice of his. It was obvious the stranger wasn't happy with any of the prizes on offer.

'I'll take one your sister will miss more!' he told the brothers. Then he disappeared.

When Magdalen's husband arrived home, he found his wife waiting for him. But the baby was dead. It had died at about the time the stranger vanished from the castle hall.

For years afterwards it was rumoured that nothing would grow in the vicinity of the castle and there were no fish to be had from the loch. The castle itself was destroyed by fire and so was Agnes. But her screams can still be heard, echoing over the area on summer evenings when the lake is calm and still. A baby's wails have also been noticed coming from the bank, although investigators never find any trace of an infant. It's part of the mystery of the place and a reminder of that day long ago when the lake rose up and yielded its own unexpected visitor.

The Green Ghost

Why are ghost ladies invariably green, grey or white? Well, I'm not sure of the answer to that one, though I must agree red or yellow would certainly make a change. No self-respecting castle seems to be without their green, grey or white lady, however. So I've had a look at all the various 'ladies' who exist, and decided that the one at Stirling Castle merits a mention. She's very green, apparently, as are the faces of those who see her, if I'm to believe everything I read. Her identity is something of a mystery, though.

The green lady is certainly well known. There are several reports to the effect that she likes to flit about the castle corridors, appearing in the most unexpected places, generally terrifying the wits out of those who see her. In some accounts she's said to be the ghost of an attendant of Mary Queen of Scots, a lady who probably likes to do a bit of haunting herself.

The story here is that the lady sensed her mistress, the queen, was in danger one night. She rushed into the royal bedroom and found the draperies on the royal bed were on fire. And so she saved the queen's life. At least from that particular fate!

What's more, the queen, being a bit psychic herself, was soon busily informing everyone of the prophecy she'd been given by none other than Nostradamus himself that her life would be endangered by fire while she was at Stirling Castle. This was greatly cheering for the green lady, and evidently had such a huge effect on her that she then took it upon herself to warn any guests of a similar fate. Her appearances are always linked to the outbreak of fire. So the story goes anyway.

What it doesn't explain, however, are the mysterious sightings of the anguished lady who has a penchant for running along the corridors and throwing herself over the battlements. In true ghost tradition, this lady is said to have jumped to her death when her father, the then governor of the castle, killed her lover, a young and handsome officer, whom she had no hope of marrying. This lady is also green, according to those who've seen her.

In the 1820s, a young sentry was found dead at his post, a look of horror on his face, not long after he reported hearing strange footsteps running up and down the battlements. Although he was the only one to be found like this, he wasn't the first to hear them, or the last. To this day, there are reports of running steps that echo across the ceilings where there are no rooms above.

Mary's lady, or the governor's daughter? You can take your pick! I actually believe in both and, given all that went on in Stirling Castle during its time, a whole lot more besides.

The Balconie Ghost

'Gone? What do you mean gone?'

'Wi' a man, sir! I couldnae stop them! I shouted, but she wouldna listen! The keys, sir! She threw me her keys. Where they fell they left a mark!'

'Fetch out the dogs!'

'But you don't understand! The mark is on granite! That's all that's left of her, sir! All that's left of your good lady wife! The man in green took her awa'!'

This was the gist of the story that rocked Cromarty some 300 years ago, concerning the local laird's rather beautiful young wife. She was a quiet girl who spoke to very few and absolutely refused to say who she was and where she came from.

Cromarty has its share of ghosts and ghostly happenings – witches, wizards and visits from the Devil. The ghost of the Allte Grande, the laird's wife from Balconie Hall, is only one, but a fascinating one just the same. And its fascination lies in the fact that although the Devil was said to make regular appearances in certain parts, this was a lady who knew him already. How, where or why was never clear. But then she fell in love with the laird. Of course, the Devil wasn't having it.

In true tradition, he showed you can run but you can't hide. Except there's a footnote to this strange tale which shows that he then did just that. And he took her with him. That's also part of the fascination.

Are the strange wailing noises that haunt the gorge of the Allte Grande ghostly echoes from her past sorrows, or is she there yet, walled up in a mysterious cavern? Who knows? As you read on you can make up your own mind.

The Allte Grande. It's a wonderful name for a river, though unusual for a Scottish one. And no doubt the laird's young wife was intrigued with it because that's where she spent all her time. The locals may have said it was haunted but that didn't seem to worry her. But then very little did. The locals, if pushed, thought she was haunted too. Her quiet, mysterious manner made them uneasy, as did the fact she wouldn't tell anyone where she was from, only that the laird had met her on his travels abroad. I believe she was probably foreign and this may have accounted for her reticence. In fact, it was likely she didn't understand a word anyone was saying.

As time passed, she did become a little friendlier. The locals commented on it. They also talked about the fact that she was more at home with the servants than the local 'bigwigs'. In particular, she liked to talk to her own maid, a Highland girl.

The two of them were walking down by the Allte Grande one evening when a dark man in green appeared and beckoned to the laird's wife. At first, she was reluctant but it was as if she was mesmerized. At least that's what the serving girl said afterwards. Then the laird's wife walked forward. The maid called her but she didn't answer. She merely turned around and threw the maid a bunch of keys. This suggested that she wouldn't be needing them any more. The keys struck a boulder and apparently made an impression on the stone, which can still be seen to this day.

The maid stooped to pick them up. When she looked up again, the laird's wife and the green man had gone. She ran round looking for them, then rushed back to the hall where I'm sure you can imagine the scene that took place, especially when she came to the bit about the man in green. A search began and continued for days but the laird's wife was never found.

Many thought the maid had brought harm to her mistress. But she was never formally accused. No body was ever found. It was suggested that the laird's wife had run off with someone from her past. No one knew what happened that day and, apart from the maid, there were no other witnesses.

Then, 10 years later, a fisherman searching the gorge for a basket of fish climbed down on a ledge and found an enormous cavern. As he stepped inside, two black dogs got up to meet him. His basket of fish was there – and so was the laird's wife! There she was sitting at a table, looking much the same as ever, only sadder. The fisherman was quite taken aback and, of course, seeing himself as the gallant rescuer of the lady, offered to whisk her back up the cliff. Only this couldn't be done. She was chained to the chair, which in turn was chained to the wall. And by now the dogs were agitated by the stranger. She told him to leave, which he did, but he vowed he'd be back.

Instead, he went straight to the laird to tell him what he'd seen. At last a witness did exist. An extensive search was mounted but ended in vain. Neither the cave nor the lady were ever found.

Legend says it was the work of the Devil and that the laird's wife is still chained in a cave somewhere in the gorge to this day. A quite chilling thought. How else could you explain the ghostly wailing that is sometimes heard in the gorge at night? Or is it just a case of strange acoustics? I don't know.

Having heard the story, I have my doubts, but am now wary of approaching strange men in green!

The Phantom Lady of Meggernie

Alright, so headless phantoms are fairly common in ghost stories, along with those who rattle chains and go bump in the night. But Meggernie castle in Glenlyon is supposedly home to a bottomless phantom. The castle is also home to a topless phantom. Put them together and I think you have a whole ghost. The story is this.

The Laird of Meggernie had a beautiful young wife who may or may not have had a lover. Even in spirit, this is apparently a woman who is free with her kisses. Whatever the truth of the matter, the laird was jealous, so he killed her in the tower and cut her body in two. It is rumoured he hid the body in a closet recess between two rooms.

To cover up what he had done, and by way of an explanation for his wife's sudden disappearance, he led people to believe she had gone overseas. He duly left 'to join her' some time later. That, he thought, would be the end of the matter. But far from it.

The laird planned to remain overseas for a few months and then return with the sad tale that his wife had died in an accident while abroad. But he couldn't settle for fear someone would discover his wife's body. The best thing, he decided, was to go back home and bury his wife's body. So he set off back to the castle in order to carry out the task.

Up to this point, things had been relatively quiet at the castle. No tales of hauntings, no tales of anything. And the laird must have thought he was going to get away with murder. The servants were naturally sorry to hear of the accident that had befallen their mistress and quite understood their master's desire to be alone in the tower.

The laird managed to remove and bury his wife's lower body in the churchyard without being seen. The upper half was more difficult, however. For some unknown reason, he was unable to remove the torso and so decided instead to seal the closet. Certain this was a good plan, he waited until everyone else had gone to bed for the night.

The following morning, the laird was found dead at the tower door. Quite how he died has never been established.

There have been countless sightings of strange goings-on. Some say they've seen a woman's upper body gliding around the corridors of the castle. She has been known to glide through walls, open and shut doors and to plant hot kisses on the cheeks of unsuspecting male visitors.

At one stage, while the tower was being repaired, a skull and the skeleton of the upper part of a torso were discovered. These have since been buried, but obviously not to the lady's satisfaction.

Despairing and in two halves, she has apparently continued to haunt the castle. With her about, let's face it, who needs any others?

The Grey Man of Ben Macdhui

It's certainly a change – not necessarily a pleasant one, given that the subject matter is ghosts – to meet a grey man instead of a lady. Having said that, I haven't actually met the grey man of Ben

Macdhui myself. If I ever do, I hope I won't run down the mountain, as some have put it, 'in a time they've never bettered'.

Exactly who the grey man of Ben Macdhui is or – more importantly – was, isn't actually known. But there are too many sightings of him to ignore. They all describe the same thing – a gigantic, grey figure who takes huge strides. In some instances, he wears a top hat. I'm not sure about the hat, but I'm told he's utterly menacing. One witness described him babbling in Gaelic.

The sightings are all accompanied by the same thing – a feeling of dread and terror. Moreover, the big man likes to pursue those who do see him, sometimes for miles. That thump, thump sound the poor unfortunates hear across bramble and rock isn't the pounding of their own hearts. It's the clump, clump of the grey man's four huge feet chasing after them.

Did I say four? Well, there were four, according to one psychic, a Mrs Joan Grant, who in 1928 visited the Rothiemurchus Forest with her husband. She didn't actually see the grey man, but she was convinced that something 'utterly malign, four-legged and obscenely human, invisible but solid' was trying to reach her. Not a pleasant thought and one that caused her to run back the way she had come in terror. Mrs Grant wasn't the first to be frightened by the grey man of Ben Macdhui. Nor the last.

Given that Ben Macdhui is so remote – one of the six peaks of the Cairngorms and the highest at that – most of those who do see him tend to be experienced climbers or naturalists. So is it just altitude sickness that makes them think they're seeing something they're not? Somehow I don't think so, or this would occur on other peaks of the same height.

A year after Mrs Grant fled from the forest, there was some correspondence about Ben Macdhui in *The Times* from people who had experienced the same thing. Some years after Mrs Grant's experience, a naturalist called Wendy Wood, who never gave the matter of being alone on Scottish mountains a second thought, froze to the spot after hearing someone speaking to her in Gaelic. Being a hardy sort, she tramped round looking for the person concerned, in case they were injured. Of course, there was no one there.

It is thought that the grey man led Wendy a merry dance round the Lairig Ghru pass before she also decided enough was enough and fled down the mountainside in a panic. Of course, it was dark and people do get frightened in the dark, but what frightened Wendy was the fact that the footsteps she believed were echoes of her own didn't actually coincide. The grey man followed her quite a way down. Not caring if she got injured in her furious flight, she just wanted to get to the bottom.

That's the kind of effect the grey man has on people. He has also been shot at and, on one occasion, he was followed by someone who thought he was a lost climber. Rather like the business with Wendy, the person stopped eventually because they suddenly realized that there were no footprints where the grey man had tramped across the mud. Not a very human state of affairs at all.

So who is the grey man? Well, that much has never been clear. But I think we have to return to what Mrs Grant said, 'invisible but solid', and assume he's some kind of phantom. He's been around too long to be human but the phantom of whom or what isn't known.

And so he remains, a sort of Scottish abominable snowman, without the snow. A strangely malign figure of the Lairig Ghru pass and Rothiemurchus Forest, seen by many – and frightened many more!

Pearlin' Jean

Is it possible to be fond of a ghost? Well, I think so, if they're the kind that don't do any harm or exude any kind of 'evil' feeling. Of course, some do, but the vast majority are literally just poor souls who haven't found it possible to move on, for whatever reason. Having said that, those who know me and my work also know that I do not fully believe in evil spirits. I'm forever preaching that we are more in danger from the living than from the dead.

Pearlin' Jean is perhaps a bit of a neglected ghost these days. Let's face it – there are just so many ghosts about! Not so long ago, however, Pearlin' had pride of place as one of the best-known Scottish ghosts. And people loved her! Well, some of them did anyway. I'm sure she frightened quite a few in her time – her wicked lover most of all – even though he seemed to deserve it.

But, on the whole, the locals who knew of her were quite devoted to her. So much so that, when the house she haunted was taken down, they worried about what was going to happen to her. Of course, she didn't disappear as quickly as that! That was in the 19th century, and she was already 200 years old by then. The word is that Pearlin' Jean has been seen many times since. I think she deserves a place here because of her fame and her story.

Near the village of Allanton in Berwickshire, on the banks of the Blackadder, stood the house of Allanbank. It was a very grand place, owned by the Stuart family. At a party one evening, Sir Robert Stuart was introduced to a beautiful French lady, a very exotic creature by all accounts, and he fell quite madly in love with her. Or perhaps I should have said 'in lust with her', because that seemed to be the extent of Sir Robert's feelings.

Her name was Jeanne and she was very naive and trusting. What she was doing in Scotland I have no idea but she wasn't there long. Sir Robert took her to France but she wasn't there long either as things transpired, because one evening he decided he'd had enough.

'Please! Please don't leave me!' she begged. 'I will do anything, anything,' the frantic creature cried, throwing herself on the floor in order to kiss his hand. In her silk gown with the 'pearlin' lace on the bodice, she was very beautiful, and she had done her hair in the style he liked, to please him. But he had seen it all so often. The stony expression she so dreaded settled on his face. He strode out of the house without a word.

The coach was already pulling away from the kerb. She rushed down the steps, her little feet echoing on the stone. She was vexed that he did not love her but she believed that if she could get inside the carriage to speak to him, she could put everything right. She could not believe that he meant to abandon her. As she reached for the carriage door, she slipped and the heavy wheels passed over her head.

Sir Robert went home. Jeanne had been killed instantly when the wheels struck her head, her lovely face crushed beyond recognition. It had been in him, he knew, to have stopped the coach. In him, too, not to have said, 'Drive on, damn you!' to the driver as she reached for the handle. In his way, he had murdered Jeanne. And, as so often happens, the victim confronted her killer.

Evening was approaching as the coach pulled up towards the archway to Allanbank. Jeanne was sitting above the archway gazing at him, with her broken head (and her broken heart). It was a vision he would see till the day he died.

Pearlin' Jean, as she came to be known, returned to Allanbank, not as the bride she had hoped to be, but as a ghost. The rustling of silk in empty hallways, the sound of footsteps walking across the floor, the shadowy sad figure wandering the grounds at dusk. These are all reported sightings of Pearlin' Jean.

Sir Robert, driven mad by her presence no doubt, made several attempts to exorcise her ghost. Pearlin' Jean, however, steadfastly refused to budge. Such was his crime that she believed he should pay for it. A portrait of her hung between Sir Robert and Lady Stuart seemed to please her for a time. But Sir Robert's relief was only temporary. When he died, the hauntings continued.

As time passed, the locals grew fond of her, although one young man going to meet his girlfriend in the grounds of the hall was a bit put out to discover that the young woman waiting for him was actually Pearlin' Jean – who seemed to want to embrace him.

The hall was demolished years later but Pearlin' Jean's presence still could be felt … and seen. Another sighting involved two young lovers. As they walked hand in hand over the grassy area where the hall once stood, the female stopped dead in her tracks. Her face white with terror, she explained to her partner that a beautiful female, dressed in pale cream silk, had walked across her path. Her face was beautiful but, as she turned, the other side revealed the most gruesome of injuries. 'Blood-stained and gaping' was how this young girl described what she'd seen. Seconds later, her partner, too, felt a hand gently caress his face. Out of the corner of his eye he caught the merest glimpse of a long, swaying skirt.

In more recent times, a young soldier, home on leave, was relaxing on an area of grass while his friends played games nearby. Their laughter and rowdiness disturbed the soldier as he tried in vain to rest. Eventually, however, he did manage to nod off into the most peaceful of sleeps. He could no longer hear his friends. As he dozed, he could smell the most wonderful aroma. He dreamt of a beautiful young woman, calling his name. A huge smile played on his lips as he slept. He seemed to be floating towards the young woman, but as he got closer, she stepped out onto the road and was hit by what looked like a carriage being pulled by a horse. He woke with a start and, although he could see his friends only yards away, he could not hear them. What he was hearing was the desperate pleas of a female which then turned into what he could only describe as a 'shrill'. The screaming subsided and once again he could hear only his friends' riotous laughter.

He has never forgotten that day and the scenes he witnessed.

I'm perfectly sure Pearlin' Jean still haunts that area. Equally, however, I feel she must surely vanish from time to time. After all, it's obvious she has unfinished business to attend to, and I'll bet Sir Robert doesn't get much peace in the afterlife either.

The Tinker's Curse or the Deil of Glenluce

While sounding like a cross between a bad Victorian melodrama and a Hammer horror film, the Deil (Devil) of Glenluce was anything but, although I don't think there's any doubt that part one went like this.

Scene: a road, the sky in the distance. A poor cottage at one side of the road, a garden at the other. Gilbert Campbell answers the cottage door to Alexander Agnew, a wandering beggar.

Campbell: No, no! Be off with you! I don't have a halfpenny to waste on a beggar like you!

Agnew: You will refuse a poor man who hasn't got even that much to his name?

Campbell: I'd say you should count yourself lucky you've at least got a name. If it proves your parents were married, then that's better than some have got, though I'm bound to tell you I don't think they were glad to beget a sorry- looking devil like yourself. Why don't you work, you lazy blaggard?

Agnew: I can't work. I've been suffering from the sickness. All I need is a morsel of bread to satisfy my hunger. Please, sir, I beg you.

Campbell: If you're sick you can't be hungry. Sick people don't eat. At least not that much. Now get you gone. Go roam the highways and find yourself a decent job and don't think to curse this house with any ill fortune. I've well heard it said what kind of man you are. The Devil himself in disguise. Well, you'll find I'm a great believer in the Almighty. One who isn't as terrified as all that by any threat of blackmail you may offer to be frightened into feeding you. Get away with you!

Agnew: Oh, I'm not the Devil. But I can curse.

Campbell: Get away! (*Pushes him towards stage right.*)

Agnew: Gilbert Campbell – I curse you.

Campbell: Or I'll set the dogs on ye!

Agnew: Ill fortune will be your master!

Campbell: Out!

Agnew: A plague shall follow you! By the demon of the well and the spirits of the hills, you shall be troubled!

Campbell: Well, so long as it's not by the stink of your rambling breath, that's something I can deal with. Now get away! (*Throws Agnew off stage.*)

Enter Jennet Campbell

Jennet:	Faither, faither, what are you doing? Who was that man?
Campbell:	Alexander Agnew.
Jennet:	But you didna send him away? Curses faither, do you not know? They say he's in league wi' the Devil. He'll bring him down upon us.
Campbell:	Hush now. That he will not.
Jennet:	But faither...
Campbell:	Let the Devil come here if he so desires. I'm match enough for him.

Whether the Devil did or didn't visit the home of the Glenluce Campbells during the 17th century, and whether Gilbert was match enough for him, isn't entirely clear. But something certainly did happen, if the resulting disturbances are anything to go by.

And what's more, exorcism had absolutely no effect. The visitor evidently enjoyed his stay and wasn't for being driven away. It was, after all, a long, cold winter, and the harsh conditions outside weren't nearly as inviting as the warmth of the Campbell's humble cottage. Moreover, the spirit being seemed to form quite an attachment to Gilbert's son Tom, so much so that it stoned him, whistled after him, destroyed his clothes and hit him with sticks. Jennet, too, came in for a fair bit of attention, though perhaps it wasn't quite so fond of her, since it threatened to throw her into the well. Obviously, it wasn't about to give up the two people it was most fond of in the world.

Gilbert didn't know what to do. Soon he was begging round the parish for families to take both Tom and Jennet in.

It seemed the disturbances lessened when they weren't around. The cynical might say he just wanted rid of them. But what extreme lengths to go to! And if he was responsible for creating the disturbances, he must have been a dab hand at it. On one occasion the house was almost burned to the ground.

Even a prayer meeting of ministers couldn't budge whatever it was. The spirit was from heaven it told them, something they positively disputed. It said it had a commission 'to annoy the family' and that if it had a spade it would dig a grave for itself. Whether it would was never proven, since no one hastened to oblige. In the event, though, graves were very nearly dug for a handful of local women when the spirit pronounced them witches. Fortunately, Glenluce didn't become the Salem of its day. But just the same, things were nasty for a time.

The spirit stayed a while, defeating everyone's best efforts to remove it. Every day it dished out beatings to each member of the family, so that generally they weren't to be seen without black eyes and broken teeth – the kind of thing that would certainly involve welfare workers asking all kinds of questions today. But times were different then. It seemed it would never go, yet it did, in a way that really convinced people that Alexander Agnew was in league with the Devil. It vanished when he was hanged at Dumfries on a charge of atheism.

So perhaps there is something in the old business of laying a curse after all.

The Martyrs of Murder Moss

This makes such a good title, I don't like to change it, although I do have a confession to make. The martyrs were more like murder victims. But at least they died for love, which seems as good a reason as any to call them martyrs. Like some of the other stories in this book, this one happened a long time ago – 250 years to be precise. But it's a good example of how conscience can get the better of us in the end. Or was there more to it than that? And was local lad Geordie O' the Mill forced to take his own life by forces he couldn't contain? I'll let you be the judge. The story goes like this.

Geordie O' the Mill was a handsome man – rich, strong and mysterious. The kind you'd think would have many of the local girls queuing up to marry him. But he was also dark, quiet and had a habit for disappearing for days on end. No one knew where he went but he certainly knew the district. The year was 1745, a time of great political upheaval in Scotland, and it may have been that Geordie spied for the English. No one liked to say. Where he lived in Bowden near Selkirk was certainly border country. So spying wouldn't have presented him with many problems, and he would have been able to cross back and forth quite easily.

Geordie was in love. His black, somewhat forbidding eye had fallen on a young woman called Kirsty, who wasn't a stranger to men like him. Her father was in a class of his own when it came to fending off her suitors. So Kirsty had none – except for Geordie.

It seemed that he alone made the grade where such things were concerned. And to be fair, Kirsty was quite happy. Geordie was, after all, handsome and rich, if a little sullen. No doubt she thought she could change him and his melancholy habits, and win the approbation of the other women in the village for doing it. At any rate, the couple became engaged and set a date for their wedding.

Things were going very well till a man named Will Hob came back to the village. He had gone away some years before as a boy and returned as a handsome and rich man, like Geordie. But there the similarity ended. Will was all the things Geordie wasn't in terms of his charm. And soon Kirsty had fallen head over heels in love with him. The engagement with Geordie was broken off. Kirsty, it was announced, would marry Will.

For his part, Geordie took things very well. But even then he may have had other plans. Will certainly never liked him and made this plain, although Geordie was always very polite to him. On the eve of the wedding, all Kirsty's friends were gathered at her father's house for a 'shindig' when the distant sound of galloping horses and shouting reached them through the storm outside. The storm, of course, is an integral part of Scottish weather and ghost stories. On this occasion, it certainly played its part by adding to the confusion. The villagers thought the English raiders had arrived and rushed out onto the moors to hide, Will and Kirsty among them. They were on the same horse when, suddenly, the shape of a mounted man loomed up before them. It was Geordie. 'Oh! Save us!' cried Kirsty. 'You know your way about these moors!' 'Right you are,' said Geordie. 'I know of just the place where you'll never be found.' And he was right. These were ominous words. They were never found. The young lovers were never seen again.

When Geordie came home the next day, it was with the tale that the lovers were on their way to Leith. They were frightened, he said, and had galloped off eagerly enough, thinking they would be safe there. Kirsty's father, however, didn't believe him. He looked for his daughter, even going as far as Leith. There was no trace.

The whispers started. It was said that Geordie had brought the English to the village and handed the young couple over to them so that they would be taken away and imprisoned. That seemed the most plausible explanation. But then Kirsty's handkerchief was fished out of one of the pools in a swamp area of moorland. And things became more unthinkable. Of course, she might have dropped it at some other time. But the villagers didn't think so. She and Will were last seen with Geordie, so the blame fell on Geordie's head. He was a murderer. Only, without the bodies, it couldn't be proved.

Geordie was ostracized. From then on, no one spoke to him. Well, certainly no one human. But rumours started of whispers and sighs at the pool where the handkerchief was found, whispers and sighs that followed Geordie wherever he went. More and more, that was to the pool, as if some ghostly hand wanted to draw him back there and confront him with what he'd done. His health deteriorated. He became haunted and morose. Eventually, he disappeared. He was last seen riding for the swamp and that was where he was eventually found, submerged to his waist, his eyes protruding in terror and quite, quite dead.

So what drew Geordie there? Was it just chance or guilty conscience? Or did the murdered Will and Kirsty really haunt their killer to the extent that he felt obliged to jump into the swamp? What did he see there that caused him to look as he did when he was found?

These questions will perhaps never be answered. But on dark nights for centuries after, it was said that the whispers of 'Geordie, Geordie' could be heard. And, just occasionally, among the rushes and black pools of what came to be known as Murder Moss, the phantom figure of a young woman could be seen, flitting silently, as if even then peace could not come for one who had met such a brutal end.

The Pass of Killiecrankie

Where Jacobite history is concerned, the lost causes and bloody battlefields of Glencoe, Sherriffmuir and Culloden certainly gave the average ghost-story writer plenty to be going on with. The pass of Killiecrankie yields up quite a crop of stories. The Jacobite leader, Grahame of Claverhouse of Bonnie Dundee song and bonnet fame, was himself the subject of many myths. The most scorching was that he was in league with the Devil. It's hardly surprising, then, that the area is reputed to be haunted. According to legend, Dundee was dispatched with a silver bullet.

Dundee was often called the De'il (Devil) by his enemies, and he had many of those. But to his friends, he was known as a fair man who felt passionately about the Stuart cause in Scotland and wanted to do his best to enlist their help.

Perhaps that was why he decided to visit one of them – Colin Lindsay, who was under house arrest – and implore him one last time to join the Highlanders. Nothing wrong with that, you will say, except that it was on the morning after the battle. Dundee had already been dead for hours. Colin Lindsay was, however, so certain it was Dundee that he got out of bed and talked to him. He got quite a shock when Dundee faded away through the wall. He thought Dundee had come to free him. Then he realized he was talking to a ghost. It was something that haunted him for years. Not Dundee himself, but the thought that he had appeared like that, as if he was still very much alive.

On the eve of the battle, it seems that Dundee himself also witnessed an apparition. As in all good battle stories, his second-in-command, Cameron of Lochiel, didn't want Dundee to fight. 'It will be my last,' said Dundee. And it certainly was, though not perhaps as Dundee was hoping or meaning. He was, however, apparently warned about the hazards of fighting by a man who stood at his bedside, blood pouring from a wound to his head, and saying, 'Come with me.' He did not add, 'if you want to live', as this was a line yet to make its appearance a few hundred years later in films, but it was plain that this was what he meant. At least, this was according to Cameron of Lochiel, with whom Dundee discussed it. But Dundee did not want to 'go with it', apparently, or maybe he couldn't be bothered getting out of bed, because he just turned over and went back to sleep.

So the figure was forced to shake its gory head once more and go through the whole performance again. This must have been done with a little more panache as, on this occasion, Dundee fetched the guard to complain that someone was in his tent. 'That's not possible, sir. We've been guarding it and no one's gone in,' they told him, which may or may not have made Dundee's beautifully curled hair rise a little. He had just got back into his bed when the man appeared and went through his little routine again. This time he was adamant that Dundee come with him, but he may have had quite enough of the idea of letting him live, because he merely waved airily at the plain of Killiecrankie and indicated he was going to meet Dundee there.

Dundee did not live. Nor did he sleep again that night, which was hardly surprising. Whoever the figure was, he probably wasn't used to having such an awkward customer. And if he was death, he certainly had to bide his time. Dundee waited the whole of the next day till the sun was sinking and blinding his opponents' eyes before charging down from the hills and into the pass.

Every 27 July, on the anniversary of the battle, a red glow hangs over the pass, as if this moment is being repeated. So many people say anyway – too many to ignore. It's a phantom light, they say. Then there's the story of the lady who walked down the path and met the Highlander. She thought he was a tour guide and even had a little chat with him. We must hope he didn't have blood pouring from his head, or ask her to come with him, because there were actually no tour guides in the gorge that day.

In a much earlier sighting, the Highlander was thought to be just that – someone visiting the gorge in Highland dress – but Highland dress of 300 years ago. The sound of heavy panting has also been reported, which may be that of the government army running for their lives. If the jump at least one of them took over Soldier's Leap is to be believed, then they were certainly desperate men as well as potential long-jump champions. But then, maybe the figure chasing them had blood pouring from its head. Who knows? The pass certainly has stories to tell, given the events associated with it and the nature of the deaths of those who perished there.

Culloden

Visit Culloden on a dull, grey day when the Scottish weather is doing its worst and it's not hard to believe the place is haunted, although there may not be the sightings of ghosts that you would expect. Personally, I think that depends on how you define ghosts – as individual spirits or some kind of overall presence. In some respects, the silence is atmospheric enough to send shivers up the most sceptical of spines. I think it's the kind of place that would frighten ghosts away. The battle was a killing field. 'I never saw such slaughter,' one war-hardened lieutenant-colonel wrote to his brother five days after the event. 'Our men gave no quarter.' Nor was much given afterwards to the Highland clans who had supported the Bonnie Prince – Charles Edward Stuart. The Jacobites were to be squashed by all means available, and inevitably this was what happened. It wasn't only men who died at Culloden – a whole cause died too and, for many a Highlander, a way of life.

The Bonnie Prince himself is quite a restless spirit. Perhaps this is not surprising, as he was a man whose insistence on fighting there brought the Highlands to its knees. His ghost is so restless that it manages to haunt several places at once, which is unusual. None of these are reputed to be Culloden, from which he managed to flee. They are, however, the places he stayed on his travels, and he certainly managed to spread himself about. The sheer number of haunted rooms would indicate that he is doomed to relive his steps during that fateful campaign.

Although I've said that Culloden is too brooding a place even for ghosts, ghosts have been seen there, particularly at the cairn itself – the memorial built to commemorate those who died on the moor. Several reports talk about strange lights moving about the cairn at dusk but there are others who claim that the shadowy form of a Highlander haunts both the cairn area and the nearby Highlanders' graves. One woman who came upon him said she first saw the figure standing at the cairn itself. He was dark-haired and handsome, she remembered, and dressed in tartan plaids. Thinking he was part of some historical re-enactment, she came forward to take a photograph but stumbled over a stone. When she looked again, the figure was gone. She went round the other side, thinking she would find him there, but there was absolutely no sign. In the split second she took her eyes off him, the figure had vanished into thin air. She didn't see how anyone real could have done that and promptly took to her heels.

'Dark-haired and handsome' might seem like wishful thinking on her part, but in a separate sighting, a dark-haired, handsome man in very dirty red tartan was seen lying on top of a mound, looking as if he was dead. There doesn't seem much doubt that he was, and what this other woman was seeing was a ghost. The figure's clothes were old fashioned, and looked as if he had been sleeping in them for weeks.

On yet another occasion, a girl of 13 followed a man along a path to the cairn. 'It was a very dull day,' she said years later, 'but I remember distinctly that he was wearing a red tartan plaid. As I walked behind him, I didn't think anything of it. Believe me, he looked like a real person. But then, when I got to the end of the path, he was gone. The last I saw was of him ducking his head to get round a tree branch. When I realized this I ran back to get my parents.

'I never told them what I thought I'd seen. The funny thing was I wasn't frightened. The figure wasn't sinister and I didn't think he was going to harm me. I didn't want people to laugh, though, so I didn't tell anyone at that time. However, I'm pretty certain the man wasn't real. He was of medium height with dark hair. I never saw his face. As I said, he was in front of me on the path. Maybe he was someone dressed up but I don't think they tended to do things like that at historical sites at that time. At least I never saw anything like it anywhere else.' The girl, now a woman in her 40s, also remembered clearly the feelings of unease she had near the old Leanach cottage, still situated on the battlefield today. 'I had such a feeling of being shut in there, I couldn't stand it. I just knew people had died there and it was horrible.' In fact, 30 soldiers of Prince Charles's army – some of them wounded – holed up in a barn adjoining the cottage for two days but were eventually killed when it was set on fire.

Echoes of the past? Well, almost certainly. An event of such savagery is bound to leave its own mark. That may be in the creeping silence, howling wind, the enveloping mists that lie about the lonely mounds, or even in the face of the man who waits by the cairn for a ghost army and a cause that has long been laid to rest.

Walking Walter

The Abbotsford saga could easily have been a book in its own right. A writer possessed by a dream. A house constructed in instalments. Rooms rising one by one from another stroke of the pen, a name, a legend, a knightly deed that inspired its author. A rich man facing ruin in the greatest financial drama to hit the literati of the time. The six years standing between him and the grave that saw him lose his dream home but turn out a stream of bestsellers. The bestsellers that drove him into his grave but not before his dream house was returned to him, albeit briefly.

Fate did indeed play Sir Walter Scott a cruel hand. For 10 years he wrote with great intensity to make Abbotsford his 'baronial castle'. Then, just a year after its completion, it was taken from him when his co-partners failed to come up with £117,000 – a stupendous sum in these days. Quite an amount today, come to that. It's no wonder that his ghost is said to roam the house, particularly his beloved dining room where he died, just a few months after his creditors had restored the house to him. For six years he had turned out book after book in an effort to raise the cash. He succeeded only to lose it again, this time to death.

Sir Walter was not a poor man. Any struggling authors among you might well be astonished to know he received an advance of £19,000 for his *Life of Napoleon*, which was better known in Scotland than anywhere else, France included. He was also making £10,000 a year in royalties. But he had a dream – a common human failing – and that dream was Abbotsford. A small farm when Scott first bought it. A turreted mansion full of relics and armour by the time he had finished. Or rather, by the time it had finished with him. And it did finish him. By the time he won it back in 1830, he was a sick man.

Sir Walter died in bed in the dining room, one of his favourite rooms. From the window he could see the River Tweed. His health had been ruined not only by the financial disaster which had overtaken him, but the force within which drove him to win the house back. His books are huge affairs. And while it is true that he had a readership for them – rejection slips very definitely aren't part of the Abbotsford mementoes – it must have been daunting to know that he had to keep churning out stories and hope that a fickle public wouldn't turn their backs on him. He had, after all, lost so much.

So does his ghost haunt the dining room? Well, a shadowy, silent figure has been seen in just that room, walking back and forth as if in deep thought. And I would say this is very probably Sir Walter. Perhaps not as he was in the house itself in his last few months there. But as he was when he was working desperately – like a sort of 'thought transference'. The energies that people generate during such times of stress often remain after they die and are then picked up by others. Just as some of us can generate these energies, so others are sensitive to them. This often explains why some people see nothing at all, while others see everything!

Scott reported that while the original farmhouse was being altered, he kept hearing 'violent noises'. Sounds that suggested the furniture was being dragged about were heard in the new part of the house. Like so many of his heroes, Sir Walter was no coward. He reached for 'Sir Beardie's broadsword' and went to investigate, but nothing could be found. The ghost was said to be George Bullock who was originally in charge of the rebuilding. But even then, that story has a strange side to it because George was still alive the first time the disturbances took place. He died when they were at their height.

So perhaps other things haunt Abbotsford. And given the array of jail keys and executioner's swords that Sir Walter proudly accumulated, that wouldn't be surprising. 'My Delilah', he called his beloved house when he first lost it, and this it certainly proved to be in more ways than one. But was the house really that or did something darker prowl there during his time, making sure misfortune came to those who got in its way?

Mary King's Close

Plague! A quite horrifying disease. One that swept Europe many times down the centuries, decimating entire populations with its symptoms of fevers and boils. In Edinburgh, as in most other cities, the infection rampaged through the overpopulated streets, killing most who were unfortunate enough to develop it within hours of their first tell-tale sneeze. Quite a shocking thought nowadays to a generation reared on antibiotics.

The parliament, being quick to look after its members in a time of crisis, wasted no time in relocating to Stirling, where they could continue to govern the country. That was much more important than bringing in measures to deal with the sick and the dying. But measures were instigated in a desperate bid to halt the disease. And one of these was to seal off the infamous Mary King's Close, a bustling, overcrowded, unsanitary street, the remains of which are now situated beneath the City Chambers.

It was thought that this would solve the problem, or at least help it. The incidences of plague were certainly worst there. No doubt in their ignorance of how the disease was actually spread, people thought this would contain it. And as it was, the plague *did* pass – probably of its own accord but not before having felled great numbers of the population. The close, however, remained sealed.

About 40 years later, it was reopened. Ignoring the possibility of any stray germs lurking in its grim and dirty corners, Mr Thomas Coltheart moved his family in. He was the first to notice the quite chilling atmosphere in their new home; the severed, venerable and grey-bearded head of a man that floated round the living room; the sobbing little girl with plague pustules all over her face; and the procession of headless animals in the corridors. Quite why they were headless, I can't say, since that's not a symptom of plague, so far as I know!

It was, however, all very harrowing for Thomas. So much so that he is reputed to have quickly fled. But not before other residents began claiming that they too were being visited, and not just by their friends eager to see their new home. Severed arms, cold spots, strange noises – these were very much the order of the day for anyone who stayed there. The plague may have left but it in its wake was something far worse, so far as the occupants were concerned – a set of spirits who had possibly fallen victim to it and left their sufferings behind for all to see.

Then Mary King's Close was damaged by fire – so badly damaged that most of it had to be demolished. Whatever was left didn't settle the dead, and ghost stories have persisted. There are too many to ignore, so much so that a sort of 'spot the spook' tour now runs. Visitors and guides have reported hearing strange noises. The little girl ghost has been seen so often that some people actually leave sweets and toys for her. A dog and a woman in black are probably the next most common in terms of sightings.

But if you are going along in the hope of taking a photograph, forget it. For some strange reason, cameras are big trouble in Mary King's Close, either working by themselves or failing to work at all. Oh, and wrap up, if you're in any way in tune with the spirits. The 'cold spots' in Mary King's are horrendous. This is all perfectly in keeping with such a haunted place and one that has seen such suffering. It's almost as if the spirit of the plague itself walks there.

The Fyvie Five

A family curse, a secret room, a haunted chamber, a phantom trumpeter – it all sounds a bit like Glamis Castle and its many famous ghostly occupants. But Fyvie Castle in Aberdeenshire is similarly haunted by a variety of apparitions – ones that really do go bump in the night. They have such fascinating histories attached to them, they must make the castle a close second to Glamis in terms of what goes on there. And if you choose to visit, you'll certainly be following in some very famous footsteps. William the Lyon, Alexander II, Edward I of England, Robert the Bruce and the Marquis of Montrose have all passed through its ancient portals. Not as ghosts of course. The Fyvie spirits have nothing to do with any of them.

Fyvie has stood for a long time, no thanks to Thomas the Rhymer who took time out from cavorting with the Fairy Queen to curse it. Its visitors book is quite impressive and so are its ghosts – something that would probably disappoint Thomas, who was pretty specific in his hope that the castle would be doomed. Of course he called on a bad day, and perhaps some higher power made allowances for that fact, but certainly the rest of his prophecy seemed to come true. The direct line of the Preston family who held the castle at that time did die out after two generations, exactly as the Rhymer said. And the castle and estate have changed hands constantly ever since. While Thomas's ghost doesn't haunt the castle – he was in fact last seen heading for fairyland with his queen – his words certainly do. So it's worth taking a look at that story first.

In his day, Thomas the Rhymer was a very famous man – a seer, whose gift of prophecy allegedly came from the Queen of Elfland herself, with whom he was in love. It was said that she gave him a tongue which could not tell a lie – something that in itself could be quite a curse at times – and that among the things he foresaw were the crowning of Robert the Bruce and the Battle of Flodden. He was also a poet, bard and wizard.

Thomas visited Fyvie at a particularly inconvenient moment. Sir Henry, the then owner, was busy demolishing a monastery. With a degree of enterprise and zeal common to men of his time, he was using the stones to construct a new part of his own home. This was quite a weighty task and three of the stones fell in the river. Sir Henry was somewhat enraged by this and by the fact that Thomas, the well-known rhymer and poet of Ercildoune, had just appeared at his gates.

'Give me shelter for the night, won't you?' asked Thomas.

'Get lost,' said Sir Henry, or words to that effect.

'Well,' said Thomas, 'you can build all you will, but if you don't get the three stones out of the river, the property will never descend in a direct line for more than two generations.'

This was very daunting for Sir Henry to hear. Daunting, too, for those who had gathered to hear the words of the poet, largely because they would be given the task of dragging the river to get the stones and haul them back out again. Apparently, as Thomas spoke, a violent storm burst over the castle and everyone was soaked, except him. This wasn't because, being a seer, he'd had the foresight to bring along an umbrella. The spot where he was standing was dry too. It seemed that Thomas did have powers. Sir Henry was very worried.

Eventually, as in all the best challenges, two of the stones were found. One had moisture on it and still 'weeps' to this day, no matter how dry or warm the weather is. But the third was never found and so the curse continues. The Meldrums, the Setons, the Leiths and the Gordons have all held Fyvie, but never for longer than two generations.

This has made for an interesting history and, as in all the best castles, a fascinating history of ghosts too. One of the ghosts that haunts Fyvie is that of Lilias Drummond, the wife of Alexander Seton who, in certain accounts, died not at Fyvie but in Fife. Lilias, a beautiful woman and loving wife, had the misfortune to produce a line of girls – something that wasn't much use to a husband obsessed with a male line. In this respect, it could be said that Lilias fell victim to the curse. At any rate, the word is that he starved her to death and proceeded to marry Grizel Leslie a few months after.

Lilias – not surprisingly – was simply furious. 'Dame Lilias Drummond', she carved into the stone window ledge of the wedding chamber, making a lovely surprise for her erring husband on his wedding night. In addition to demonstrating her mastery of graffiti, Lilias began making appearances on the stairs leading to the chamber, as well as in the room itself. For a time, these seemed to herald the death of various owners of the castle, and it is therefore fortunate that the building is now held by the National Trust for Scotland. Moreover, Lilias is not the only female phantom to wander the castle precincts.

Another figure, variously reported as being grey – Lilias is said to be green – has been frequently reported gliding noise-lessly through walls and stairwells, terrifying all who come into contact with her. No one knows who she is, or rather was, but she was particularly active in the 1920s and 1930s in the gun room.

The story is that a group of workmen was called to the castle to deal with a persistent fungus that was growing on the walls there. They did a little renovation work, finding a secret room with the complete skeleton of a woman in it. Another unfortunate Fyvie wife? Well, it's possible. But certainly the Grey Lady liked being left alone. According to some accounts, the hauntings increased until the bones were put back. Legend also has it that this hidden chamber was not the only one at Fyvie, that there is another, kept locked.

As if it's not enough having a grey and a green lady vying for the visitors' attention, Fyvie also has a musical ghost. Some say it's a drummer. Some say it's a trumpeter. Perhaps it's a very talented player of two instruments, or there are two ghosts.

The trumpeter is said to be the ghost of Andrew Lammie, who did actually play the trumpet at the castle and fell in love with Agnes Smith, the daughter of the local miller. By all accounts, Agnes must have been very beautiful because the Laird of Fyvie also had his eye on her – for his mistress. Whether or not Agnes's parents approved of this isn't known, but they certainly weren't keen on Andrew. When the laird found out that the apple of his eye had a canker in it in the shape of his own trumpeter, he had Andrew seized and transported off to the West Indies as a slave.

Andrew managed to escape, however, and he came back to Scotland, desperate to find the woman he loved. But she was dead, either of a broken heart or poisoned by her parents for rejecting the laird. Andrew died soon after, not surprisingly broken by all he had suffered. Before he died, he cursed the laird and swore to play his trumpet before the death of every

Fyvie Laird from then on. That is, apparently, more or less what happened. In addition to that, Andrew – like all good artistes – sometimes enjoys being seen. Those who see him, however, don't necess-arily enjoy the experience.

No wonder, then, that the castle is run by the National Trust. Three ghosts and two curses would certainly take some living with, for even the stoutest of hearts!

Abergeldie Kate

Here's one I personally find very interesting. Being a bit of a 'seer' myself, I can't help finding the histories and fates of those with similar abilities fascinating. In the past, the ability to 'see' things was very often regarded with the utmost suspicion. Women who could do so were generally thought of as witches, and Scotland's record of persecution of this hated sisterhood is horrific. Between 1563 and 1737, at least 1500 women were tortured and executed, often for doing no more than 'looking squint' at a neighbour. Women were expected to behave in a proper moral and Christian fashion at all times, and those who went beyond these bounds for any reason could find themselves accused. Well-documented reports abound of their trials. The case of the North Berwick witches, in particular, caused a sensation in its day. But the story that interests me most is that of Kittie Rankie of Abergeldie Castle, largely because she wasn't a witch at all. I don't even think she could 'see'. She just happened to say the kind of common-sense thing we all do at times. But it was the wrong thing, in the wrong place, at the wrong time, as this story goes to show. And Kittie paid for it with her life.

Abergeldie itself, in keeping with all of Scotland's grand houses, has a bloody history. At one stage, the seven sons of Gordon of Knock were murdered by Forbes of Strathgirnock, who promptly stuck their heads on their spades as a warning not to cut peat on his land. Abergeldie was also burnt by the Mackenzies in 1592. But these are all quiet spirits, content to rest.

The one who haunts Abergeldie is Kittie. She was a French girl who was working at the castle as a maid at the end of the 16th century when witch-hunting fever was at its height. Possibly the fact she was foreign didn't help her, since it meant that she was different. And being different in those days was tantamount to being a witch.

Anyway Kittie, whose real name was Catherine Frankie, was busy doing her work one day when the mistress started complaining that her husband hadn't come home. She asked Kittie why and Kitty, to all intents and purposes, replied that he was probably 'dallying with other women'. How Kitty knew this I don't know, unless he had already been dallying with her – always a distinct possibility in these stories and the most likely explanation for what followed. Or perhaps he was found to be 'dallying' after what appears to have been a chance throwaway response. Whatever the truth of the matter, Kittie was imprisoned on the mistress's say-so and placed in the castle dungeon, accused of witchcraft.

At this time it was virtually impossible, once a charge was made, to escape the awfulness of the sentence that followed. Kittie was burnt at the stake, her dying screams quite terrible to hear. And I think it's quite safe to say that, had she had any gift for prophecy, she would certainly have seen where opening her mouth was going to get her and kept it firmly shut.

But that was not the end of the matter, as the family was about to discover. Kitty soon came back to Abergeldie in phantom form. At times, she looked as young and lovely as ever. At others, she definitely appeared to be a bit on the char-grilled side. For hundreds of years, she has been seen at regular intervals, mainly in the tall clock tower but also in other parts of the castle. Thumps, bumps and mysterious 'ghost' noises can also be laid at her door. Having suffered so terribly at her end, she also likes to warn the family when any misfortune is going to happen to them by ringing a bell, so that they can be prepared. That's the 'cosier' way of looking at it!

Given her fate, I doubt I'd be so nice about it. But maybe that's just me!

The Melrose Monk

While castles tend to provide an abundance of lady ghosts of varying benevolence and hue, men certainly find their niche in churches and abbeys up and down the land. Mad monks, malevolent monks and medieval monks are actually quite plentiful, making some places very haunted indeed. Melrose Abbey has two spirits haunting it, as well as the heart of Robert the Bruce buried in the nave – a trifle gory to say the least.

One of the ghosts isn't actually a monk at all, while the other – well, let's just say he was certainly a very strange one, unless drinking blood was the order of the day in religious orders then. One could almost be tempted to ask if they'd run out of Communion wine. For so holy a place, it's strange that Melrose hasn't got religious ghosts. The monk who haunts the cloister area has actually been seen to slither along the ground rather like a snake. When he lived isn't known for certain but the story is that he led a particularly violent life, dabbling in the black arts, despite the vows he had taken.

Although vampire legends are generally associated with Eastern Europe, this monk evidently became some kind of early version of Bram Stoker's fictional count. Before too long, he had taken to rising from his tomb and flitting abroad each night to sink his teeth into the necks of unsuspecting local virgins, one of whom just happened to be the abbess of the nearby convent. Scotland might have become the next best thing to Transylvania – indeed the area might have been overrun with vampires – had one of the other monks not decided enough was enough and, in best vampire tradition, waited with an axe one night. This was to cut off the blood-thirsty monk's head as he climbed out of the tomb.

I would think that must have caused quite a sensation in local circles. It put an end to dastardly deeds – well, for a while anyway. Obviously the monk wasn't able to deal with a slithery ghost, which is what replaced the vampiric monk. Not a tale for the fainthearted! But then neither is the other story associated with Melrose, the story of Michael Scott. Sir Michael, I should add, of Balwearie.

Sir Michael was a very clever man, a 13th-century scholar whose main interests were in science and philosophy. Perhaps he was in many ways a victim of his time, in that these interests soon led to people claiming he was a warlock, one who indulged in necromancy and possessed a book of spells.

Whatever the case, people feared him and rumours spread. Despite people's feelings about him, when he died in 1292 he was interred in the abbey on the south side of the chancel. But either he wasn't too happy with it or with them because his spirit soon began haunting this spot. Many people confess to feeling uneasy when they stand anywhere near his grave. Chilliness, cold spots and a general unpleasant sensation are other things that are noticed by people who know nothing about the grave or the remains it contains. So maybe some of the legends about Sir Michael do have substance to them. Or perhaps he doesn't like being buried in Melrose because of the slithery ghostly thing that slides across his tomb!

The Brolass 'Braw-lass'

'I am searching the moors and the bens,
All the spots where I courted my dear,
I am searching the mountains and glens,
But he is not here, not here.'

A singing ghost? Well, it is possible. Given that some of them have been known to speak, scream and sob, bursting into song shouldn't be beyond the capabilities of the occasional ghost. Especially if they've good reason to, and it seems the Brolass ghost does. Betrayal, murder, a family curse, ill-starred lovers and death

– it doesn't come much better than that. Romeo and Juliet in the Mull district. And did I say the Brolass ghost, meaning there's only one? That was very silly of me. In fact, there are two and they're sisters, but not on speaking or even howling terms. The story is this.

Elizabeth and Margaret MacLean were two of the most beautiful girls in Mull and as such had no absolutely no problem finding suitors. Elizabeth in particular because she also had an easy-going temperament, much more so than the hard-to-please Margaret. Their father was a tacksman, a person who leased ground and then sublet it to others, so he was quite active in the community and he soon got fed up of Margaret's stubbornness. Elizabeth had married the first man who proposed to her. Why couldn't Margaret do the same?

Well, the reason for this was quite simple. Margaret had a secret. In the best Shakespearean tradition, Margaret was in love with a member of a rival clan. Not the Montagues in this instance but the Macdonalds. There was no way the couple could be allowed to marry as things stood, but Margaret secretly hoped circumstances would change, as they so often did between the clans. She believed the enmity would pass. Then she could tell her parents that she was actually betrothed. In the meantime, in a storyline used by writers since time immemorial, she pretended to be hard to please and found fault with every young man who came to call.

This was all very well till Elizabeth decided to worm the truth out of her. 'You can tell me, Margaret dearest. Aren't we sisters, after all?' Then she went straight to her husband. To be fair to Elizabeth here, it was evident that she did this because Margaret was now planning to elope and she feared this would kill her parents. But Elizabeth's husband used a claw hammer to crack a nut. He rounded up Margaret's suitors, telling them of the plan and arranging for them to ambush the pair.

In the ensuing scene, Margaret's lover was stabbed to death in front of her terrified eyes. 'Ah me!' she is alleged to have said, after throwing herself on his corpse. 'The dignity of the Macdonalds. The conceit of the MacLeans.' She then ran away.

Margaret was seen again. Seen by many in fact. For weeks she ran about the moors, a bit like Cathy in *Wuthering Heights*, sobbing and crying. 'Have you met my lover?' she asked of everyone she met. At times she sang, 'My mother's chair is empty, empty and cold. My father, who loved me, sleeps in death. My sister, her promise broken, all has told, I am without kin, without lover. I have only breath,' her pure, trembling voice echoing round the hillside. She couldn't eat or sleep and eventually she died, by this time mad with grief, but not before she could add:

'Sister may ill befall all that you loved best,
May neither rain nor dew bless the soil you till,
May no child of yours want your arms in rest.
May your cattle find no food upon the hill.'

These things very much came to be the case. Elizabeth's husband left her. Her parents died, despite what she had done to prevent that. They were brokenhearted over Margaret's end. Although her father had once sublet land, Elizabeth lost her home and was forced to beg for food and money from her neighbours in order to survive. She died at last, a broken woman, hungry and cold, unloved and alone. Margaret's curse had indeed come home to roost.

But even in death, that hasn't been the end of the matter. The area of Brolass where the family lived is said to be haunted by Elizabeth's ghost. A tall woman has been seen on a number of occasions, wandering about, wringing her hands. Is she repenting of her actions? Or is she fondly imagining that Margaret's neck is between them? Does she hate her for the awful ruin her life became?

Chillingly, Margaret's ghost also haunts the area. Her voice, sweet and pure, has been heard singing the words of her song over the area she last roamed, as a poor, grief-crazed girl.

Let's just hope the two never meet!

The White Dove Ghost

'Natalie. May God forgive us.'

Just sometimes you come across a story that really stands out. The ghost may be gone. Maybe he or she was only ever seen once. But the appearance itself was of such a quality, the facts surrounding it so strange, that it qualifies for an entry in its own right. This one could have stepped straight off the pages of M.R. James, that great ghost story-teller. In fact, it reads more like fiction than fact. But personally I found it very hard to resist, even though The White

Dove Hotel has gone now and the ghost appeared only once. Who Natalie actually was and what happened to her nobody knows – only that she must have met a very sticky end and, as with all good ghosts, came back determined to have her revenge. And that, she did. Here's how.

The White Dove Hotel was in Aberdeen – a busy place with a varied clientele. It was visited at one stage by an actress called Miss Vining who, it was thought, had come from abroad. That was certainly the impression she gave to the few guests she talked to, and she didn't talk to many. She fell ill a day or so after her arrival. In fact, she fell very ill. No one knew what was wrong with her. She was too tired even to speak and her temperature was high, so a doctor was fetched.

The doctor didn't know what was wrong with Miss Vining either. He did, however, think that whatever it was had been contracted abroad, possibly in the tropics. By now Miss Vining's temperature was so high, he felt she shouldn't be left alone. He sent for a nurse and she moved into the room to look after the sick woman.

The nurse didn't like the atmosphere in the room. Indeed, from the start she sensed a strangeness, which she put down to the fact that Miss Vining was raving with delirium and a storm was now raging outside. It was, at any rate, a very 'odd' sick room, she felt. She did, however, do everything she could to make Miss Vining comfortable, confidently believing that once her temperature came down, she would begin to recover. And once she had sponged her patient's forehead and taken off some of the blankets, she sat down in the chair to read. I'm just hoping it was a nice, pleasant tale, because what happened next certainly wasn't.

The nurse looked up from her book and there sitting across the bed from her was a little girl. She was seated very quietly, not moving in any way, her hands arranged in her lap. On her head was a large hat which covered her face. The nurse was taken aback.

'Who are you and what are you doing here? This is a sick room. You can't come in here. Now off you go!' she said, and began to stand up to shoo the child away. But as she did, the child raised a hand. The nurse found she couldn't move. She felt as if she was riveted to the chair, which in turn was riveted to the floor. And her patient needed help. She could see that. Only the little girl wouldn't let her go to her. Instead, she raised her other hand and the nurse fell asleep.

When the nurse woke up, the girl was gone. This was something of a relief. But Miss Vining's temperature had risen even higher and the doctor was brought back. When he heard about the visitor and why the nurse hadn't been looking after her patient, he was annoyed. It seemed he blamed the nurse for the poor state his patient was in. 'Lock that door in future. Let no one in,' he said, privately thinking the nurse was making the story up.

Well, the nurse did as she was told. She made absolutely sure the door was locked and she was the only person alone in the room with Miss Vining. So she got the most terrible fright when she looked round to see the little girl was back. Again, the arm was raised, again the nurse was held to the spot. Only this time she wasn't tired.

The nurse was forced to watch as Miss Vining deteriorated before her eyes, tossing and turning and calling out for water. The nurse begged the little girl to let her help but the girl shook her head. And so Miss Vining died. She died and the child made for the window.

Realizing she was free at last, the nurse leapt forward and grabbed at the child. Catching her hat, she knocked it to the ground. Then she saw what she hadn't been able to see before. The girl's face was that of a corpse. Her throat had been cut and her face was contorted by death. She was, the nurse noticed – or at least she had been – a very beautiful girl, Indian in appearance. But it was all too much for the nurse, and she fainted.

Later, when Miss Vining's body had been removed and the staff were packing up her belongings, they came across a photograph – a picture of a very beautiful little Indian girl. When they showed it to the nurse, her face turned white. It was the girl she had seen in the room. On the back of the photograph, these words had been written:

'Natalie. May God forgive us.'

Who Natalie was and what she had to do with Miss Vining, nobody knows. But one thing is clear – she came back from beyond the grave to exact her own revenge, and after she did, she was never seen again. Whatever drove her, it drove her to one thing – the death of Miss Vining. However much the latter appealed to God to forgive her, it is certain that one person never could – Natalie, the phantom child with the special powers, who refused to rest in peace.

The Lustful Laird of Littledean

'Gie me a wife frae Hell. That's what I want. For still she'll be a warmer ane than you.'

What is it about Scotland's ghosts that makes them almost fall into two categories – either weeping women or lustful men? I'm not quite sure. Maybe as a race the Scots are just an amorous, bloodthirsty lot. Who knows! Littledean Tower in Roxburghshire has a varied history. The site is said to be the birthplace of John Duns Scotus, a 13th-century theologian and Franciscan priest, who had the rare distinction of being beatified by Pope John Paul II in 1993, even though he had been branded a wizard and a warlock in 1296 or thereabouts. It is also the haunt of a ghost on horseback – one allegedly lustful laird who occupied more than the site in the 17th century.

I'd like to say I'm sure his reputation was impeccable. But given the amount of drink he consumed, servants he abused, family he mistreated and Covenanters he persecuted, this doesn't seem likely. His wife's name was Margaret, and let's just say she had her hands full. She was, however, a particularly stoical woman, one who put up with her remarkable indignities in an 'unremarkable' way. By that I mean she never made any remarks at all. To all the insults that were heaped on her head, she just said nothing.

At least she just said nothing for a long time. But one evening, the laird had some friends over for drinks, as was his way – a raucous evening with flowing drinks. He got hold of her and demanded, 'What do you mean, keeping yourself up here, out the way of us?' as if the answer to this wasn't perfectly obvious. 'Get down the stairs. Fill the cups of my friends.'

Of course Margaret wasn't doing any such thing, and the laird became steadily more vicious. 'Well then, I'll kick you down the stairs,' he said. Margaret was pushed and beaten so badly, it was amazing that she still managed to say nothing. But she did, even when the laird dragged her all the way down to the bottom step. He slapped and jostled her in front of his friends, who were delighted to see the 'sullen beldame' brought down. Eventually, Margaret did speak, but only after her husband had pushed her away saying, 'Gie me a wife frae Hell. That's what I want. For still she'll be a warmer ane than you!' Margaret had decided enough was enough.

'You'll live to regret those words,' she told him quietly, chilling words, in a chilling situation. The laird, of course, didn't believe a word of it and carried on as if nothing had happened. That very evening, he saddled up and rode all the way through the woods. They were dark and deep, and at the far side was a little cottage. The laird reined his horse. The door was open and sitting inside was a woman. Young, of course, and incredibly beautiful, enough to put poor Margaret in the shade. And the laird, being a lustful sort of fellow, got off his horse. Well now, wasn't this lady just the finest thing he'd ever seen? Or was ever likely to. And just sitting there spinning in her bonnie wee cottage. Imagine such a beauty being a plain, simple spinner!

He crept closer and the woman saw him. Or maybe she had seen him all along. Perhaps she wanted him to walk into her trap. Who knows? Anyway, she lifted the thread and, with a maniacal laugh, snapped it in two. This might have told the silly laird something, especially if he'd read his Greek legends. But evidently he had been far too busy drinking and carousing for that. Anyway, at that moment his horse bolted and he was dragged off. So that was the end of his amorous intentions for that evening. He was dragged so far and for so long that it was almost the end of them for life, come to that.

This didn't make him forget the woman. On the contrary, he was back the next evening searching for her. Evidently the amount he'd had to drink had speeded his recovery. Of his brutal dragging through hedge and bracken, he felt not a thing. Indeed, it almost seemed to have spurred him in his determination to find his new amour. That maniacal laugh of hers had quite tickled his fancy, and his fancy was to make her his very own.

Of course he didn't find her. Well, not straight away. It took a little time and a great deal of frustration, but he did in the end come upon her as she was standing in a moonlit glade – of course! And before very long, he was doing a lot more than just watching her from a distance. Stalking, I believe we call it now. The affair was, by all accounts, an absolute scandal – a real 'confessing on the church stool before the eyes of the startled congregation' type of thing. Not that the laird confessed. He was no doubt too grand for that. But he was certainly a happy man. His wee amour was a feisty woman, strange and beautiful in the extreme, just the kind to see a man right. And as for Margaret – well, it was all the better that she got to hear of it. The day she took off her wedding ring and threw it in his face was one of the happiest of his whole existence. 'Goodbye Margaret,' he thought. 'Now at last I can marry the woman of my dreams.'

Unfortunately, what he didn't see, to coin a certain phrase, was that this was also going to be 'in his dreams'. Before she left the house, Margaret sent two men to find out exactly who the laird had been meeting in the moonlit glade by the wandering stream, and they came back with some startling news. It was a hare.

Before any charges of bestiality come to be laid at the laird's door, I think I should add that the hare was also a woman – a woman who became a hare.

While Margaret was trying to take in this stunning discovery, who should come home but the laird. He was in quite a state. Apparently, something had chased alongside his horse – a hare. And when he tried to chase it away, several others had swarmed round him, so that he was forced to ride in the direction of Midlem, a village known to house several witches. He'd had to draw his sword – something Lady Margaret thought was quite different from what he had been drawing of late. The hares had jumped all over him and his horse. It was very frightening. He might have been thrown, for goodness sake, he shouted at her. Fortunately, he had managed to chop the paw off one of the treacherous beasties, or goodness knows where he would be now, because they had run off, every last one of them, when he did that. But even then, that wasn't the end of the matter. The paw had sprung up in the air. It had landed on his belt, or sword sheath, or whatever it was he was wearing. He was past caring.

'Look there it is!' he remonstrated, flinging it on the table. 'There! There! There!'

And Margaret stared. Of course she stared. So did everyone else because what the laird had flung on the table
wasn't a hare's paw. It was a woman's hand, severed neatly
at the wrist and no doubt dripping with blood.

The laird brought his sword back out. His own hands were
shaking by this time but he speared the hand and started for
the river. If only he could get rid of the hand he felt he could
put this distressing incident behind him. Somehow or other
he had become confused, bewildered. There had been a mix-
up with what he had seen. This wasn't a woman's hand he was
throwing in the river. It was an animal's paw. That was only
how it looked to him because he was a man possessed.
Possessed by love. It was true that when he first met the
woman, he hadn't thought so. There had been other forces
then. That was the thing he didn't understand. But now he did
and he could see. Margaret was leaving him. That was all this
was. She was leaving him and he was free. In all his life he had
never known that feeling – what it was to have the thing he
loved within his grasp. That was why he must put this hand
away, throw it as far as he could into the water. When he did
and he heard it fall, dropping with a dull, leaden splash into
the water, he knew he could laugh about it. And he did.

'That was my hand you took from me,' someone said in a
voice not quite human. He stepped back. Surely he recognized it? Surely he had heard it before in recent months,
when he had been bewitched, slipping out at all hours like a
guilty boy to meet his love? The woman he would have given
up everything for.

'Yes. It is me,' she said to him, 'and that was my hand. Now
I'm afraid it will be with you forever.'

And so the laird ran home, ran home even with the hand back in his pocket. He threw it out of the window; he threw it on the ground. Still it followed him. That night when he went to bed, it was there, under the pillow. Not even fire could destroy it. Cowering now, almost mad with terror, he climbed into bed and pulled the blankets over him. What the morning would bring he had no idea. He only hoped that the sun rising might bring an end to this terrible nightmare.

The laird didn't get up the next morning. Lady Margaret, by now sorry for his condition, sent the servants to wake him. The door was locked. It had to be broken down eventually because no matter how they pounded on it, the laird didn't answer. The reason for this was soon revealed. He was lying on the floor quite dead. Morning had come but not an end to the nightmare, if the look on his face was anything to go by. The marks on his neck showed clearly that he had been strangled, strangled by an anonymous hand. The woman from hell had had her revenge it seemed, and that was the end of the Laird of Littledean.

But not quite. This is a ghost book after all so it wouldn't do to leave the story there. A woman from hell was what the laird wanted, and the word is he's still looking. On moonlit nights his horse can be heard breathlessly galloping over the land nearby. The laird is still at his frantic search for the woman who eluded him. Just remember if you're a female travelling alone, you have been warned to stay well away!

Black Andrew of Balnagowan

Andrew Munro, or 'Black Andrew' as he came to be known, was indeed a man of many parts. He seemed to feel the need to share one particular part round most of the ladies in the district. Without their consent, of course, which is probably how he came by this name. Rape was his speciality, as was murder on occasion. Not that Andrew probably saw it like that. He was, after all, a landed gentleman and, historically speaking, landed gentlemen were occasionally notorious for adhering to a particular concept: 'droit de seigneur'. Andrew was certainly a chief exponent of it.

While it's wrong to look at people of his time with our modern eyes, Andrew's contemporaries gazed at him and were equally horrified. Even by their 16th-century bloodthirsty, brutal and lawless standards, Andrew took a bit of beating. The chief of the Ross clan eventually hanged him from a window of the castle. He was probably hoping that would be the end of the matter, but Andrew obviously wasn't that kind of person. Indeed, giving his rampaging nature, it's doubtful he even noticed he'd been flung of out the window in the first place, a noose firmly attached to his neck. That's also possibly why he comes dancing out of dusty ghost-hood the minute a pretty lady visitor arrives at the castle.

Andrew didn't actually live at Balnagowan himself. That was owned by the chief. There had, however, been so many complaints about the general rapaciousness of his behaviour, the chief felt obliged to act. This, in itself, could be termed 'rich', coming from a man whose own relatives had suffered various periods of imprisonment for terrorizing the local community, trying to sink James VI's ship by witchcraft, poisoning, murder, incantation and sorcery. But evidently these deeds paled into insignificance when held up next to Andrew's. Or maybe this was just a good old case of the pot calling the kettle black. Who knows? But the chief captured Andrew and brought him to the castle, there to dispatch him by the best means available – a rope out of the window.

Andrew has continued to walk the corridor ever since, clumping up and down, probably looking for more women to ravish. So do be warned if you're young and female, won't you? And also be sure to cover up. Andrew liked his female servants to go about their tasks naked, something that must have been quite horrendous, given the Scottish climate. Not that they were probably allowed to be cold for long!

Despite the chief's intention to stick to the letter of the law concerning Andrew and win over the local people with his heroic act, the reputation of the Rosses suffered slightly when the castle became the haunt of another ghost – a young woman with auburn hair and green eyes.

It is said she is the ghost of a princess who, in true Scottish tradition, was murdered there. I just hope it wasn't by Andrew!

The Skeleton of Skibo

'No Andrew, I dinnae think you should do that.'

'But you promised. You promised,' Andrew's fingers dug into her neck. Grisel stared back at him.

'Promised?' she cried angrily. 'I never said I would. Get away from me, Andrew Martin! Get away or I'll scream! I'll scream, I tell you. Let go!'

'Scream all you like,' Andrew said. He didn't know why, but it seemed funny all of a sudden. 'There's no one to hear you.'

She did scream then. Her face was all contorted, and perhaps it was the sight of it that made him panic. But when he looked again she had broken away. 'Please! Please!' she was sobbing and he could see that her hair was loose. Her hands battered on the door. 'Don't,' he kept saying. 'Don't! No one will hear.'

But she kept screaming and he was afraid that someone would. That was why he took her by the throat again. 'No! No!' she was shrieking and struggling about. 'Let me go! I never said I would!' He then reached for her throat. He had to. It was to stop her shouting. His hands clasped the little thin reed that was her neck. They grasped it and her eyes went wild with terror. He saw them but still it didn't stop him.

'Shut up!' he said. 'Shut up!' She was on the floor and there were strange muffled noises coming from her mouth, like a sort of gurgling. He squeezed the top part of her face near her eyes and knocked her head back against the floor. He did it several times.

'Shut up!' he was still saying, and she was quiet then, a kind of strange quiet he'd never heard before. He let go of her face and her head dropped back, right back on the stone of the hall. Where it lay, there was blood, lots of blood. It was framing her head, a bit like a halo. Only this halo was red. He stared at it for a moment and his eyes – big, dark and strange-looking – stared back at him.

'Grizel!' he said. 'Grizel!' But she didn't answer, and after he had gazed at her for a long time, he knew what he had done. The *big eyes told him. 'You've killed her.' They said. 'You damn bloody fool. You've killed her, stone bloody dead.'*

Whether the ghost at Skibo was called Grizel or not – and whether her killer's name was Andrew for that matter– isn't generally known. She was apparently a local girl, however, one who was silly enough to visit the castle one day – unchaperoned, of course, since this was probably for a lover's tryst. It is thought these events may have taken place at the end of the 17th century.

It was one that went horribly wrong when her lover murdered her, although it was never actually proved. What actually took place isn't known. The girl was never seen again, though. Skibo was her last port of call. The castle keeper was the only one there, so I don't think it's stretching credibility too far to say he had a hand in her disappearance. His guilt was never proved, although the word is he left Skibo shortly afterwards to work elsewhere.

It's very difficult to prove that a murder has taken place when no body is found, and this was very much the case here. The only kind of proof was that it was suddenly haunted by a dishevelled, half-dressed young girl, screaming her head off, or what was left of it. But eventually a body was found. It was hidden in a wall and only came to light when the castle was renovated. Scotland's builders must be a hardy lot given the amount of skeletons that turn up in this way!

This seemed to prove a point but this was years after the girl's death, so it was too late to do anything about it, except give the bones a decent burial. This happened in due course and the hauntings stopped immediately. The partially assaulted girl was never seen again. Rather than revenge, it seemed this was all she wanted. Having said that, I've no idea what happened to the manservant. Even if he did come back there, I imagine he'd find it quite changed. Present-day Skibo was only built in 1898, so he'd probably have difficulty finding his way around.

The Wraith of Rait

While certain places can boast of a headless phantom, Rait has its own speciality – a handless one. For hundreds of years, this ruined old hall-house has been the haunt of a young female ghost, decked out in a bloodstained dress and wringing her stumps together.

Legend has it that her hands were most horribly hacked off by her own father. Rumour also has it that the dress is a bridal gown and her demise was part of one honeymoon she never banked on. Poor girl! She was, by all accounts, in love, and the object of her desire was a Mackintosh. She was also a Cumming. They were at war with the Mackintoshes so, of course, this was a love that could not be.

The story is that her father was as furious as any father could be when he heard what his daughter was up to with the son of his sworn enemy. But he pretended to be nothing short of delighted. Marry the Mackintosh boy? Why, of course! What a grand way to patch up those territorial differences! Why not have the feast here?

You can almost sense what's coming next, can't you, because of course his daughter believed him. The invitations

– such as they were in the far-off days of 1524 – went out. Everyone was delighted, especially the Mackintoshes. That was because they'd no idea the Cummings really planned to shut the castle door once they were inside and pick them off en masse. They really thought the hand of friendship was being offered so it was a big surprise when they learnt that the wedding feast was a ruse and it was a funeral they were going to be attending – their own.

How did they know? Well, the girl must have found out and somehow warned them. So it's said anyway, although it's equally possible the whole thing was a shock to her too, that she knew nothing about it and the Mackintoshes just happened to arrive for the 'do' armed to the teeth. At any rate, quite a battle took place over the hors d'oeuvres, and the Mackintoshes fled. But not before a large number of Cummings had been pinned to the floor with broadswords through their backs, spleens and intestines.

When he saw the extent of his losses, the girl's father was beside himself. Whether the girl was to blame or not didn't matter. He chased her through the castle in all her finery, up the stairs and along various corridors. Eventually, sick with terror, the girl climbed out of a window. She was probably trying to drop to the ground when her father stuck his head out and hacked at her hands, cutting them off. She fell straight to the ground and was killed instantly – not a nice story at all. So it's no wonder she haunts the place.

The Mackintoshes – probably including her lover – did have their retribution, eventually killing her father at Balblair. But even this didn't stop the girl, who's had quite a penchant for wandering round the castle ever since, possibly looking for her lost love. I don't think she'll find him now. The best part of 500 years is a long time to do your searching, and that's how long she's been around. Or maybe she's looking for her hands so she can get a better hold of him! Who knows? But she's reputedly a gruesome ghost and not one you'd want to meet on a dark night!

The Headless Horseman

Alright, so we've had phantom horsemen already. Do enough digging and the country's probably covered by them. But headless phantom horsemen are another matter and suitably ghoulish to merit a write-up all of their own. I rather like this one, in so far as it's possible to express feelings for a headless ghost! Like many other Scottish tales, it's a good one, full of the usual family squabbles. The quarrel was between the MacLaines and took place in 1538.

This particular branch of the MacLaines lived in Moy Castle in Mull, a very plain, ordinary dwelling by all accounts, them being the poor relations to the MacLeans of Duart. Although it wasn't up to much, which was perhaps part of the problem, it was good enough for the family to live in. Iain the Toothless, the MacLaine chief, and his only son, Ewen of the Little Head, lived in it very happily together, despite their strange names, until Ewen decided to take a wife.

In true Scottish tradition, she was a nag, the kind Robbie Burns later devoted poems to. A predisposition for 'keeping up with the Joneses' was also one of her failings, except that, living in Mull, there weren't any Joneses around. There were the MacLeans, however, possessors of an extremely grand castle. When she saw it, Ewen's wife realized she had married the poor relation. She began to complain immediately. The bulk of these complaints concerned their wedding present from Iain the Toothless – a summer crannog at Loch Squabain.

'I'm not going in that,' she said. 'Not over our dead bodies. Get you up to the castle and do something about it!' So Ewen the Put Upon did. He rode all the way up to Moy Castle and told the old man that this wasn't good enough. The Toothless, who was evidently also the Brainless because of what happened next, was enraged. He hauled out his sword. Ewen of the Little Head did the same. There was a bit of a battle and soon Ewen wasn't of the Little Head any more, nor the Big One either. In fact, he wasn't of any head at all. When the Toothless swung his sword, Ewen's horse bolted. The horse rode for two miles with Ewen's headless body still on its back, before anyone managed to stop it.

One shudders to think of this sight in the bright country-side that morning. Although I have to add that it's a sight that has been seen many times since. Ewen has continued to ride through Glen Mor, probably because his death was so sudden and so terrible. By all accounts, the horse simply bolts wildly through the glen, as it must have done the day its rider was slain. The sightings usually accompany the death of one of the MacLaines – from natural causes, I'll add quickly. Not that this makes those who see Ewen feel much better, or rather those who see Ewen's body. No one's ever seen his head since the day his father hacked it off.

As I've already said, killing his son wasn't the cleverest thing for the Toothless to do. An interesting footnote to this tale is that MacLean of Duart, in the best family tradition, then seized the lands, so that in addition to being the Toothless, Iain was then also the homeless. He was imprisoned in Cairnburg Castle, the idea being that this would prevent him producing a new heir, since his only female companion was a deformed dwarf. This didn't stop Iain. With his name the chances are it was a match made in heaven, and soon she found she was pregnant.

How can I say these things about them both? Well, before any of you throw up your hands in horror thinking I'm being unkind, perhaps I should just draw your attention to the new baby's name – Murdoch the Stunted.

Earnest Ernie, the Shackleton Spectre – Discovery Point, Dundee

'Ponies! That's what did for him and me. Wretched damned ponies. Not that I'm for wanting folk to compare us, you understand. I had my fill of that when he was a man alive. But ponies! They don't take to the ice the way a dog does. A gale raging at a hundred miles an hour is nothing to a dog. Set on one another, drag their neighbour on, down a crevasse in a moment, if you let them. But they'll go. Man and dog, as if they were always made to work together. Ponies lick the salt sand. Kills them in the end. And that's not what you'd call "a lot of comfort" when you have to pull the sledges yourselves.

'I suppose in a way you might say it's ironical. Probably the only thing Scott and I never fought about. And we fought about plenty, let me tell you. Those wardroom stories you've probably

heard, him and me at one another's throats most nights – well, they're true. Maybe not in every word. Now that would be a lie if I were to say so. But what credence they lack can only be explained by one fact. Scott was a gentleman. You know there were things about Scott's expeditions I could see were damned foolhardy to say the least. Only you couldn't tell him that. You could try. But trying and succeeding are two very different things, as I think you'll agree. We both wanted the Pole, and you might say I tried at that too. It was Scott who beat me out of it. I rather lost my head about it because I didn't succeed. The second time it was Mongolian ponies. But the first time, now that was Scott. Secretly I didn't wonder he wasn't glad about the scurvy, no matter the tears that stood in his eyes when he told me. The state of my feet was bad, it's true. Those last few miles we crossed, the toes must have been black from the feel of them. Or maybe I should say the lack of feel in them because that had gone long before. But when he asked me, I replied heartily I could go on. Even with the scurvy and the blood coming up as it was doing, I felt there was a chance. "You shall need to go back," he said. "Not in a hundred years," I told him. "I cannot take the risk," he said. That was when the tears stood in his eyes. He then began a rambling discourse about the dreams and hopes of the party and how none of us would get further etc., if I insisted on coming on. I must say, for a gentleman he cried quite a bit. Then he said it was the gentlemanly thing to go back. There would be other chances. I had to agree of course. What else could I do, with the others standing round watching? The coughing was bad, but not so bad I couldn't have gone on for their sakes. But to have it made out I was ruining their chances, that was something I wasn't prepared to do, or to have.

'Anyway, Scott had the final word. He was the leader, after all, and one should never underestimate the power of a leader. I came home. It wasn't what I wanted, but I thought I would try again. As things turned out, that was a bit of a dream too. You know the kind of thing where the second state is worse than the first because I was closer then, might even have made it if it hadn't been for the ponies. That's life isn't it? Not to have your dreams. Still, keeping trying, that's the thing. That's what I believe anyway. Keep trying. Forget the ponies and forget Scott.'

The South Pole. Looking at these three stark words it's hard to comprehend the terrible passions they aroused at the start of the 20th century, when men were prepared to risk their lives in what seems to be an insane slog to reach it. Amundsen was the first in late 1911, but not before Scott had made two attempts, the second ending in bitter tragedy when he and his men died on the return journey in a tent just 11 miles from a food depot. They had finally reached their goal, only to read the words, 'Welcome to 90 degrees' written in Amundsen's hand. That it was 90 degrees was already known to them. That Amundsen had somehow got there before them and staked his claim in glory, was not.

Then there is the story of Shackleton. Invalided home in 1903 at Scott's insistence when he was within 530 miles of the Pole, he later returned to Antarctica and might have been the first to succeed. Only the insufficient pulling power of the ponies let him down. With 97 miles to go, he was forced to turn back. In fact, the Pole was always to remain one of his dreams. In 1922, 10 years after Scott, he made an ill-starred return, dying of a heart attack.

Small wonder, then, given the drama associated with the Pole, that the research ship which carried Robert Falcon Scott and Ernest Shackleton on the Antarctic expedition of 1903–4 is reputed to be haunted by the latter's ghost. It is said that despite the nightly contretemps with Captain Scott, Shackleton was very fond of the ship, the *Discovery*. This was to the extent of claiming that, if there was an afterlife, he wanted to spend it in the narrow and winding corridors below decks. So perhaps that explains some of the curious incidents which have taken place on board since the boat returned to Dundee in 1986. Noises, footsteps that don't trigger the alarm, flickering lights and cold spots at the door of Shackleton's cabin have all been noticed by staff at various times. But that isn't all, and is Ernie entirely to blame? Other schools of thought actually attribute the noises and chilly atmosphere to someone else.

Charlie Bonner, a young seaman who was overcome by the noisy rapture of a New Zealand audience, climbed the topmast to great acclaim and plunged 100 feet when part of it snapped. Not to such great acclaim, one imagines, since he was done to death by the iron roof of a deckhouse. George Vince is another likely contender for the position of *Discovery* ghost. Just a few months after the unfortunate Charlie, he was skiing back to the ship in Antarctica when he got a bit lost and went flying off the end of an ice cliff. This was something that also involved a bit of a drop – in George's case, right into the ocean. George survived the drop by all accounts but drowned instead.

What makes those involved with the *Discovery* believe that the ghost is neither of those, however, is the fact that

Shackleton's ghost has been sighted. 'That is most definitely him,' one young lady said, after looking at some archive photographs. 'He was sitting in the corner of the wardroom. I saw him.' In fact, according to reports, she did more than that. She spoke to him, probably thinking he was a volunteer guide.

Then there was the young Dutch volunteer guide who stepped on board one day to be greeted by a figure in Arctic clothes. And this figure wasn't a dummy – the ones placed at strategic points. The young man ran the proverbial mile to get away and is possibly running still! Unlike Shackleton, who vowed to be back when Scott sent him home in 1903, what this man had to say was quite different. 'I'll never be back,' he told the other crew members.

Were they playing a trick? Apparently not. With its winding corridors and low lighting, the *Discovery* isn't the kind of place to play tricks. The moment always comes when someone is left alone there, and that's when the lights flicker and the footsteps can be heard walking up and down. That's when Shackleton comes out and takes his ghostly revenge, looking for his rival, perhaps in the hope of continuing an ancient quarrel or settling a few scores. If you should see him, there's one thing you shouldn't mention – ponies!

The Ringcroft Horror

The idea of a house possessed by evil spirits is nothing new. America may have the Amityville Horror but in Scotland in 1695, a disturbing pamphlet was published by a local clergyman

called Alexander Telfair. It concerned the alarming happenings at
the house of one of his parishioners, an Andrew Mackie, who was
a mason by trade. Such was the nature of these disturbances that
Andrew and his family were eventually driven out. The house fell
into disrepair and has long since disappeared. Looking at what
went on, maybe that's just as well. After all, it's not every day you
meet the Devil in your barn, now is it! This is the story.

The Mackie family had lived for some time in the Rerrick
area of Kircudbrightshire where they had a small piece of
land. As well as being a mason, Andrew also farmed and
kept a number of animals. One morning, going round to the
back of the house, he discovered that one of his cows had
somehow got loose. Nothing unusual in that, except that it
was hanging from a beam. Andrew was disturbed. For some
time there had been incidents where his animals were
moved about and their tethers cut. He thought he had an
enemy. But obviously, given the position of the cow, this
enemy would have needed superhuman strength.

About a week later, someone came into the house and
tipped over a basket of peat while the family were asleep. The
peat was set alight. Had it not been for Andrew's quick
thinking, the house would have burned to the ground. By
now the family was concerned. Who had they crossed and
why? Two days later, some stones were flung at the house.
Andrew fetched in the Reverend Monteith. By now the family was frightened to go out. One of the stones had broken a
window and was lying in the middle of the floor.

'Do you see that stone?' Andrew asked the minister. 'Well,
I've picked it up and it feels only half as heavy as it should.

Lift it for yourself and see.' But Reverend Monteith never got the chance. The stone suddenly lifted itself in the air and smashed against the ceiling, then hit the Reverend on the back. This was enough for the Reverend Monteith. He fled.

Now all kinds of things started happening. Andrew's children came screaming to him with tales of the figure that sat by the fireside. 'It wears a cloak!' they said. As in the best Hollywood tradition, not only did it wear a cloak but it also needed something to carry. A shepherd's crook was taken from the kitchen. What it was going to do with it is less clear, but you can imagine it stalking the countryside claiming lives. Who knows what carnage might have followed had the enterprising Andrew not discovered the crook in the locked and shuttered loft and burned it.

It was now time for the Reverend Telfair to step in and exorcize the presence. But he promptly stepped out again when it threw a shower of stones at him. Being a brave sort of man as well as a minister, he came back. 'I will deal with this,' he told Andrew, but the spirit thought otherwise. In the resulting battle, the minister and Andrew were whacked by sticks, stoned and had furniture thrown at them. Nor was the spirit having any prayers. 'Whisht!' it repeatedly shouted at Andrew's children as they knelt down to pray.

By now, news of the disturbances at Ringcroft, the farmhouse, was spreading. Ministers and neighbours were coming from near and far to view the phenomenon. The spirit, possibly delighted with its fame, obliged with several stone-throwing and peat-hurling sessions. It knocked on walls. It scratched people across the face. No one left without being terrified out of their wits. Then, as if things were coming to a head, several even stranger events took place.

Mrs Mackie, noticing that a slab in the kitchen was loose, lifted it to find several bloodstained stones. This in itself wasn't that surprising, given the amount that had been hurled about. But with these stones was a piece of flesh wrapped in an old bit of paper. That night, a burning hot stone was placed on the children's bedclothes. A letter written in blood was left on the kitchen table. No one could understand what it said. Then the house went on fire. Andrew and his family, driven out, had to live in their stable.

It would be nice to report that, with no house left to haunt, the Ringcroft spirit moved on. This wasn't the case, however. Some of Andrew's neighbours came by to help the family. With the exception of the children, no one had seen the spirit, or presence, or whatever it was that was causing the problem. As the neighbours stepped into the barn, however, they did. Each one described the same thing – a black shape that grew in size till they thought it would fill the building. This was, of course, before they fled for their lives. After that, Andrew's sheep shelter was gutted by fire and that was the end of the disturbances. As quickly as it had come, the presence disappeared. To this day, the matter has never been fully explained. What haunted the place and why isn't known. Only that it was, and that for the residents of that tiny farming community, it was a terrifying experience.

The St Andrews Spectres

As with many other apparitions, the exact identity of the ghostly lady who haunts this historic ruin isn't known. But her appearances are well-documented. Moreover, she's not alone. Being so old a building, the cathedral can lay definite claim to two ghosts, both of whom are said to be friendly. Not with each other I'm sure, since one is a monk. Having the ghost of a monk in a cathedral isn't that unusual, and given the fact that St Andrews Cathedral was once the largest and most magnificent building of its kind in Scotland, it would only be surprising to learn that it's entirely spectre-free. What makes the St Andrews monk so interesting, however, is that he's of the 'Caspar' variety – so entirely friendly and helpful, he could qualify for a good citizen award.

Some accounts state that the man was murdered in what is known as St Rule's Tower – a part of the building which was actually built before the cathedral itself went up – but given his eagerness to help visitors up and down the winding staircase, the chances are that he might have met with an accident there instead. Perhaps he was even overcome by the magnificent views from the top. Who knows?

Whatever his fate, it seems he's as real as the bricks to many of the tourists who've used the staircase over the years. In some instances where a tourist has stumbled, he's actually come to their side and tried to take their arm. If you encounter him, there's apparently no need to be frightened and run away screaming because he'll probably stand aside to let you pass, his manners are just so impeccable. And he's not likely to follow you outside either. The tower is his 'haunt', so to speak. He just wants to be sure you enjoy your visit and leave safely.

The 'White Lady' is much more likely to accost you in the grounds. As in all the best ghost stories, she is very mysterious and beautiful, not to mention well-dressed. Many of those who have seen her describe her as wearing a white veil and gloves. It's only unfortunate that her story isn't known because she's been around for at least 200 years, having been seen by the sober and the not-so-sober, so I'm told. What is known is that in 1868 a sealed vault in the tower was opened and six coffins were found. The mummified body of a young woman wearing a white veil and gloves was also discovered, so the chances are she and the White Lady are one and the same. Even then her identity wasn't clear. So whoever she is, it seems she haunts the cathedral ruins because her grave is there.

The Dark Dungeon of Dunnottar

'At Dunnotter, they were received by George Keith of White-ridge, sheriff-depute of the Mearns. This large company was thrust into a dark vault underground, one of the most uncomfortable places poor people could be in. It was full of mire, ankle deep and had but one window towards the sea. So throng were they in it that they could not sit without leaning upon another. They had not the least accommodation for sitting, leaning or lying and were perfectly stifled for want of air. They had no access to ease nature and many of them were faint and sickly. In this miserable vault about a hundred of them were pent up all this summer and it was a miracle

of mercy that they were not all killed. When soldiers brought in
barrels of water, they would pour it into the vault to incommode
them the more. Considerable numbers of them died and no won-
der.' (Wodrow)

Writing about the sufferings of the Covenanting prisoners
who were brought to Dunnottar Castle in 1685, Wodrow was
perhaps a little colourful. He was, after all, the historian of
the Kirk of Scotland and its sufferings, and suffering was certainly what the Kirk did in its long history. The Whig's vault,
where this incident took place, isn't actually underground
and it's not quite so dark and airless as Wodrow would have
it either. In fact, it has several windows through which hand-
fuls of more daring prisoners attempted to escape. It's also
doubtful if parts of the lower vault, which Wodrow mentions
later in his account, could have held anything like the numbers he claims. What is certain, however, is that during
Monmouth's rebellion against the crown, some 167 men and
women were held in the castle for roughly nine weeks.
Although there were some concessions towards the end of
that time, the larger part of that period was spent in the
vault. Nine died and twenty-five escaped through the afore-
mentioned window. Fifteen of them were promptly recap-
tured when the alarm was raised, and tortured with lighted
matches.

Given this dark episode, which is only one of many in
Dunnottar's long history – William Wallace is said to have
burnt 4000 Englishmen within its walls – it's really no surprise to learn that the castle has its fair share of ghosts.
Although personally, I'm a bit suspicious about that number

of Englishmen. It seems to me that it's not just Wodrow being fanciful there!

Aptly, given that Wallace was portrayed on screen by Mel Gibson, the castle was also used to film *Hamlet*, in which Gibson also starred as the doomed prince, prodded by his father's ghost to thoughts of revenge. So Dunnottar's association with ghosts certainly stretches right across the board. There are also wonderful stories connected with the smuggling out of the Scottish crown jewels and the private papers of King Charles I, which had been brought to the castle for safe-keeping in 1651. But ghosts are what we're concerned with here and, in keeping with its history, various ones have been seen.

The Whig's vault itself is said to contain quite a few apparitions. These have been seen on various occasions, largely when there's an unsuspecting tourist or two about. But despite the cellar's grim history, one of Dunnottar's most persistent and best-known ghosts seems to have nothing to do with it. The figure of a girl, dressed in a dull plaid dress, is frequently witnessed in the brewery. Maybe she just likes it better there. Or maybe that was where she worked. She has, however, been seen on too many occasions to ignore. Apparently, she apparently always follows the same path, leaving by the doorway, then vanishing into space.

Other ghostly apparitions seen in Dunnottar include a young hound and a tall Scandinavian man. The latter seems quite likely, given the length of time the castle has stood on its high cliff, looking out to sea. And it's possible he's even some reminder of the far-off Viking days. Benholm's Lodging is also haunted by a noisy bunch. They've never been seen, only heard, always locked in some interminable meeting. Perhaps they are clamouring for a mouthful of ale while they debate the fate of the prisoners – who knows!

The 'Green Mass' – St Mary's Steeple, Dundee

'There's the church and there's the steeple. Open the gates and there's the people.'

He wanted to go home, to breathe the clean sea air as it swept from the river and lingered over the plants that trailed by the door, the growing patch of turnip and kale his mother had planted. But that was gone now. 'Now! Now! Now!' came the order, and he was on his feet, struggling for a hold on the steaming pot of pitch as it was dragged to the slit of a window and upended, recalling as he clawed his way forward what it was that had woken him from his dream. That sound, that booming sound of cannon shot pounded against the walls of his home, shattering the quiet night.

'Roundheads! Bloody, bastard Roundheads!' the voices had shouted, the skinny faces contorted with fear and blood. 'Run! Run for God's sake!'

'It's because they cannae take the town!' his mother had said. 'They're going to blast us out and kill every one of us! Run!'

He had lost her then. It was in the confusion and he had prayed. 'Please God, help me! Help us!' All that night he had prayed. Now he knew a different sort of prayer. The kind that came from the blackened seams of his clothes, from his entrails every time he heard the words, 'Come on lads! More pitch!' and knew he must not make a fool of himself in front of the other men. As the hammering on the door increased, however, he knew. It was only a question of time before it gave in completely. Then they would all be at the mercy of Monk's men, or the Almighty – whatever the choice was.

Suddenly it did not matter much. He was too cold and frightened to think otherwise. There was a shaft of light and he was running towards it. Something had grazed the cloth on his shoulder, cutting it open so that the blood sprayed in an open fan across the room and he was too surprised by the sight of this to do anything more than stare. Then it was around him – the smell, the terrible smell, filling his senses with thoughts of death. In his eyes, his nose, his mouth, the smell of musket fire rolling in, so that at first, though he had embraced it, he was choking now on its acrid depths, unable to speak, unable to say what he most wanted to: 'I am coming Mam, I am coming home.' Then he was falling, falling, through a swaying patch of turnip seed, to what he knew to be her arms.

Few cities could have wiped out their past as thoroughly as Dundee. Take a stroll through the centre and what you'll find predominantly are plaques. 'This is the site of the Dundee castle'. 'Mary Shelley slept here'. Or wander a little further to where the ghosts of the 'palais grands' still haunt the shady roads along the river front and you'll find most of them replaced by signs saying 'information technology'. It's that kind of place, one where new jostles old and even the visions of the 'dark satanic mills' are fading.

Dundee does, however, have a long history. Despite its more northerly position, it fell to the English as often as

Berwick and has had its share of sackings too, largely due to the gall of the population. When the Marquis of Montrose sent his drummer into the town to demand its surrender during the Civil War, some of the residents locked him up – an act which led to the town being ransacked and burned. When General Monk insisted that its citizens lay down their arms and stop defending Charles II, they invited him to lay down his and join them. All in all, the resulting siege was quite an affair – another instance when the town and its people paid dearly for their failure to be submissive and were forced to rise from the ashes of adversity.

Given all this, it's a miracle the town stands at all. But it does. Most impressive are its two landmarks, one natural, the other man-made – the Law Hill round which it gathers its skirt of houses, and St Mary's Steeple. The latter is the oldest church tower of its kind in Scotland – something of a record given the bloody history that has been enacted around it, not to mention the way the town keeps taking itself to bits, the surrounding Overgate area in particular. And the atmosphere in the steeple can be grim. But is it haunted? Well, I wouldn't be surprised.

To begin with, it more or less stands on a graveyard. Every so often, excavation in the vicinity throws up mass graves, which could be those of plague victims or Monk's massacre. Its hallowed precincts were once used as a jail. Before the gallows were built, condemned prisoners were actually shot in the vaults, which seems a slightly surreal touch, I must add, and perhaps the most multiple use of a church I've ever come across. Then, of course, there's Monk's siege. When he at last broke through the city walls, the carnage in the streets was terrible. No quarter was given and many of the citizens, women and children included, retreated to the tower where they took their last stand. They were hoping to hold out, even though the odds were stacked against them, and the tower must have seemed as good a place as any to do it. But they didn't succeed, despite a large amount of heroics. Look round the foyer as you step inside and you can almost picture it piled high with dying men and women.

The clock tower is reputed to be haunted by a green apparition, a sort of shapeless mass that's neither male or female and just hangs there in the air. You can't touch it and it won't touch you. Some of those who've seen it say that it's just dust motes in the light. Others say, 'No. Something's there. You just can't afford to think about it with all those stairs to get back down!'

Given the history of the place, I'm not sceptical. I think they could be seeing a sort of tortured mass of ages of pain and suffering.

The Dame of Delgatie

It isn't known whether or not the spirit who haunts Delgatie Castle – a suitably forbidding 14th-century pile near Turriff – was a lady of quality. But courage was very much in her line, if the story of her exploits is anything to go by. Beautiful and 'spirited', in more ways than one, she apparently defended the castle against attack. The only problem is that she has since felt obliged to repeat her antics. So if you should visit this place – beware!

Delgatie is a lovely place with a long history of association to the Scottish crown. Sir William Hay of Delgatie was standard-bearer to the Marquis of Montrose at the battle of Philphaugh. Although they were on the losing side, Sir William did manage to sneak the standard off the field and to Buchanan Castle. This was before he was caught and executed at Edinburgh castle in 1650.

Delgatie's 'dame' is called Rohaise, an unusual and lovely name, which is possibly to do with the Hay family. She's so well known there, a whole room has been dedicated to her, and her appearances are certainly of the interesting kind. During the Second World War, she drove out a whole group of battle-hardened soldiers, who happened to be stationed there. This was on two occasions. It's possible, given her history, that she believed they had war-like intentions so she wasn't taking any chances. Men, on the whole, don't tend to feature much in her 'good books'. In fact, she views them with so much suspicion, she often visits those who are brave enough to stay in the 'Rohaise room' – and it's not for the kind of affectionate kisses other female ghosts bestow. I suspect she may have been brutally treated during her spirited defence of the castle, hence her dislike of the opposite sex and tendency to disturb them. At any rate, she's not a gentle ghost. The soldiers she drove out were terrified, particularly when a search of the castle revealed there was no one there.

Delgatie was also the scene of a horrific accident in the 1880s when a coach driven by Lady Fanny Ainslie plunged off the Bridge of Turriff. What was she doing driving? Apparently, she was headstrong and had insisted on doing so, something that resulted in the actual driver, a certain Charles Arthur Scofield, being crippled for life.

At least that's the story as it's given. Could it be that horse and driver took one look at the Lady Rohaise ...

The Hanged Man of Ayrshire

Hotels and boarding houses often have their fair share of ghosts. This isn't always to do with the volume of people passing through. Sadly, there are people who choose the unfamiliar surroundings of a hotel or boarding house to end their lives. But while they themselves are no more, their spirits linger.

This proved to be very much the case in a boarding house in Ayrshire, near the famous racecourse. One spectral visitor was a lingering presence, making himself known by standing at windows, opening and slamming doors, rearranging furniture, stepping in front of the owners – often to their horror – and also creating what they described as a 'graveyard' smell.

The owners were able to identify their ghost. Any claims that they were making up the story to attract more business can be quickly dismissed as the ghost was that of a man who had hanged himself in one of their rooms. And such was the level of disturbance that the couple decided to sell the property. Sharing their house with living people was obviously one thing, but a member of the spirit world was quite another. Eventually, they felt the house was too unhappy for them.

The hanged man was from Australia, but was Scottish by birth. Initially, he came to stay for a few weeks, 'To have a holiday,' he said. His wife had sent him over with quite a sum of money. Later it transpired that this was to get rid of him. He suffered problems with alcohol abuse, problems so severe that, within a short space of time, the money was gone. His wife paid the bill for his lodgings from then on. It was clear the marriage was over, that there was nothing for him here or in Australia. Before he hanged himself, he left a note saying that this was the only way to straighten everything out and asking the proprietors to contact his wife. So far as they were concerned, when they did that it would be the end of the matter.

Two days later, as the owners stepped from their car, their late guest was back. He was standing at the lounge window staring at them. Both saw him and were white with shock. It was some time before they felt able to go into the house. When they did, the room was empty but upstairs in the room where the man died, they could hear the sounds of furniture being moved about. They called in a friend who worked as a psychic. When she arrived at the house she also saw their late guest and described him perfectly. As the disturbances continued, seemingly without reason, the house was blessed by a local priest. And after this, as if the whole thing was connected with how the man died, the problems stopped.

As for the couple concerned, they were never troubled by ghosts again. Perhaps this is as well. What they put up with at the hands of this particular one was enough to last each of them a lifetime!

The Severed Hand of Dyce

Sounding vaguely like something Conan Doyle or another Victorian writer might well have devoted the odd chapter to, comes this story from Dyce – itself an unfortunate name in the severed-hand stakes. It was sent by a client who remembered quite clearly the terror she felt at the sight of the hand when she was just four years old. Little wonder really. This is almost more of a horror story than a ghost one. Strangely enough, no one else ever saw it. But it did have an owner.

Little Alice was lying in bed one evening in the farmhouse owned by her mother and father. The house itself was large and comfortable and Alice had no reason to be afraid. No bad things had ever happened there, so far as she was aware. Her parents, too, found that, on the whole, the farm had a pleasant atmosphere, except for one of the sheds. That was sometimes cold and dank, even on a hot day, but as it was a farm building, they didn't think anything of it. Everything, so far as they knew, was fine, both in the house and out, so they were quite alarmed on this particular evening to hear shouting coming from Alice's room. They hurried up the stairs and threw the door open. Alice was in terrible distress. Sweeping across the ceiling of her room was a hand, she said.

This in itself might have been quite an entertainment. Alice had been put to bed earlier than usual that night, her parents fancying a little longer to themselves. And her mother might have been forgiven for thinking Alice's imagination was working overtime, had it not been for the state she was in.

The fact was she wouldn't be pacified. Of course, they had to pretend, the way parents do, to look for what was frightening Alice. But Alice assured them that the moment they opened the door, the hand had disappeared, so there was no point looking. Alice's parents didn't know what to make of it. Eventually, they decided she had been dreaming.

The next night, however, the hand was back, sweeping back and forth across the ceiling of Alice's room. It was large and bloodstained, severed at the wrist with a gaping hole. Alice was terrified, cowering under the covers screaming. The hand never came near her but that wasn't the point. For nights on end it paraded across the ceiling in its grotesque and bloody fashion till Alice couldn't stand to be in the room any longer. For the sake of peace, her parents were forced to move her. Although they had never seen the hand, they were convinced that what she saw was more than a dream or childish fantasy.

At that stage, they had no idea about the history of the farm and the young man who had been killed when his hand was trapped in a threshing machine. The accident happened in the shed, the one that sometimes felt so cold. That much Alice's father learned from his neighbours, when eventually he spoke to them about the strange goings-on.

The bedroom Alice slept in had been the young man's room, but no one had ever complained of seeing the hand in it before. Alice was the first and perhaps the only one, possibly because of her youth, since young children can sometimes be susceptible to spirits. At any rate, after her room was moved, she never saw the hand again, which was perhaps as well. There's definitely something creepy about the idea of a severed hand roaming about, and I don't think I'd like to be the person called in to get rid of it. Who knows? It might just take them by the throat!

The Gale of Inverurie

A cottage in Inverurie in Aberdeenshire is the haunt of a tele-phone-answering spirit, a Gaelic speaker at that. How do people know? Well, there's not a Gaelic speaker in sight – not of the cottage anyway. The owner doesn't know a word. But what the spirit actually does is speak to those who ring up in Gaelic. So clearly, too, that those who speak to him think the person they're talking to is real. They're quite understandably spooked to dis-cover he's not. So is the owner. When she goes out, she always leaves the answering machine on. Although the incoming calls are logged in the telephone memory, there are never any messages – nothing on the answering machine at all. The telephone has clearly been answered, but not by her.

This spirit also likes walking up and down the hallway. He's been seen there a number of times, and not just by the owner. Visitors have twice reported seeing a man walking down the hall into the living room, then through the wall into the cottage next door.

On one occasion, the ghost even tried getting into bed with a visitor, snuggling up to her back, no doubt because he was somewhat cold. The woman in question wasn't afraid, so she said anyway. She believed the ghost didn't mean any harm and wanted her to stay calm. When she did manage to sit up, the presence moved then seemed to vanish out of the bed again.

However, the ghost wasn't quite so friendly on another occasion. Plainly tired of having other people sleeping in his bed, the spectre tried to pull the offending person out. Their dog was with them in the room and cowered in the corner. It was dark and the person couldn't see well but they were clear about one thing – whoever was trying to move them out spoke what sounded like Gaelic, and they seemed angry.

The cottage owner isn't too happy about the uninvited guest, although it would seem that the man, whoever he is, views himself as the owner and everyone else as intruders. He's been asked to go by various sources, but so far resists all attempts to move him out. Obviously, he's a stubborn old gent. Or perhaps he just doesn't understand. It's possible that anyone asking him to go should do it in his own language. Does anyone know any Gaelic?

The Bride of Baldoon

You can take your pick of the versions of this sorry tale. All equally bloodthirsty and horrible, they concern Janet Dalrymple, who found fame not only as a ghost but as Lucia Di Lammermoor, or in plainer terms, the Bride of Lammermoor, the quite mad heroine of opera and literature. Sir Walter Scott described how the door of the bridal chamber was broken down to reveal the bridegroom drenched in blood, the bride cowering in the corner, quite insane. Not the kind of thing one would expect, but then the sounds coming from inside weren't normal either – shrieking, hideous laughter, wild, echoing screams. A rollicking time was certainly being had by all, but it wasn't the sort of thing that made for a happy family life. The bride died shortly afterwards, utterly insane, and the bridegroom – well, we'll come to him in a minute.

No matter which account of the first-night frolic you accept – and we'll come to that too – the facts leading to the wedding day are always the same. Janet Dalrymple was the eldest daughter of Sir James Dalrymple. She was deeply in love but the object of her fancy, Archibald Rutherford, didn't meet with her parents' approval. He was poor – virtually penniless in fact. This enraged the Dalrymples who were known for counting their money the way insomniacs do sheep. This was the 17th century when daughters did as they were told. Janet had no choice in the matter. It was up to Sir James. And his choice for her was David Dunbar, the Baldoon son and heir.

The couple were married in the Kirk of old Luce. Her two brothers took her to church, no doubt to ensure she arrived there. Both, however, noticed that her hands were as cold as ice, although it was a hot summer's day.

After the wedding meal took place, Janet and her new husband retired for the night, and it is here that the stories start to differ. Whichever one you choose, they are all suitably bloodthirsty. In the first, Janet stabs her new husband with the dagger she has concealed in her wedding dress and he is found drenched in blood. She is insane. In the second, David stabs Janet when she refuses to give him what he is expecting. She is drenched in blood and he is insane. In the third – in the best bedroom-farce tradition with a bit of murder thrown in – Archibald turns up and stabs David, then jumps out of the window. In the fourth, the Devil himself stabs David and torments Janet, who was silly enough to have sold her soul in the hope of marrying Archibald.

Even Sherlock Holmes would be kept guessing what happened that night! Personally, I favour the first version, reckoning that the poor girl was insane with unhappiness and the thought of being touched by the unappetizing David. But whichever you favour doesn't matter. What does is that Janet died shortly afterwards and her ghost began to wander the grounds in a white nightdress stained with blood, and that time itself has not caused the volume of these sightings to 'die' down.

Baldoon castle is now in ruins, with little left but the gateposts, but some say Janet still walks pathetically around the area where the castle stood. Apparently, she is most active on the anniversary of her death, 12 September. I would have thought she was more likely to re-enact the anniversary of her wedding night, but this doesn't seem to be the case.

I said I'd tell you more about David Dunbar. Well, he recovered sufficiently in all departments to want to take the plunge again, this time with a daughter of the Earl of Eglinton. Evidently he survived the experience in that she didn't produce any surprises on their wedding night. He was killed instead falling off his horse in 1682. In true romantic tradition, Archibald, the impoverished lad who Sir James turned down on poor Janet's behalf, never married. He died in 1685, 16 years after her. Sadly, for whatever reason, the sightings of Janet indicate that, in death as in life, they are not destined to be together.

Barnbougle Castle

'And ever, when Barnbougle's lords
Are parting this scene below,
Come hound and ghost to this haunted coast
With death notes winding slow.'

*Sounding remarkably ghost-like – well, I think the word 'bougle'
might prove to be a Scottish kind of spook! – Barnbougle Castle
would give Arthur Conan Doyle's famous book* The Hound of the
Baskervilles *a run for its money in the doggy haunting stakes! The
legend goes right back, much further than the one attached to the
fictional Baskerville family. In fact, it's one of the oldest I've come
across, dating right back to the Crusades.*

The hound in question was allegedly owned by one Sir
Roger Mowbray. Being a faithful sort of dog, it followed him
everywhere. Sir Roger planned to fight in the Crusades with
the Red Cross Knights – a problem for his doggy follower,
but not for long. Apparently, the dog was so devoted to him,
it followed him right to the ship and looked so utterly
piteous, doing all sorts of whimpering and howling, that Sir
Roger took it on board.

For years – and the Crusades did last for years – Sir Roger
and the dog went everywhere together. But then in one battle in Syria, Sir Roger and his faithful companion were killed.
At that moment, a bugle rang out from the old tower in
Barnbougle Castle, followed by the baying of a hound.

From then on the area was alleged to be haunted by Sir
Roger's companion. Although the howling sends shivers up

the spine, the dog itself is said to be harmless. That's if you're not a Barnbougle laird. The dog has howled sufficiently often just prior to the death of certain lairds to allow the story to weave itself into legend, much as the poem above suggests. Hound Point nearby is also named after the faithful hound, which no doubt thinks it is doing all these lairds a big favour, letting them know when their clogs are going to be popped!

Perhaps this is because it failed to warn Sir Roger. I'm not sure. But it is a nice story and, in the ghost stakes, makes a change from all the green ladies and lustful men who seem to populate Scotland's 'otherworld'!

Index

Abbotsford 225–7
Aberdeen 104, 242
Abergeldie Kate 234–6
Agnew, Alexander 212–14, 215
Ainslie, Lady Fanny 275–6
Airth Castle 64–9
Alec's Exam 5–7
Alexander II 230
Allanbank 210
Allte Grande 201–2
Antartica 261–2
The Ardvreck Ghost 195–8

The Bakery 144–6
The Balconie Ghost 200–3
Baldoon Castle 281–3
Barnbougle Castle 284–5
Bellshill 72
Ben Macdhui 205–8
Black Andrew of Balnagowan
        251–2
Blackadder 209
Bonner, Charlie 262
Bothwell Brig, Battle of 62
The Bride of Baldoon 281–3
Bride Beth 130–3

And the Bride Wore 164–7
Brodie, Deacon 193
The Brolass 'Braw-lass' 238–41
The Brooch 14–16
Broughty Ferry 116–18
Bruces 54, 65–7, 230, 236
Buchanan Castle 275
Bullock, George 227
Burns, Robbie 257

Cairnburg Castle 259
Cairngorms 206
Cameron of Lochiel 220
Campbells 212–15
My Captain 56–60
The Car that Moved 172–4
Charles I 270
Charles II 62–3, 273
Charlie, Bonnie Prince 222–5
Civil War 273
Coltheart, Thomas 228
The Council Tenant 69–72
Crawford, Earl Beardie 191
Cromarty 201
Crusades 284
Culloden, battle of 219, 222–5

Cummings 255–6

Dalrymple, Janet 281–3
The Dame of Delgatie 274–6
The Dancing Couple 74–6
The Dark Dungeons of
    Dunnottar 268–71
Dearly Loved David 26–8
The Deil of Glenluce 212–15
Delgatie Castle 274–6
Discovery 262–3
I Don't Know What It Is 161–4
Douglas, Lady Janet 192
Drummond, Lilias 232
Dumfries 215
Dunbar, David 282–3
Dundee 56, 140, 262, 271–4
Dundee, Bonnie 219–21
Dunnotar Castle 268–71
Dyce 278–80

Earnest Ernie 259–63
Edinburgh 60, 193, 227, 275
Edward I of England 230
The Elephant Man 30–3
Elfland, Queen of 230
English 216, 218, 272
ER Was Never Like This
    154–6
Ewen of the Little Head 257–8

Fairwind 187
Fairy Queen 230
Falkirk 64
Fife 69, 232

First World War 50, 99–100,
    125, 138
Flannan Isle 186–90
Forbes of Strathgirnock 235
Forth 64
France 100, 209, 226
The Friendly Ghost 119–21
Frith Woods 181
The Fyvie Five 229–34

The Gale of Inverurie 280–1
Geordie O' the Mill 216–19
The German Soldiers 54–6
Ghost or Not? 141–4
The Ghost Who Never Was
    72–4
The Ghost Who Wanted To Go
    Upstairs 113–15
The Ghost Who Was Scared
    90–3
Gibson, Mel 270
Gibson, W.W. 188–9
Glamis Castle 190–3, 229, 230
Glasgow 60, 101, 133, 150,
    152, 178
Glen Mor 258
Glencoe, battle of 219
The Glencourse Ghost 181–3
Glenluce 212, 214, 215
Glenlyon 204
Go Back for Alison 39–42
Gordons 232, 235
Grahame of Claverhouse 219
Grant, Joan 206–7
Grassmarket Ghost 193–5

The Green Ghost 199–200
Green Lady 199, 232, 233, 285
Green Man 201–3
The Green Mass 271–4
Grey Lady 192, 199, 205, 232, 233
The Grey Man of Ben Macdhui 205–8

The Hanged Man of Ayrshire 276–7
The Haunted Dog 108–11
The Haunted Motorbike 156–8
The Haunted Office 150–2
Hay, Sir William 275
The Headless Horseman 257–9
Hebrides 190
The Hero Ghost 18–20
Hesperus 188–9
Hob, Will 217
The House is Empty Now 148–50

Iain the Toothless 257–9
Inverurie 280–1
The Iron Mask 60–3

Jacobites 219, 222
James II 62–3
James VI 252
Jarron, Magdalen 195
Jean Paul II, Pope 245
Jersey 128
Jim, My Gay Spirit 33–5

Killiecrankie 219
Kircaldy 69
Kirk O'Shotts 60–1

Lairig Ghru 207–8
Lammie, Andrew 233
Leiths 232
Leslie, Grizel 232
Lindsays 192, 220
loneliness 33–5, 46, 65, 138
Lothian 148
The Love that Never Died 167–9
The Lustful Laird of Littledean 245–50

McAvoy, James 72–4
Macdonalds 239, 240
Mackenzies 235
Mackie, Andrew 264–6
Mackintoshes 255–6
MacLaines 257, 258
MacLeans 239–41, 257–9
Mad Earl 193
The Maid from Broughty Ferry 116–18
Malcolm, King 191
The Man Who Went To His Own Funeral 42–4
Marshall, Thomas 187
The Martyrs of Murder Moss 216–19
Mary King's Close 227–9
Mary Queen of Scots 199, 200
Meggernie 204

The Melancholy Motorcyclist 133–5

Meldrums 232

The Melrose Monk 236–8

Midlothian 181

Monk, General 272, 273

Monmouth, Duke of 62–3, 269

Monteith, Reverend 264–5

Montrose, Marquis of 273, 275

Mowbray, Sir Roger 284–5

Moy Castle 257–8

Mull 239, 257

The Mum Who Came To Say Goodbye 111–13

The Mum Who Wanted To Be Remembered 51–3

Munro, Andrew 251–2

Murdoch the Stunted 259

The Mystery of the Trophy Room 121–3

Napoleonic wars 181

National Trust 232, 234

Neilston 54–6

Newport-on-Tay 125

The Noble Nurse 99–101

Nostradamus 199

Not One But Two 49–51

The Not-So-Holy Nun 28–30

Occupant of the Locked Room 192

Ogilvys 192

Old Course Hotel 85

The Orphaned Imp 81–5

The Pass of Killiecrankie 219–22

Pearlin' Jean 208–12

The Persistent Papa 46–9

Peter Put the Kettle On 44–6

The Phantom Bandstand 95–9

The Phantom Fisherman 152–4

The Phantom Lady of Meggernie 204–5

The Phantom Letter 175–7

The Phantom Nanny of Airth Castle 64–9

Philphaugh, battle of 275

The Piper Alpha 12–14

The Polish Guest 88–90

That Poor Plumber 86–8

The Pregnancy 9–12

The Proud Mother? 159–61

Radio Clyde 60, 61

Ralston, Andrew 193

Rankie, Kittie 234–6

The Reassuring Spirit 178–80

Renfrew 164

The Ringcroft Horror 263–6

Robert the Bruce 54, 65, 230, 236

Rosses 251, 252

Rothiemurchus Forest 206

Roundheads 271

Rutherford, Archibald 282–3

Safe To Go Back In The Garden 137–8

The St Andrew Sceptics 267–8
St Andrews 85
St Mary's Steeple 271–4
Scott, Captain Robert Falcon 260–3
Scott, Sir Michael 237–8
Scott, Sir Walter 225–7, 281
Scotus, John Duns 245
Second World War 55, 107, 108, 165, 275
Selkirk 216
Seton, Alexander 232
The Severed Hand of Dyce 278–80
Shackleton, Ernest 259–63
Sherrifmuir, battle of 219
He's Sitting There 138–40
The Skeleton of Skibo 252–5
Skibo 252–5
Smith, Agnes 233
Our Soldier 125–8
South Pole 260–2
Stevenson, Robert Louis 193
Stirling 169–72, 199–200, 228
Stoker, Bram 237
Strathmores 193
Stuarts 209–10, 212, 219, 222–5
Sun 55, 58, 70
The Supermarket Ghost 128–30
Sweet Caroline 23–6

Tay, River 56
Telfair, Alexander 264–5

Thomas the Rhymer 230–1
The Tidy Ghost 20–2
The Times 207
The Tinker's Curse 212–15
Together Forever and Ever 93–5
Tweed, River 226

The Vase 1–4
The Victoria Doll 76–81
Vince, George 262
Vining, Miss 242–4

Walking Walter 225–7
Wallace, William 65, 269–70
Wartime Sweethearts 35–7
We Do Have a Ghost. I've Seen Him 140–1
Weirs 194–5
What a Waste of a Life 85–6
The Wheelchair 16–17
The White Dove Ghost 241–4
White Lady 199, 268
William the Lyon 230
Wodrow 269–70
The Woman in White 101–3
Wood, Wendy 207
The Wraith of Rait 255–7

Yellow Bubble Car 7–9
You Met My Mother 103–8

The Gift

The Story of an Ordinary Woman's
Extraordinary Power

Mia Dolan

The extraordinary life story of psychic and clairvoyant, Mia Dolan, the new Betty Shine.

Mia Dolan is one of the UK's most eminent and extraordinary psychics whose work has taken her from private readings to 'ghostbusting' to psychic demonstrations in front of hundreds of people. Her abilities have made her one of the most sought-after psychics in the country.

An ordinary woman brought up in a working-class family on the Isle of Sheppey, she had her first out-of-body experience at the age of 12 when she was sexually assaulted by a local teenager. At the age of 22 her spirit guide began to talk to her and showed her how to use her clairvoyance as well as providing fascinating insights into the nature of the Afterlife. Mia's life has been touched by tragic experiences – she foresaw the murder of her own brother and her son died while still only a teenager.

In *The Gift* Mia describes how her psychic ability developed, and the more dramatic readings that she has given, including the man who came to ask her where his missing wife was – she knew instantly that she was dead, and the body was later found exactly as Mia described.

'I want people to know there is more to life than what we call reality, more than what we can see – and it is not as far beyond our reach as we imagine. It is ordinary, everyday, here and now, in this minute. And it is magical, a gift.'

Make
www.thorsonselement.com
your online sanctuary

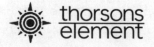

Get online information, inspiration and
guidance to help you on the path to physical
and spiritual well-being. Drawing on the integrity
and vision of our authors and titles, and with
health advice, articles, astrology, tarot, a
meditation zone, author interviews and events
listings, www.thorsonselement.com is a great
alternative to help create space and peace
in our lives.

So if you've always wondered about practising
yoga, following an allergy-free diet, using the
tarot or getting a life coach, we can point you
in the right direction.

thorsons
element